LEWI
Intern

ted

-77

LEWIS CARROLL has been a popular author for a long time. His *Alice* books are among the world's most read, most frequently quoted, and most regularly translated works. Despite this popularity, studies of Carroll were infrequent until 1960, the year Martin Gardner published his *Annotated Alice*. Since then, Carroll scholarship has burgeoned.

This bibliography will fill the critical gap of information about Carroll publications written during the significant post-1959 period. It attempts to include and annotate everything written by or about Lewis Carroll that has been published since 1959 in any language in any country. The book will make scholars aware of the excellent studies of Carroll and his art published in foreign languages, and it will provide collectors with information on the many fine translations of his work. The more than 1500 entries cover all aspects of Carroll's life and art, including his literary works, his photography, his work on logic, and his relations with other Victorians.

The information in the bibliography is organized under four headings: Primary Works; Reference and Bibliographical Works and Exhibitions; Biography and Criticism; and Miscellaneous—including Dramatic and Pictorial Adaptations and Discussions of Translation. The author gives unusually full bibliographical entries, with descriptive annotations.

# Lewis Carroll

## AN ANNOTATED INTERNATIONAL BIBLIOGRAPHY 1960 – 77

*by*

*Edward Guiliano*

Published for the
BIBLIOGRAPHICAL SOCIETY OF
THE UNIVERSITY OF VIRGINIA and the
LEWIS CARROLL SOCIETY OF NORTH AMERICA by the
UNIVERSITY PRESS OF VIRGINIA, Charlottesville

THE UNIVERSITY PRESS OF VIRGINIA
Copyright © 1980 by the Rector and Visitors
of the University of Virginia

*First published 1980*
Library of Congress Cataloging in Publication Data
Guiliano, Edward.
   Lewis Carroll: an annotated international
bibliography, 1960–77.

   Includes index.
   1. Dodgson, Charles Lutwidge, 1832–1898—Bibliography.
Z8234.8.G86      [PR4611]        016.828'809        80-13975
ISBN 0-8139-0862-0

Printed in the United States of America

# Contents

# Acknowledgments

One of the continuing gratifications I have had during the years I have worked on this bibliography has been the encouragement and generous assistance I have received from dozens of people around the world. No one has helped or sustained me more than my wife, Mireille, whose training in and gift for languages have been invaluable.

I want to thank two friends, teachers, and colleagues, Professors Richard A. Levine and William S. Peterson for their help and encouragement. William Peterson's Robert and Elizabeth Barrett Browning bibliography provided me with the idea for this bibliography and frequently served as a model. Richard Levine's advice and encouragement were instrumental in bringing this project to fruition.

Stan Marx deserves my deepest thanks. He graciously opened his home and his superlative Carroll collection to me for days at a time.

Joseph Brabant, Denis Crutch, John Davis, Selwyn Goodacre, David Schaefer, and Byron Sewell checked one of the earlier drafts of this bibliography against their own extensive Carroll holdings. Their diligent efforts are warmly appreciated. Their aid, with that of Stan Marx, has made this listing much more accurate and extensive than would have otherwise been possible.

Alice Berkey, Professor Nina Demurova, Professor Peter Heath, Nobuhide Suda, Professor Reinbert Tabbert, and Professor Bela Toth went to great lengths to provide me with substantial amounts of information, and for this I am grateful to them.

I am also indebted to Ruth Berman, Professor Lucia Binder, Professor Morton Cohen, Professor Klaus Doderer, Martin Gardner, Sonja Hagemann, Jolanta Hatwig-Sosnowska, Professor Izabela Lewanska, Carla Poesio, Kaija Salonen, Professor Shin-ichi Yoshida, and many others who go unnamed.

The majority of the people I have acknowledged are either members of The International Children's Literature Research Society, The Lewis Carroll Society of North America, and/or the Lewis Carroll Society (England). I owe additional thanks to the members of the Lewis Carroll Society of North America. In 1975 the Society published my annotated Carroll bibliography for 1974, which represented a trial use of the format adopted in this bibliography.

I wish to thank the reference staffs of the libraries at the State University of New York at Stony Brook and the New York Institute of Technology for helping me locate and secure copies of numerous books and articles. In all, the staffs of more than twenty libraries aided me. I especially want to thank Sally Leach and Erika Wilson of the Humanities Research Center, the University of Texas, for their repeated efforts in my behalf.

# LEWIS CARROLL: An Annotated International Bibliography, 1960–77

# Introduction

Lewis Carroll has been a very popular author for more than one hundred years. His *Alice* books were immediate best-sellers and have remained among the world's most popular, most frequently quoted, and most regularly translated literary works. Since 1960 Carroll's already high reputation has soared to ethereal heights, leaving his admirers to contemplate in awe the strength of its flight as editions, translations, and studies of his works multiply.

The keen critical interest in Carroll that now exists is a recent development. In 1935 William Empson began his seminal study of the *Alice* books, published in *Some Versions of Pastoral,* by remarking that it seems "a curious thing that there has been so little serious criticism of the Alices, and that so many critics, with so militant and eager an air of good taste, have explained they would not think of attempting it." As this bibliography clearly demonstrates, that attitude has now disappeared. In the history of Carroll studies, 1960 is pivotal. Since 1960 increasing numbers of people have discovered the richness of Carroll's work and have turned unabashedly to the study of his art and life. It is now common to find articles on Carroll's literary works, his work on logic, and his photography in the most erudite scholarly journals. Carroll's position within the universities has also become secure. His works are now found regularly on required-reading lists for courses in Victorian literature, children's literature, freshman English, linguistics, logic, philosophy, and the history of photography. In 1960 Martin Gardner published his *Annotated Alice,* and this book, which has both opened and entered many doors, can be credited for substantially aiding the recent surge of critical and popular interest in Carroll. Also during the period covered in this bibliography, the celebrations of the centenaries of his three most popular works, *Alice in Wonderland, Through the*

*Looking-Glass,* and *The Hunting of the Snark,* helped increase interest in Carroll's life and art.

This book is designed to fill a critical need for information about Carroll publications during the significant post-1959 period. Possibly because Carroll studies has only recently earned a widespread legitimacy in scholarly circles, and also perhaps because Carroll publications pose a special and difficult set of problems, bibliographers have not kept pace with the growth of interest in Carroll. Since he is such a popular genius with such varied talents, valuable writings treating him not only appear in a broad range of major publications but are liable to turn up in obscure publications, some of which are privately printed. Also, important writings about him are published in many countries besides Britain and America and in many languages besides English. Carroll's following is international, and his art is a part of the cultural heritage of many non-English-speaking nations. *Alice in Wonderland* has been translated into more than fifty languages. Part of my aim in compiling this checklist was to make scholars aware of the excellent studies of Carroll and his art published in foreign languages and to provide collectors with information on the many fine editions of Carroll's works that have appeared in translation around the world.

Currently a standard bibliographical reference work on Carroll is *The Lewis Carroll Handbook* (B62:2 in this listing), edited by Sidney Herbert Williams and Falconer Madan and revised by Roger Lancelyn Green. In 1979 it was reissued with further revisions by Denis Crutch. The *Handbook* deals primarily with the writings of Lewis Carroll, including the variant editions and auction histories of the manuscript materials. It contains only a limited checklist of writings about him, and virtually all the materials catalogued are British or American publications. For information about translations of the *Alice* books, the standard reference is Warren Weaver's *Alice in Many Tongues* (B64:2). Unfortunately Weaver's compilation leaves off just when interest in Carroll began to pick up rapidly around the world, and it has become dated as much new information has come to light. At the time of his death in 1978, Warren Weaver had just begun working on a revised edition.

In compiling this book, I have attempted to consider for inclusion absolutely everything written by or about Lewis Carroll that was published in 1960 through 1977 in any language and in any country. Naturally I cannot claim to have been successful in tracing and recording every publication. I am confident, however, that I have traced much valuable information about a far greater number of Carroll publications than anyone previously had known existed.

My bibliography does not follow the format of previous Carroll bibliographies. I have treated primary and secondary material similarly—which is, in part, a reflection of the increasing interest in the critical discussion of Carroll's works that marks the 1960–77 period.

I have organized the information I have collected on Carroll publications under four section headings: Section A. Primary Works; Section B. Reference and Bibliographical Works and Exhibitions; Section C. Biography and Criticism; and Section D. Miscellaneous—Including Dramatic and Pictorial Adaptations and Discussions of Translation. I have done so to make this a workable handbook. Certainly there are other patterns of organization that might have served as well; however, no pattern of organization is without some drawbacks. The bulk of the entries I have made fit comfortably under one umbrella or another, yet a substantial number are equally suited for more than one section. Where does one place a brief biographical piece noteworthy only for a letter or a few photographs that are published for the first time? Does one give a new critical introduction to a primary work a separate listing? I have not made multiple entries. Where does one place an article on the problems of translating Carroll's works? The study of the success or failure of a particular translation certainly can throw new light on the original. Does it belong with the biographical and critical articles? Sometimes this is the case; generally, I have treated such discussions as I have treated serious discussions of illustrating Carroll's works or of adapting them for the stage or for the motion-picture screen and have placed them in Section D. I have also had to consider carefully whether or not to subdivide the section on primary works. Should I separate the English works from the translations, the self-contained works from those that are collected in other titles?

Overall, I have tried to select the fewest workable categories and have relied upon indexing and cross-referencing to compensate for any weakness inherent in my system of organization.

I have worked to examine or to verify via a reliable person every item in this listing, and I have met with excellent results.

Many of the rules adopted in the compilation of the bibliography should be apparent; a few of the most important rules that I have attempted to observe can be summarized as follows:

1. In Section A, titles are arranged alphabetically by the name of the editor, translator, or illustrator—except for the case when the illustrator is the original illustrator (e.g., Tenniel). Titles without identifiable key names—other than Carroll or the original illustrator—are listed first. In the other sections, titles without identifiable key names are listed alphabetically.

2. In Section A, illustrated editions are in black and white unless otherwise identified, and all editions are hardcover unless otherwise identified. I have used the terms *hardcover* to designate all forms of editions bound in boards and *paperback* for all varieties of soft-cover editions. I have included information about binding only in Section A; it is of interest to the collector, and may be valuable when identifying editions. I do not promise that information about bindings is complete. I simply have recorded the editions I have seen with soft covers. It should be remembered that in Europe, and elsewhere as well, it is an increasingly common practice to bind books only in soft covers, with library volumes and some private copies being bound subsequently in a universal hardcover.

3. In cases of simultaneous or subsequent publication by two publishers in more than one location, notably British and American editions of the same book, I have listed both publishers and have tried to cite first the publishing house or city from which the title originated.

4. Only substantially revised editions are given separate entries.

5. Information about reprints of books first published after 1959 is listed under the title's first entry. Modern reprints of significant books by or about Carroll are listed under the first year covered in this bibliography in which a reprint appeared. Subsequent reprints are recorded under the first entry. Information about reprints of articles in books, when it was available to me, is indicated following the article's initial entry and through cross-references. Reprints that have appeared since 1959 of articles first published prior to 1960 are recorded.

6. Academic theses are listed under the year in which the abstract is published in *Dissertation Abstracts International;* if an abstract has not been published, a thesis is listed under the year in which it was accepted.

7. Book reviews are listed under the item in question and are arranged by date. Occasionally a review may be important enough—particularly a longer review essay—to merit a separate listing. Reviews are cited only for books dealing primarily or exclusively with Carroll. Listings of reviews are representative rather than comprehensive.

8. Films and, in general, dramatic presentations are not listed, although reviews of them are.

9. I have tried to make my coverage broad yet selective. Recording every instance that Lewis Carroll's name is evidenced in a book or in an article would have diminished the value of this work for scholars and students. There is also little value in reporting every instance when "Jabberwocky" is anthologized. On the other hand, it is valuable to record the appearance of a primary work in a particularly revealing context—say, a series of Carroll photographs in a history of photography or a selection of his poems in an anthology of nonsense poetry. Encyclopedic entries and passing references to Carroll in books about Victorian literature and other topics associated with Carroll have been

excluded except when the entries were, in my judgment, significant. My *see index* notation is limited to books that contain more than a passing reference to Carroll. I have used the *see index* notations when the references to Carroll were too diverse to identify adequately.

10. I have not recorded parodies, more "Alice" stories, retellings, substantially abridged versions, coloring books, recorded versions, published musical adaptations, and similarly related items. If I judged such an item to have special merit or appeal, I have included it in section D.

11. As is the standard practice, articles and notes in serial publications have been given separate entries; those in anthologies and *Festschriften* are listed following the bibliographical entry for the book in which they appear. However, in the cases of *Bandersnatch* (England) and the *Knight-Letter* (America), the periodic newsletters of the two major Carroll societies—newsletters that contain much valuable information about books, plays, films, and Carroll ephemera as well as news of the societies—I have not listed each note separately. I have simply listed the newsletters annually; although in rare instances, particularly significant notes are also entered separately.

12. Throughout this checklist I have tried to give unusually full bibliographical entries. Although it is not standard practice to include volume numbers for weekly serial publications, I have often included the number, since I found it useful and sometimes necessary when tracking down many publications in this listing. Similarly, I have often included numbers and months for scholarly journals when volume and year are all that is normally required. I have not used abbreviations for titles, except in two cases: I have used the standard abbreviation *WMG* when citing cross-references in *The Lewis Carroll Handbook,* and I have used *JJLCS* to designate *Jabberwocky: The Journal of the Lewis Carroll Society* (England), including the years when it was subtitled *The Lewis Carroll Society Magazine* (1969–72). I trust the reader will forgive me for the very rare instances when I was unable to com-

plete an entry (e.g., lacking a page or volume number). This usually resulted from working with clippings or notes in one of the many libraries and collections that I used or with those sent to me from contributors around the world.

13. I have tried to ensure that current standard transliteration and romanization practices have been observed. Since much of this work was performed by correspondents abroad, however, I cannot attest to its complete accuracy. In some instances the bibliographical information came to me in a translated form. I have entered the material in that form, noting its original language.

14. Throughout I have tried to make my annotations descriptive and not evaluative.

15. When writing about Carroll or cataloguing his works, one must choose repeatedly between his real name, Charles Lutwidge Dodgson, and his pseudonym. Since it is Lewis Carroll that is famous—like George Eliot and Mark Twain—Lewis Carroll is used throughout this work to denote the man and the artist. Occasionally, however, it has been necessary to make a critical distinction between Carroll and Dodgson.

*Annotated International Bibliography*
1960–77

# Section A. *Primary Works*

## 1960

**A60:1]** *Alice's Adventures in Wonderland* and *Through the Looking-Glass.* Illustrations by John Tenniel. Foreword by Horace Gregory. (Signet Classics.) New York: New American Library; London: New English Library, 1960. Pp. 238, hardcover and paperback.

Frequent reprintings: 1962 (3rd), 1964.

**A60:2]** *Alice's Adventures in Wonderland.* Illustrations by John Tenniel. London: Sir Isaac Pitman & Sons, Ltd., 1960. Pp. 154.

The 7th impression of a shorthand version first published in 1909—the so-called New Era Edition.

**A60:3]** *The Humorous Verse of Lewis Carroll.* With illustrations by John Tenniel and others. New York: Dover, 1960 (paperback); London: Peter Smith [1961] (hardcover). Pp. 445.

Reprint of *The Collected Verse of Lewis Carroll* first published in 1932 by Macmillan, London, copyright 1933 (*WMG* 306).
   Reprinted: New York: Dover; London: Constable, 1973, paperback.
   Reviewed by: Anne Clark, *JJLCS,* 2, No. 3 (Autumn 1973), 7; Peter Conrad, *New Statesman,* 86, No. 2231 (21 December 1973), 946.

**A60:4]** *Lewis Carroll's Alice in Wonderland and other favorites.* Illustrations by John Tenniel. New York: Washington Square Press, 1960. Pp. xiv + 274, paperback.

Includes *Through the Looking-Glass* and *The Hunting of the Snark.* Edition first appeared in 1951.
   Frequently reprinted, including in 1963, 1965 (9th printing), and 1971.

**A60:5]** Baram, Bella, trans. *Aliza b'erez ha-pelaot.* Tel Aviv: Massadah, 1960. Pp. 87, illustrations.

Hebrew translation of *Alice in Wonderland.*

**A60:6]**  Bušyna, G., trans. *Alisa v krajini čudes.* Kiev, Ukrania: Rad. pis'mennik, 1960. Pp. 247, illustrations.

Ukranian translation of *Alice in Wonderland.*

**A60:7]**  Cunha de Giacomo, Maria Thereza, trans. *Alice no reino del espelho.* Illustrations by Oswaldo Storni. São Paulo: Melhoramentos, 1960. Pp. 137.

Portuguese translation of *Through the Looking-Glass.* Reprinted in 1961 (labeled 4th ed.), 1962, 1963, 1964, 1966 (still labeled 4th ed.), and 1971 (5th ed.).

**A60:8]**  Dragic, Nada, trans. *Alice in Wonderland.* Belgrade: Mlado Pokolenjo, 1960. Pp. 140.

Title and text in Croatian.

**A60:9]**  Echavarri, Luis, trans. *Aventuras de Alicia en el pais de las maravillas / Al otro lado del espejo y lo que vio Alicia alli.* 2nd ed. Illustrations by Chikie. Buenos Aires: Ediciones Peuser, 1960. Pp. 272.

Spanish translation of *Alice in Wonderland* and *Through the Looking-Glass.* Two books bound in one.

**A60:10]**  Erten, Azize, trans. *Alis harikalar ülkesinde.* 3rd ed. (Büyük Çocuk Kitaplari: 10.) Istanbul: Varlik Yayinevi, 1960. Pp. 119, illustrations, paperback.

Turkish translation of *Alice in Wonderland.* Translation appeared in 1943. Reprinted in 1961, 1967 (pp. 120).

**A60:11]**  Gardner, Martin, ed. *The Annotated Alice: Alice's Adventures in Wonderland and Through the Looking-Glass.* Illustrations by John Tenniel. Introduction and notes by Martin Gardner. New York: Clarkson N. Potter, 1960. Pp. 352.

Other English editions, usually with slight revisions, are: London: Anthony Blond, 1960, 1964 (revised); New York: Meridian [New American Library], 1963, paperback; Cleveland: World Publishing, 1963, 1968 (pp. 345), 1971; Harmondsworth, England: Penguin, 1967 (new edition), 1970 (revised), 1971, paperback; London: Nelson, 1975; New York: Bramhall House [a division of Clarkson N. Potter], [1962] © 1960.

Reviewed (all editions) by: Joseph Carroll, *Nation*, 190, No. 26 (25 June 1960), 556–58; Alan Pryce-Jones, *New York Herald Tribune Bookweek*, 17 July 1960, p. 1; Earle F. Walbridge, *Library Journal*, 85 (1960), 1794–95; Naomi Lewis, *Victorian Studies*, 4 (1960), 170–73; *Times Literary Supplement* (letters), 14 January 1965, p. 27, 28 January, p. 72, 18 February, p. 132, 1 April, p. 255, 6 May, p. 356, 9 September, p. 782; Naomi Lewis, *New Statesman*, 71 (20 May 1966), 741–42; Marghanita Laski, *Listener*, 74 (1967), 917, 919; Benny Green, *Spectator*, No. 7632 (5 October 1974), p. 439.

**A60:12]** Han, Nak-Wong, trans. *Alice in Wonderland*. In *Collection of World Juvenile Literature*. Illustrations by John Tenniel. Seoul: Kae Mong Sha, 1961, XII, 1–132.

Title and text in Korean. Volume also includes translations of Oscar Wilde's *The Happy Prince* and two short stories by Katherine Mansfield. Reprinted in 1962, 1963, 1966, and 1968 (12th ed.).

**A60:13]** Hüttenmoser, Anita, trans. *Alice im Wunderland*. 2nd ed. Illustrations by Robert Högfeldt. Stuttgart and Zurich: Artemis, 1960. Pp. 124.

German translation of *Alice in Wonderland*. Translation first copyrighted in 1947.

**A60:14]** Lobato, Monteiro, trans. *Alice no país das maravilhas*, 9th edition. São Paulo: Brasiliense, 1960. Pp. 143, illustrations.

Portuguese translation of *Alice in Wonderland*. Translation first appeared in 1931.

**A60:15]** Maghidson-Stepanova, G. K., trans. *Alice in Wonderland*. Leningrad: Publishing House of the Ministry of Education of the RSFSR, 1960. Pp. 76.

An English adaptation for the 6th form of English students; includes a vocabulary on pages 62–76.

**A60:16]** Maraja, ill. *Alice à travers le miroir*. Milan: Fabbri, 1960. Pp. 63, color illustrations.

French translation of *Through the Looking-Glass*. Abridged text.

**A60:17]** Olenič-Gnenenko, Aleksandr, trans. *Alisa v strane* *čudes*. Illustrations by A. G. Mosina. Rostovna-Donu, USSR: Rostovskoe knizhnoe izd-vo, 1960. Pp. 114.

Russian translation of *Alice in Wonderland*. This more or less literal translation first appeared in 1940 and was reprinted in 1946, 1958, 1960 (see next entry), and 1961.

**A60:18]** _____, trans. *Alisa v strane čudes.* Illustrations by V. Alfeevsky. Introduction by V. Vazhdaev. Moscow: Publishing House of Children's Literature, Ministry of Education, 1960. Pp. 143.

**A60:19]** Peake, Mervyn, illus. *The Hunting of the Snark.* London: The Reprint Society, 1960. Pp. 46.

Special issue of the edition first published in 1940 by Chatto & Windus, London.

**A60:20]** Pintong, Nilawan, ed. *Alice In Wonderland. Youth's Weekly* (Bangkok), 4, No. 203 (21 September 1959), 26f.: weekly until 8 February 1960.

Title and text in Thai. Translation published in twelve successive weeks; the same Tenniel illustration is repeated in each issue.

**A60:21]** Semenović, Luka, trans. *Alisa u zemlji čuda.* Belgrade: Mlado, 1960. Pp. 135.

Serbian translation of *Alice in Wonderland*. Translation appeared in 1951. Edition appeared in 1959 and was reprinted in 1963, 1964 (with much type reset), 1965 (3rd ed.), 1969 (4th ed.), and 1972.

**A60:22]** Soydaş, Leylâ, and Bige Atasagun, trans. *Alice (Alis) harikalar diyarinda.* Istanbul: Hamle Matbaasi, 1960. Pp. 90, illustrations.

Turkish translation of *Alice in Wonderland*. Reset and published in 1964 in Istanbul by Iyigün Yaÿinevi. Reprinted in 1965, 1966, and 1967 in paperback.

**A60:23]** Tanaka, Toshio, trans. *Fushigi no kuni no Arisu.* Illustrations by John Tenniel. Tokyo: Iwanami Shoten, 1960. Pp. 213.

Japanese translation of *Alice in Wonderland* aimed at fifth and sixth classes of elementary school. Translation first appeared in 1955. Volume 95 of Iwanami's Children's Library. Reprinted in 1968, seventeenth printing in 1973.

**A60:24]** Thomas, M. W., and G. Thomas, eds. *Alice's Adventures in Wonderland*. Illustrations by Lewis Carroll and Douglas Hall. (Junior Classics.) London: Hutchinson, 1960. Pp. 96.

Abbreviated text.


# 1961


**A61:1]**  *Alice in Wonderland: Comprising the two books / Alice's Adventures in Wonderland and Through the Looking-Glass.* Illustrations by John Tenniel with ten color plates by Donald E. Cook. New York: Holt, Rinehart and Winston, 1961. Pp. xii + 276.

Reprint of the edition published in 1923 and 1957.

**A61:2]**  *Alice In Wonderland.* Illustrations by John Tenniel. New York: Scholastic Book Services, 1966. Pp. 159, paperback, brown-and-black illustrations. Misplaced; see A66:3.

**A61:3]**  *Alice in Wonderland.* Illustrations by Lewis Carroll. Prefatory note by Roger Lancelyn Green. (Everyman Paperback.) London: Dent; New York: Dutton, 1961. Pp. 111, paperback.

A portion first appeared in the Everyman series in 1929. Preface first added in 1961 paperback edition. Reprinted in 1966, 1972, 1974, and in 1976 with an updated bibliographical note.
    Reviewed by Anne Clark, *JJLCS,* 2, No. 3 (Autumn 1973), 9.

**A61:4]**  *Alice in Wonderland.* London: The Children's Press, 1961. Pp. 152, illustrations [Harry Roundtree].

Often reprinted.

**A61:5]**  *Alice's Adventures in Wonderland.* Illustrations by John

Tenniel. London: Folio Society, 1961. Pp. 113, line drawings in red, slipcase.

**A61:6]** *Alice's Adventures in Wonderland / Through the Looking-Glass.* Illustrations by John Tenniel, eight redrawn in colour by Diana Stanley. (Children's Illustrated Classics.) London: Dent; New York: Dutton, 1961. Pp. 246.

Edition first appeared in 1954. Reprinted in 1966, 1972 (in an imitation leather binding), 1975 (as a Janson Book), and reissued by Dent in 1977 as part of their paperback series "A Children's Illustrated Classics Paperback."

**A61:7]** *The Complete Works of Lewis Carroll.* Illustrations by John Tenniel. Introduction by Alexander Woollcott. (Nonesuch Library.) Chester Springs, Pennsylvania: Dufour, 1961. Pp. xiv + 1165.

Reissue of 1939 edition published by Random House in New York and the Nonesuch Press in London (*WMG* 313). *The Complete Works of Lewis Carroll* was first published in 1936 by the Modern Library, New York, and reprinted in 1937 by Random House, New York.

Other reprints: London: The Nonsense Press, 1966. Pp. xiv + 1165 (1939 ed.); New York: The Modern Library, n.d. [196?]. Pp. xiii + 1293 (1936 ed.); New York: Vintage, 1976. Pp. xvi + 1293, paperback (1936 ed.); the 1936 edition was also reprinted in England by Wildwood House in 1973, but this edition was withdrawn due to copyright infringement.

**A61:8]** *Liisa ihmemaassa.* Helsinki: Kynäbaari, [1961]. Pp. 114, illustrations.

Finnish translation of *Alice in Wonderland.*

**A61:9]** *Through the Looking-Glass and what Alice found there / The Hunting of the Snark.* (Dolphin Books.) Garden City, New York: Doubleday, 1961.

**A61:10]** Aardweg, Ankie, trans. *Alice in Wonderland.* Amsterdam: Van Holkema en Warendorf, 1961. Pp. 113, illustrations.

In Dutch.

**A61:11]** Afezolli, Maqo, trans. *Liza në botën e çudirave.* Illustrations by John Tenniel. Introduction by Bedri Dedja. Tiranë, Albania: N. I. Sh. Shtyp, [1961]. Pp. 143, paperback.

Albanian translation of *Alice in Wonderland.*

**A61:12]**  Backhouse, G. W., illus. *Alice in Wonderland.* London and Glasgow: Collins, 1961. Pp. 128.

Reprint of earlier edition.

**A61:13]**  Bay, André, trans. *Alice au pays des merveilles. De l'autre côté du miroir.* Illustrations by Sempé. Preface by André Maurois. Paris: Club du libraire, 1961. Pp. 271 + xvi.

French translation of *Alice in Wonderland* and *Through the Looking-Glass.* Bay's first translation of *Alice* appeared in 1948, and his first translation of *Through the Looking-Glass* (with H. Parisot) appeared in 1949.

**A61:14]**  Ch'üan, Fan, trans. *Alice in Wonderland.* Illustrations by John Tenniel and others. Hong Kong: Jih-hsin Book Co., 1961. Pp. 86.

Title and text in Chinese. Reprint of earlier edition. Reprinted in 1967 in paperback by Daily News Book Store, Hong Kong.

**A61:15]**  Collingwood, Stuart Dodgson, ed. *Diversions and Digressions of Lewis Carroll.* New York: Dover; London: Constable, 1961. Pp. xiv + 375, paperback.

Modern reprint of *The Lewis Carroll Picture Book* published in London in 1899 by T. Fisher Urwin *(WMG 287).*

Another reprint without alteration: *The Lewis Carroll Picture Book: A Selection from the Unpublished Writings and Drawings of Lewis Carroll, Together with Reprints from Scarce and Unacknowledged Work:* Detroit: Gale, 1971. Pp. xv + 375.

The Dover edition was subsequently reprinted as *The Unknown Lewis Carroll: Eight Major Works and Many Minor* with thirty-four photographic portraits taken by Carroll and now in the Parrish Collection at Princeton University added to an otherwise unaltered text.

**A61:16]**  Ema, Shoko, trans. *Fushigi no kuni no Arisu.* Illustrations by Taizo. (Jido Meisaku Zenshu No. 37.) Tokyo: Kaiseisha, 1961. Pp. [6] + 190 + [6], part color illustrations.

Japanese translation of *Alice In Wonderland*. Volume 37 of "Collection of Masterpieces for Children."
Reprinted in 1963, 1964, and 1971.

**A61:17]** Garg, Kishor, trans. *Achraj lok*. Illustrations by John Tenniel, except for frontispiece & title page. 3rd ed. Delhi: Rani Prakashan, 1961. Pp. 80.

Hindi translation of *Alice in Wonderland*. Translation first appeared in 1956. Sixth edition, 1965.

**A61:18]** Gülsoy, M. Z., trans. *Aynalar dünyasi: Alis' in başka serüvenleri*. (Çocuk klâsikerie: 44.) Istanbul: Varlik Yayinevi, 1961. Pp. 53, illustrations, paperback.

Turkish translation of *Alice in Wonderland*. Reprinted in 1966.

**A61:19]** Inove, Hideko, trans. *Fushigi no kuni no Arisu*. Illustrations by John Tenniel. Tokyo: Kaibun-Sha, 1961. Pp. 235, paperback.

Japanese translation of *Alice in Wonderland*. English / Japanese parallel text. The English version is annotated.

**A61:20]** Lobato, Monteiro, trans. *Alice no país do espelho*. 3rd ed. Illustrations by John Tenniel. São Paulo: Brasiliense, 1961. Pp. 134.

Portuguese translation of *Through the Looking-Glass*.

**A61:21]** Mu-yün, Huang, trans. *Alice in Wonderland*. Hong Kong: Friendly Book Co., 1961.

Title and text in Chinese.

**A61:22]** Olenič-Gnenenko, Aleksandr, trans. *Alisa v strane čudes*. Illustrations by V. V. Vasilieff. Habarovsk, Siberia: Khabarovskoe knizhnoe izd-vo, 1961. Pp. 135.

Russian translation of *Alice in Wonderland*. Translation first appeared in 1940.

**A61:23]** Papy, Jacques, trans. *Alice au pays des merveilles / Ce* *qu'Alice trouva de l'autre côté du miroir.* Illustrations by John Tenniel. Paris: J. J. Pauvert, 1961. Pp. [x] + 457 + [v].

French translation of *Alice in Wonderland* and *Through the Looking-Glass.*
  Reprinted in Paris: Secle-Régine Deforges, 1977. Pp. 457, paperback.

**A61:24]**  P'ei, Wang, ed. *Alice in Wonderland.* Hong Kong: Tsin Hsiu Press, 1961. Pp. 93.

Abridged English version with notes in Chinese and a vocabulary.

**A61:25]**  Roundtree, Harry, illus. *Alice in Wonderland and Bruno's Revenge.* London: Thomas Nelson & Sons Ltd., 1961. Pp. 158.

Twentieth reprint of the edition first published in 1925. Includes two essays (anonymous) "On thinking it over" and "The writer of the stories."

**A61:26]**  St. Lo Conan Davies, E. V., trans. *Elisi katika nchi ya ajabu.* London: Sheldon Press, 1961. Pp. 111 + [i], illustrations, paperback.

Swahili translation of *Alice in Wonderland.* New impression offset from 1940 first edition. Reprinted in 1965, 1966. Translator subsequently listed as St. Lo De Malet.

**A61:27]**  Singh, Samšer Bahadur, trans. *Äscharya lokmen Alice.* Illustrations by John Tenniel. Delhi: Rajkamal Prakasăn, 1961. Pp. 160, hardcover deluxe edition.

Hindi translation of *Alice in Wonderland.*

**A61:28]**  Skoumalovi, Aloys and Hana, trans. *Alenka y kraji divů a za zrcadlem.* Illustrations by Dagmar Berková. Afterword by Adolph Hoffmeister. Prague: Státni nakladatelstvi dětské kniby, 1961. Pp. 245, part color illustrations.

Czech translation of *Alice in Wonderland* and *Through the Looking-Glass.*

**A61:29]**  Soper, Eileen A., illus. *Alice in Wonderland.* London: George G. Harrap and Company Ltd., 1961. Pp. 128.

Fourth reprint of an edition first published in 1948.

**A61:30]**    Temkov, Slavčho, trans. *Alisa vo zemjata na čudata.* Skopje, Yugoslavia: Kultura, 1961. Pp. 111.

Macedonian translation of *Alice in Wonderland.*

**A61:31]**    Tsuchiya, Yukio, trans. *Fushigi no kuni no Arisu.* Tokyo: Kaiseisha, 1961. Pp. 117–221, cream-and-tan illustrations.

Japanese translation of *Alice in Wonderland.* Volume (pp. 230) includes *Peter Pan* and an essay on Barrie and Carroll, pages 222–30. Reprinted in 1964.

**A61:32]**    Vera, Pilar, trans. *Alicia en el país del espejo.* Illustrations by Maika. Barcelona: Mateu, 1961. Pp. 207, paperback.

Spanish translation of *Through the Looking-Glass.*

**A61:33]**    Vyas, Kant, trans. *Alice in Wonderland.* 3rd ed. Delhi: Rajpal & Sons, 1961. Pp. 95, illustrations in gray, blue, and white.

Hindi translation of *Alice in Wonderland.* A 96-page edition entirely reset but apparently using the same woodblocks for the illustrations was subsequently published in Delhi by Shiksha Bharati in 1968 in paperback.

**A61:34]**    Yakobovitch, A. L. *Alisa b'erez ha-pelaot.* Illustrations by A. Shrberk. Tel-Aviv: Isreel Publishing House, 1961. Pp. 74.

Hebrew translation of *Alice in Wonderland.* Translation first appeared in 1951.
    This is a reprint of the 1951 edition in a larger format, due to wider margins. Reprinted in 1968.

## 1962

**A62:1]**    *Alice's Adventures in Wonderland.* Illustrations by John Tenniel. London: Macmillan; New York: St. Martin's, 1962. Pp. xii + 206, part color illustrations.

Reprint of the 1927 children's edition; reprinted in 1965, 1967, 1972, 1974, and in 1977 in a slipcase with A62:6.

**A62:2]**   *Alice's Adventures in Wonderland / Through the Looking-Glass.* Illustrations by John Tenniel. Introduction by Louis Untermeyer. New York: Collier; London: Collier-Macmillan, 1962. Pp. 317, paperback.

Reprinted in 1966 (3rd), 1967 (4th), and 1975 (9th).

**A62:3]**   *Alice's Adventures in Wonderland / Through the Looking-Glass.* Illustrations by John Tenniel. Introduction by Eleanor Graham. (Puffin Books.) Harmondsworth: Penguin, 1962. Pp. 347, paperback.

First combined paperback edition of the *Alice* books by Penguin. Reprinted in 1963, 1965, 1966, 1968, 1970, 1971, 1972, 1973, 1974, 1975 (2x).

**A62:4]**   *Fushigi no kuni no Arisu.* Tokyo: Kodansha, 1962, pp. 6–82, part color illustrations.

Japanese translation of *Alice in Wonderland.* Volume (pp. 170) also includes *Dog of Flanders.*

**A62:5]**   *Through the Looking-Glass and what Alice found there.* Illustrations by John Tenniel. London: Folio Society, 1962. Pp. 131, line drawings in red.

**A62:6]**   *Through the Looking-Glass and what Alice found there.* Illustrations by John Tenniel. London: Macmillan; New York: St. Martin's, 1962. Pp. xv + 236, color plates.

Reprint of the 1927 Children's Edition; reprinted in 1965, 1968 (new printing), 1975, and 1977 in a slipcase with A62:1.

**A62:7]**   Aragon, Louis, trans. *La chasse au snark.* Paris: Seghers, 1962. Pp. 69 + [iii], paperback.

French translation of *The Hunting of the Snark.* Translation first appeared in 1929.

**A62:8]**   Buljan, Prevela Mira, trans. *Alica s onu stranu ogledala.* Illustrations by Goranka Vrus Murtić. Zagreb, Yugoslavia: Mladost, 1962. Pp. 108.

Croatian translation of *Through the Looking-Glass.*

**A62:9]** Gardner, Martin, ed. *The Annotated Snark: The Full Text of Lewis Carroll's Great Nonsense Epic "The Hunting of the Snark" and the Original Illustrations by Henry Holiday.* New York: Simon and Schuster. Pp. 111.

Other English editions are: New York: Bramhall House, n.d.; Harmondsworth, England: Penguin Books, 1967 (new edition), 1973 (pp. 126) 1975, paperback.

  Reviewed (all editions) by: Burton A. Robie, *Library Journal,* 87 (1962), 3457; *Saturday Review,* 6 October 1962, p. 41; William Jay Smith, *New York Times Book Review,* 18 November 1962, p. 26; *Times Literary Supplement,* 15 February 1963, p. 111; Jean Gattégno, *Etudes Anglaises,* 17 (1964), 199–201.

**A62:10]** Halano, K., H. Hamada, and H[avako] Muraoka. *Fushigi no kuni no Arisu.* Illustrations by Sige. Tokyo: Shogaku-Kan, 1962, pp. 79–140.

Japanese translation of *Alice in Wonderland.* Volume (pp. 253) contains *Treasure Island, Peter Pan,* and a story by Oscar Wilde.

**A62:11]** Honda, Akira, trans. *Fushigi no kuni no Arisu.* Illustrations by Kuma. Tokyo: Kodansha, 1962, pp. 9–94.

Japanese translation of *Alice in Wonderland.* Volume (pp. 437) also contains *The Wind in the Willows, Pigeon Post, Mary Poppins in the Park,* and *Sambo and the Snow Mountains.*

**A62:12]** Maghidson-Stepanova, G. K., ed. *Alice in Wonderland.* Peking: Commercial Press, 1962. Pp. 74.

Abridged English version with notes in Chinese and a vocabulary.

**A62:13]** Oven-van Doorn, M. C., trans. *Alice's Avonturen in Wonderland.* 5th ed. The Hague: Van Goor, 1962. Pp. 120, illustrations.

Dutch translation of *Alice's Adventures in Wonderland.* Translation first appeared in 1952. Reprinted in 1965 (6th ed.), 1967.

**A62:14]** Parisot, Henri, trans. *La chasse au snark.* Illustrations by Henry Holiday. Paris: J. J. Pauvert, 1962. Pp. 81 + [iii].

French translation of *The Hunting of the Snark.* Limited edition of 1,999 numbered copies, 1–30 on Pur Fil du Marais.

**A62:15]**　Strasser, Ingrid, trans. *Alice im Wunderland.* Illustrations by Brigitte Seelbach-Caspari. Wiesbaden and Berlin: Vollmer, 1962. Pp. 154 + ii.

German translation of *Alice in Wonderland.*

**A62:16]**　Sugathadāsa, K. B., trans. *Älis dutu vismalantaya.* Colombo: M. D. Gunasēna and Co., 1962. Pp. 94, illustrations, paperback.

Singalese translation of *Alice in Wonderland.* Reprinted in 1970 and 1971.

**A62:17]**　Valente, Marina, trans. *La meravigliosa Alice.* Illustrations by John Tenniel. Preface by Oreste Del Buono. Milan: Area Editore, 1962. Pp. 166.

Contains an Italian translation of *Alice's Adventures in Wonderland;* translations into Italian by Del Buono of selected Carroll letters to his child friends; background essays on Carroll's life and world (with illustrations); excerpted "testimonials," in Italian, by André Breton, Walter de la Mare, Henri Parisot, A. L. Taylor and Martin Gardner.

**A62:18]**　Walsh, David, and John Cooper, illus. *Alice in Wonderland* and *Through the Looking-Glass.* London: Ward, Lock & Co., 1962. Pp. 224.

**A62:19]**　Wong, Tsu Pei. *Alice in Wonderland / Through the Looking-Glass.* Taipei: Ta Chung Shu Chü, 1962. Pp. 283, illustrations for *Alice in Wonderland* only.

Chinese translations of *Alice in Wonderland* and *Through the Looking-Glass* printed in both ideographs and phonetic symbols.

# 1963

**A63:1]**　*Alice im Wunderland.* Munich: Südwest, [1963]. Pp. 142, part color illustrations.

German translation of *Alice in Wonderland.*

**A63:2]**  *Alice in Wonderland* and *Through the Looking-Glass*. Illustrations by John Tenniel. New York: Grosset & Dunlap, [1963]. Pp. 278.

Bound back-to-back with *Five Little Peppers*.

**A63:3]**  *Alice in Wonderland*. Illustrations by Lewis Carroll. Introduction by Guy Pocock. (Kings Treasures of Literature.) London: J. M. Dent, 1963. Pp. 192.

A reprint of an edition first published in 1930. Includes *The Hunting of the Snark* and several poems from *Sylvie and Bruno*. Often reprinted.

**A63:4]**  *Alice's Adventures in Wonderland / Through the Looking-Glass*. Illustrations by John Tenniel. Afterword by Clifton Fadiman. New York: Macmillan; London: Collier-Macmillan, 1963. Pp. xiii + 125, ix + 148, part color drawings.

Third printing in 1966.

**A63:5]**  *Alice's Adventures in Wonderland / Through the Looking-Glass*. Illustrations by John Tenniel. *The Hunting of the Snark*. (A Nonesuch Cygnet.) London: Nonesuch, 1963; New York: Frederick Watts, 1964. Pp. 292.

Reprinted in 1966; also reprinted in 1974 under the Bodley Head imprint, London.

**A63:6]**  *Circular Billiards, for Two Players*. [Cambridge, Mass.], 1963.

Broadside "Printed in this 3rd edition . . . by the Adams & Lowell House printers."

**A63:7]**  Ardanvy, José, trans. *Alicia en el país de las maravillas*. Illustrations by A. Buyll. Bilbao, Spain: Vasco Americana, 1963. Pp. 123.

Spanish translation of *Alice in Wonderland*.

**A63:8]**  Bay, André, trans. *Alice au pays des merveilles et De l'autre côté du miroir*. Illustrations by John Tenniel. Introduction by André Maurois. (Marabout géant illustré.) Verviers, Belgium: Gérard, 1963. Pp. 320, paperback.

French translation of *Alice in Wonderland* and *Through the Looking-Glass*. Bay's first translation of *Alice* appeared in 1948, and his first translation of *Through the Looking-Glass* (with H. Parisot) appeared in 1949. Reprinted in 1975.

**A63:9]** Bossi, Elda, trans. *Alice nello specchio*. Illustrations by John Tenniel. Milan: Bompiani, 1963. Pp. 170 + [vi], paperback.

Italian translation of *Through the Looking-Glass*. Contains brief introduction. Reprinted as a paperback in 1968.

**A63:10]** ———, trans. *Alice nel paese delle meraviglie*. Illustrations by John Tenniel. Milan: Bompiani, 1963. Pp. 155 + v, paperback.

Italian translation of *Alice in Wonderland*.

**A63:11]** Chih-Ken, Lin, trans. and annotator. *Alice's Adventures in Wonderland*. Hong Kong: The English Language Publishing Co., [1963?]. Pp. 143, illustrations, paperback.

Bilingual edition with English on left and Chinese on right; annotations in Chinese. Edition first appeared in 1945. Reprinted in 1965.

**A63:12]** Das Neves, Primavera, trans. *Alice no país das maravilhas*. Illustrations by Maria Barrera. Rio de Janeiro: Bruguera, 1963. Pp. 255 + vi.

Portuguese translation of *Alice in Wonderland*. Reprinted in 1966.

**A63:13]** De Rosa, Francesco, trans. *Le avventure di Alice. Nel paese delle meraviglie / Attraverso lo specchio*. Illustrations by Grazia Accardo. Milan: Mursia, 1963. Pp. 224, color illustrations.

Italian translation of *Alice's Adventures in Wonderland* and *Through the Looking-Glass*. Reprinted in 1971, 1973.

**A63:14]** Edagawa, Masayoshi, trans. *Fushigi no kuni no Arisu*. Illustrations by Yoshi Shibahara. Tokyo: Nihon-Shobo, 1963. Pp. 174.

Japanese translation of *Alice in Wonderland.*

**A63:15]**   Enzensberger, Christian, trans. *Alice im Wunderland /
Alice hinter den Spiegeln.* Illustrations by Lewis Carroll. Frankfurt
am Main: Insel, 1963. Pp. 265.

German translation of *Alice in Wonderland* and *Through the Looking-Glass.* Reprinted in 1965.
  Reviewed by Rudolph Walter Leonhart, *Die Zeit,* 6 December 1963, p. 19.

**A63:16]**   Folon, Jean-Michel, illus. *Alice in Wonderland.* In *England in Literature.* (Taming of the Shrew Edition.) Glenview, Illinois: Scott, Foresman, 1963, pp. 439–88. Color illustrations.

Reprinted in 1968 and 1973. Previously published in 1953 and 1957. Contains
annotations.

**A63:17]**   Gerili, Stefania, trans. *Alice nel paese delle meraviglie.* 3rd
ed. Illustrations by B. Bodini. Milan: AMZ, 1963. Pp. 104, color
illustrations.

Italian translation of *Alice in Wonderland.* Reprinted in 1972 (4th ed.) and in
1974 in a 116-page edition.

**A63:18]**   Håkanson, Eva, trans. *Alice i spegellandet.* Illustrations
by John Tenniel and another. Stockholm: Natur o. kultur, 1963.
Pp. v + 163.

Swedish translation of *Through the Looking-Glass.* Uniform with *Alice i underlandet,* 1959.

**A63:19]**   Hung, Yen-Ch'iu. *Alice in Wonderland.* Taipei: Oriental
Publishing Company, 1963.

Title and text in Chinese. Phonetic representation next to each chapter. Reprinted in 1971.

**A63:20]**   Koroshi, Vaso, trans. *I Liza ston paraxeno kosmo.* Ti-
rana, Albania: Naim Frashëri, 1963. Pp. 170.

Greek translation of *Alice in Wonderland.*

**A63:21]**   Kume, Minoru, trans. *Fushigi no kuni no Arisu.* Illustrations by Suzushi Yaguruma. Tokyo: Kaisei-Sha, 1963. Pp. 156.

Japanese translation of *Alice in Wonderland*.

**A63:22]**   Leone, Sergio, illus. *Alice in Wonderland*. [USA]: Wonder Books, 1963. Pp. 159, paperback.

Text slightly abridged.
   Reprinted in England by Golden Pleasure Books, 1966.

**A63:23]**   Maaløe, Christopher, trans. *Snarkejagten*. Copenhagen: Schønbergske, 1963. Pp. 77, paperback.

Danish translation of *The Hunting of the Snark*. Bilingual edition with Danish and English on facing pages.

**A63:24]**   Maraja, illus. *Alice in Wonderland*. New York: Duell, Sloan and Pearce, 1963. Pp. 110, color illustrations.

Reprint of 1957 edition published by Grosset & Dunlap, New York.

**A63:25]**   Marti, Maria, trans. *Alicia en el país de las maravillas*. Illustrations by Maria Barrera. Barcelona: Brugera, 1963. Pp. 255 + [i].

Spanish translation / adaptation of *Alice in Wonderland*. Translation first appeared in 1955. Reprinted in 1965, 1966.

**A63:26]**   Marx, Stan, trans. *Jabberwocky*. [New York: Typographic Designers, 1963]. Pp. [4].

"Jabberwocky" with parallel text in Shaw's alphabet on facing pages. Limited to 50 numbered copies.

**A63:27]**   Nakagawa, Makoto, trans. *Fushigi no kuni no Arisu*. Tokyo: Nihon Shobo, 1963. Pp. 232, illustrations.

Japanese translation of *Alice in Wonderland*.

**A63:28]**   Ohsato, Tadash, ed. *Alice in Wonderland*. Tokyo: Gakusei-Sha, 1963. Pp. 89.

English edition with extensive Japanese notes.

**A63:29]**   Robinson, Normy, illus. *Alice in Wonderland*. Glasgow

& London: Children's Press, 1963. Pp. 156.

Subsequent impressions in 1965, 1971, and 1974.

**A63:30]**   Shiraki, S., I. Ando, and N. Yanami, trans. *Fushigi no kuni no Arisu*. Tokyo: Kodansha, 1963, pp. 283–397, illustrations.

Japanese translation of *Alice in Wonderland*. Volume (pp. 414) includes *Treasure Island* and tales from Shakespeare.

**A63:31]**   Shozo, Katayama, trans. *Fushigi no kuni no Arisu*. Tokyo: Popura-Sha, 1963. Pp. 146, part color illustrations.

Japanese translation of *Alice in Wonderland* containing phonetic symbols with a few ideographs painted with phonetic symbols.

**A63:32]**   Tsubota, G., and H[anako] Muraoko, trans. *Fushigi no kuni Arisu*. Tokyo: Sanjiu-Shobo, 1963, pp. 1–72, illustrations.

Japanese translation of *Alice in Wonderland*. Volume (pp. 136) contains other stories. No. 9 on spine.

**A63:33]**   Virgili, José, trans. *Alícia en el país de las maravillas*. Illustrations by Adrienne Ségur. Mexico City: Renacimiento, 1963. Pp. 119, part color illustrations.

Spanish translation of *Alice in Wonderland* from French [Flammarion, 1949]. Second edition of 1959 publication.

## 1964

**A64:1]**   *Alice i underlandet / Alice i spegellandet*. Udevalla, Sweden: International Book Automation, 1964. Pp. 123.

Swedish translation of *Alice in Wonderland* and *Through the Looking-Glass*.

**A64:2]**   *Alice's Adventures in Wonderland / Through the Looking-Glass*. Illustrations by John Tenniel. New York: Parents' Magazine Press, 1964. Pp. 158.

**A64:3]**  *Alice's Adventures Under Ground: A Facsimile of the Original Lewis Carroll Manuscript.* Introduction by Luther H. Evans. Ann Arbor, Michigan: University Microfilms, 1964. Pp. [x] + 91, slipcase.

**A64:4]**  Appleton, Honor C., illus. *The Children's Alice in Wonderland.* London: George G. Harrap, 1964. Pp. 96.

An abridgement by F. H. Lee. First published in January 1936, and frequently since.

**A64:5]**  Barberá, Manuel, trans. *Alicia en el país de las maravillas,* 7th ed. Illustrations by Martinez Parma. Buenos Aires: Acmé, 1964. Pp. 224.

Spanish translation of *Alice in Wonderland.* Translation first appeared in 1949. Reprinted in 1967.

**A64:6]**  Buwalda, M., trans. *De Avonturen van Alice in Wonderland.* Illustrations by Maraja. Antwerp: J. J. Tijl, Zwolle, 1964. Pp. 60.

Dutch translation of *Alice's Adventures in Wonderland.*

**A64:7]**  Carruthers, Clive Harcourt, trans. *Alicia in Terra Mirabili.* New York: St Martin's; London: Macmillan, 1964. Pp. 116.

Latin translation of *Alice in Wonderland.*

Reprinted: 's-Grav, Netherlands: Van Goor, 1965, with Dutch glossary facing page 116.

Reviewed by: *Times Literary Supplement,* 8 October 1964, p. 925; John F. Gummere, *Classical World,* 58 (1964 / 65), 92–93; H. C. Schnure, *Classical Journal,* 65 (1965), 378.

**A64:8]**  Colles, Dorothy, illus. *Alice's Adventures in Wonderland / Through the Looking-Glass and Other Writings.* Introduction by Robin Deniston. London and Glasgow: Collins, 1964. Pp. 320.

Reprint of 1954 edition. See A75:8.

**A64:9]**  Cunha De Giacomo, Maria Thereza, trans. *Alice no país das meravilhas.* 6th ed. Illustrations by Oswaldo Storni. São

Paulo: Melhoramentos, 1964. Pp. 137, part color illustrations.

Portuguese translation of *Alice in Wonderland*. Reprinted in 1968.

**A64:10]**    Elfelt, Kjeld, trans. *Alice i eventryland og bag spejlet.* Copenhagen: Spektrum, 1964. Pp. 314, illustrations.

Danish translation of *Alice in Wonderland* and *Through the Looking-Glass*. Elfelt's translations first appeared in 1946.

**A64:11]**    Flon, Luz Maria Ojeda, trans. *Alicia en el país de las maravillas*. 4th ed. Illustrations by John Tenniel. Mexico City: Diana, 1964. Pp. 144, paperback.

Spanish translation of *Alice in Wonderland*. Translation first appeared in 1953. Reprinted in 1971; sixth printing 1972.

**A64:12]**    _____, trans. *Alicia a través del espejo*. 3rd ed. Mexico City: Diana, 1964. Pp. 165 + [iii].

Spanish translation of *Through the Looking-Glass*. Translation first appeared in 1953.

**A64:13]**    Garib, Iraj, trans. *Alis dar sar zamin-e-a jayeb*. (Golden Books No. 39.) Teheran: Amirkabir Publisher Talai Books / Cavin Press, 1964. Pp. 38, illustrations.

Abridged *Alice in Wonderland* in Farsi. Reprinted in 1966 and 1967 (2nd ed.).

**A64:14]**    Jurkić-Sunjić, Mira, trans. *Alisa u zemlji čudesa*. Zagreb: Mladost, 1964. Pp. 114, illustrations.

Croatian translation of *Alice in Wonderland*. Reprint of 1959 edition. Third edition (138 pages) published in 1969, 4th edition in 1972.

**A64:15]**    Mulder, Tiny, trans. *Alice yn Wûnderlân*. Illustrations by John Tenniel. Introduction by Tiny Mulder. Drachten, Netherlands: Laverman, 1964. Pp. 119, paperback in case.

Frisian translation of *Alice in Wonderland*.

**A64:16]**    Nasser, Paulo, trans. *Alice no país das maravilhas*. Illustrations by Ramon Hespanha. Rio de Janeiro: Vecchi, 1964. Pp. 61.

Portuguese translation of *Alice in Wonderland*.

**A64:17]**   Penalva, Bosch, trans. *Alice in Wonderland*. Illustrations by Maria Barrera. Brussels: D.A.P. Reinaert Uitgaven; Netherlands: G. S. Degens, 1964. Pp. 216.

Dutch translation. Reprinted in 1967.

**A64:18]**   Reedijk, C., and Alfred Kossmann, trans. *De Avonturen van Alice*. 4th ed. Illustrations by John Tenniel. Rotterdam: Ad Donker, 1964. Pp. 304.

Dutch translation of *Alice's Adventures in Wonderland* and *Through the Looking-Glass*. Translation of *Alice in Wonderland* first appeared in 1947 and *Through the Looking-Glass* in 1949. Reprinted in 1966 (5th ed.), 1968, 1971 (6th ed.), 1972, 1973 (7th ed.), 1975 (8th ed.), and 1977 (9th ed.).

**A64:19]**   Rouillard, Henriette, trans. *Alice au pays des merveilles*. Paris: Delagrave, 1964. Pp. 158, illustrations.

French translation of *Alice in Wonderland*. Translation first appeared in 1935.

**A64:20]**   _____, trans. *Alice à travers le miroir*. Paris: Delagrave, 1964. Pp. 158, illustrations.

French translation of *Through the Looking-Glass*. Translation first appeared in 1935.

**A64:21]**   Semenović, Luka, trans. *Alisa u zemlji čuda*. Illustrations by Marko Krsmanović. Belgrade: Mlado Pokolenje, 1964. Pp. 115.

Serbian translation of *Alice in Wonderland*. Translation appeared in 1951.

**A64:22]**   _____, trans. *Alisa u zemlji i za ogledala*. Illustrations by Viktorija Bregovljanin. Belgrade: Mlado Pokolenje, 1964. Pp. 152.

Serbian translation of *Through the Looking-Glass*.

**A64:23]**   Taback, Simms, illus. *Jabberwocky and More Nonsense.* (A Harlin Quist Book.) New York: Dell, 1964. Pp. [63], color illustrations.

Reprinted in 1967 by Crown Publishers in New York and in England in 1967 by Quist as *"Jabberwocky" and other Frabjous Nonsense;* also published in England by W. H. Allen & Co.

**A64:24]**   Valori-Piperno, Adriana, trans. *Attraverso lo specchio magico.* Turin: Soc. Editrice Internazione, 1964. Pp. 80, color illustrations.

Italian translation of *Through the Looking-Glass.*

**A64:25]**   Yokotami, Teru, trans. *Fushigi no kuni no Arisu.* Tokyo: Popura-Sha, 1964. Pp. 158, part color illustrations.

Japanese translation of *Alice in Wonderland.*

## 1965

**A65:1]**   *Alice in Wonderland.* Illustrations by John Tenniel and Charles Mozley. (Caxton Junior Classics.) London: The Caxton Publishing Co., 1965. Pp. 225.

Includes *Alice's Adventures in Wonderland* and *Through the Looking-Glass.*

**A65:2]**   *Alice in Wonderland / Through the Looking-Glass.* Illustrations by John Tenniel. Introduction by C. L. Bennet. (Airmont Classics Series C179.) New York: Airmont, 1965. Pp. 256, paperback.

**A65:3]**   *Alice in Wonderland / Through the Looking-Glass.* Illustrations by John Tenniel. Introduction by Roger Lancelyn Green. (Everyman Library No. 836.) London: Dent, 1965. Pp. xv + 335.

First included in Everyman Library in 1929. The introduction is new.

**A65:4]** *Alice's Adventures in Wonderland.* Illustrations by John Tenniel. London: Macmillan, 1965. Pp. 177.

The People's Edition, first published in 1887, and frequently reprinted since.

**A65:5]** *Alice's Adventures in Wonderland.* Illustrations by John Tenniel. New York: Random House, 1965. Pp. x + 150.

"A centennial edition." A reprint of a 1946 edition. Boxed in a slipcase with *Through the Looking-Glass,* A65:8.

**A65:6]** *Alice's Adventures Under Ground.* Introduction by Martin Gardner. New York: Dover, 1965; New York: McGraw-Hill; London: Peter Smith, 1966. Pp. xi + 90 + [19], paperback (Dover), hardcover (McGraw-Hill, Peter Smith).

Modern reprint, with new introduction, of the 1886 facsimile edition published by Macmillan and Co., London (*WMG* 194). The photographs of the manuscript, however, are directly from Carroll's manuscript in the British Library.

Reviewed by: Marghanita Laski, *Listener,* 74 (2 December 1965), 917, 920; A. O'B. Murphy, *Library Journal,* 111 (15 May 1966), 2688; *Time,* 8 October 1966, p. 118; Naomi Lewis, *New Statesman,* 71 (20 May 1966), 741–42.

**A65:7]** *Arithmetical croquet for two players, by Lewis Carroll.* [Cambridge, Massachusetts: Adams & Lowell Press, 1965.] Pp. [4], paperback.

First separate printing.

**A65:8]** *Through the Looking-Glass.* Illustrations by John Tenniel. New York: Random House, 1965. Pp. x + 166.

A reprint of a 1946 edition. Boxed in a slipcase with *Alice's Adventures in Wonderland,* A65:5.

**A65:9]** Ardic, Nurettin, trans. *Alis harikalar diyarinda.* Istanbul: Rafet Zaimler Kitap Yayinevi, 1965. Pp. 159, illustrations, paperback.

Turkish translation of *Alice in Wonderland. Alice* appears on pages 3–136. Translation previously appeared in 1956.

**A65:10]**   Avery, Gillian, ed. *Unforgettable Journeys: An Anthology*. London: Gollancz, 1965.

Contains a reprint of "Isa's visit to Oxford" (*WMG* III; 1979 ed., 209a).

**A65:11]**   Bosch, Cora, trans. *Alicia en el país de las maravillas*. Illustrations by Boris Kriukow. Buenos Aires: Atlantida, 1965. Pp. 117 + [iii].

Spanish translation of *Alice in Wonderland*. Second edition 1967.

**A65:12]**   Brink, André P., trans. *Alice se avonture in wonderland*. Illustrations by John Tenniel. Introduction by Die Vertaler. Capetown: Human & Rousseau, 1965. Pp. 128.

Afrikaans translation of *Alice's Adventures in Wonderland*. Reprinted in 1966 (2nd ed.), 1970 (3rd ed.), and 1972.

**A65:13]**   Flandre, Guy, trans. *Alice au pays des merveilles*. Illustrations by Gilly. Paris: Charpentier, 1965. Pp. 192. Part color illustrations.

French translation of *Alice in Wonderland*.

**A65:14]**   Goldman, Lazar, and Stefan Gečev, trans. *Alisa v stranata na čudesata / Alisa v ogledalnija svjat*. Illustrations by Petur Chuklev. Sofia, Bulgaria: Narodna mladež, 1965. Pp. 212.

Bulgarian translation of *Alice in Wonderland* and *Through the Looking-Glass*.
   Combined 3rd edition of *Alice in Wonderland* and 2nd edition of *Through the Looking-Glass* published in 1969.

**A65:15]**   Goodall, J. S., illus. after Tenniel. *Alice in Wonderland*. London: Blackie & Son, 1965. Pp. 124.

**A65:16]**   Green, Roger Lancelyn, ed. *The Works of Lewis Carroll*. Illustrations by John Tenniel. Introduction by Roger Lancelyn Green. London: Hamlyn, 1965. Pp. 1130.

In addition to imaginative literary works, includes letters, essays, mathematical puzzles and the journal of a tour in Russia in 1867. Bibliography.
   Reprinted: Feltham, Middlesex: Spring Books, 1968.

**A65:17]**   Güvenc, Kismet, trans. *Alice harikalar ülkesinde.* Illustrations by John Tenniel. Ankara: Türkiye Cumhuriyeti Millî Eğitim Bakanliği Ankara Üniversitesi Basimevi, 1965. Pp. 121, illustrations.

Turkish translation of *Alice in Wonderland.*

**A65:18]**   Lapienytě, J., trans. *Alisa veidrodžio karalystěje.* Vilnjus, Lithuania: Vaga, 1965. Pp. 149, illustrations.

Lithuanian translation of *Alice's Adventures in Wonderland.*

**A65:19]**   Meneses, Maria de, trans. *Alice no país das maravilhas.* Illustrations by Figueiredo Sobral. Lisbon: Portugália, [1965]. Pp. 121, part color illustrations.

Portuguese translation of *Alice in Wonderland.* Fifth edition, 1966.

**A65:20]**   Montemagno, Vito, trans. *Alice nel paese delle meraviglie.* Illustrations by Red B. Stimson. Bologna: Capital, 1965. Pp. 147, color illustrations.

Italian translation of *Alice in Wonderland.* Translation appeared in 1952. Reprinted in 1967, 1970, 1975.

**A65:21]**   Muraoka, Hanako, trans. *Fushigi no kuni no Arisu.* Illustrations by Sige. Tokyo: Kaisei-Sha, 1965. Pp. 124.

Japanese translation of *Alice in Wonderland.* A short essay on Carroll appears on pages 122–24.

**A65:22]**   Naylor, Leonard E. *The Irrepressible Victorian: The Story of Thomas Gibson Bowles.* London: MacDonald, 1965.

Contains extracts from previously unpublished Carroll letters; see index.

**A65:23]**   Papadachc, Frida, trans. *Peripetiile Alisei în tara minunilor.* Illustrations by Mabel Lucie Attwell. Bucharest: Tineretului, 1965. Pp. 142, color illustrations.

Rumanian translation of *Alice's Adventures in Wonderland.*

**A65:24]**   Rohlicek, Karel, illus. *The Mock Turtle's Story.* (A Beaver Dime Book.) Fredericton, New Brunswick, Canada: Brunswick Press, 1965. Pp. [xii], paperback.

**A65:25]**   ———, illus. *The Walrus and the Carpenter.* (A Beaver Dime Book.) Fredericton, New Brunswick, Canada: Brunswick Press, 1965. Pp. [xii], paperback.

## 1966

**A66:1]**   *Alice In Wonderland.* Illustrations by John Tenniel. Introduction by Woodrow Wyatt. Banbury, England. Banbury Books, [1966?]. Pp. 159, paperback.

Also contains twenty-five color plates from the Jonathan Miller BBC TV version.

**A66:2]**   *Alice in Wonderland.* Illustrations by John Tenniel. Mt. Vernon, New York: Peter Pauper Press, [1966?]. Pp. 161, illustrations in red.

**A66:3]**   *Alice in Wonderland.* Illustrations by John Tenniel. New York; London; Richmond Hill, Ontario: Scholastic Book Services, 1966. Pp. 159, paperback, brown-and-black illustrations.

Second edition 1972, 3rd edition 1974.

**A66:4]**   *Alice in Wonderland.* London: Bancroft, 1966. Pp. 112.

Frequently reprinted, including in 1972.

**A66:5]**   *Alice in Wonderland.* (The Royal Series.) London: Ward, Lock & Co., 1966. Pp. 160, illustrations.

**A66:6]**   *Alice's Adventures in Wonderland.* Illustrations by John Tenniel. (A Legacy library facsimile.) Ann Arbor: University Microfilms, 1966. Pp. 192, blue-and-white or brown-and-white illustrations.

Stated to be from 1886 Macmillan setting but is from 1897 6s. edition, without preface. Companion volume of A66:10.

**A66:7]**   *Alice's Adventures in Wonderland / Through the Looking-Glass.* Illustrations by John Tenniel. (Papermac P53.) London: Macmillan; New York: St. Martin's, 1966. Pp. 285, paperback.

Reprint of edition which appeared in 1958 as part of "St. Martin's Library." Reprinted in 1968, 1971, 1973, and 1975.

**A66:8]**   *Fushigi no kuni no Arisu.* Illustrations by John Tenniel. Tokyo: Obunsha, 1966. Pp. 269, paperback.

Japanese translation of *Alice in Wonderland*. English / Japanese parallel text.

**A66:9**   *The Nursery "Alice."* Illustrations by John Tenniel. Introduction by Martin Gardner. New York: Dover; New York: McGraw-Hill, 1966. Pp. xi + 56 + [7], color illustrations, paperback (Dover).

Modern reprint, with a new introduction, of the 1890 edition published by Macmillan and Co., London (*WMG* 215). Includes reproductions of the cover designs and additional material from the original edition as end matter.
   Reviewed by: A. O'B. Murphy, *Library Journal,* 92 (1966), 871; Thomas Lask, *New York Times Book Review,* 6 November 1966, part 2, p. 68; *Times Literary Supplement,* 25 May 1966, p. 445.

**A66:10]**   *Through the Looking-Glass and what Alice found there.* Illustrations by John Tenniel. (A Legacy library facsimile.) Ann Arbor: University Microfilms, 1966. Pp. 224, blue-and-white or brown-and-white illustrations.

Companion volume of A66:6.

**A66:11]**   Amir, Aharon, trans. *Alice in Wonderland.* Tel Aviv: Mahbarot lesifrut, 1966.

Title and text in Hebrew. Translation first appeared in 1951; reprint of edition published in 1958.

**A66:12]**   Carruthers, Clive Harcourt, trans. *Aliciae per Speculum Transitus.* New York: St. Martin's; London: Macmillan, 1966. Pp. 135.

Latin translation of *Through the Looking-Glass*. Companion volume of A64:7.

Reviewed by: A.N. Bryan-Brown, *Listener*, 76 (26 September 1966), 471; *Times Literary Supplement*, 6 October 1966, p. 925; John F. Gummere, *Classical World*, 60 (1966 / 67), 168–69; G. Paul and W. Ready, *Library Journal*, 92 (1967), 778.

**A66:13]**  De Velcia, Eugenio, trans. "Trans Speculum et quae Alicia Ibi Invenerit." *Vita Latina*, No. 28 (July 1966), pp. 41–64.

Latin translation of the first three chapters of *Through the Looking-Glass*.

**A66:14]**  Duzel, Bogomil, trans. *Alisa vo zemjata na čudata*. Skopje, Yugoslavia: Kultura, 1966. Pp. 122, illustrations.

Macedonian translation of *Alice in Wonderland*.

**A66:15]**  Elfelt, Kjeld, and Mogens Jermiin Nissen, trans. *Alice i eventyrland*. Illustrations by John Tenniel. Copenhagen: Spektrum, 1966. Pp. 144, paperback.

Danish translation of *Alice in Wonderland*. Elfelt's first translation of *Alice* appeared in 1946.

**A66:16]**  Gattégno, Jean, and Ernest Coumet, eds. and trans. *Logique sans peine*. Illustrations by Max Ernst. Paris: Hermann, 1966. Pp. 291, paperback.

French translation of *Symbolic Logic* (extracts). Reprinted in 1968 (pp. 288 + [iv]) and 1972 (3rd revised ed.).

Contains an essay by Gattégno entitled "La logique et les mots dans l'oeuvre de Lewis Carroll" in which he looks at the importance of logic during the last years of Carroll's life, and how he used a "fun" aspect of logic in the *Alices* and the *Sylvie and Bruno* books. In these works games rather than story matter. Carroll's game (language and logic) is a description of the traps in which we fall when we reason poorly. Also shows how Carroll uses words to create a climate of dream. Pp. 9–43. Coumet contributes an article entitled "Lewis Carroll logician" in which he assesses Carroll's work on logic within the tradition of logic as it was evolving in Carroll's day. Coumet finds several elements of Carroll's work that can be considered modern by today's standards. Pp. 255–88.

Reviewed by: Jean-Blaise Grize, *La Quinzaine Littéraire*, No. 24 (13 March 1967); *Revue des deux mondes*, 16 (15 August 1967), 635.

**A66:17]**   Giglio, Tommaso [AW + TTLG], and Oreste Del Buono [letters], trans. *Alice nel paese delle meraviglie e nel mondo de specchio / Lettere scelte di Lewis Carroll*. Introduction by Oreste del Buono. Milan: Rizzoli, 1966. Pp. 255 + [i], paperback.

Italian translation of *Alice in Wonderland* and *Through the Looking-Glass* and selected letters of Lewis Carroll.

**A66:18]**   Heeresma, Faber, trans. *Alice in Wonderland*. Illustrations by John Tenniel. Antwerp: Zuid-Nederlandse Uitgeverij; Amsterdam: Centrale Uitgeverij, 1966. Pp. 158, paperback.

In Dutch. Also contains *Through the Looking-Glass*. Reprinted in 1967.

**A66:19]**   Kölling, Fritz, trans. *Alice im Wunderland*. Illustrations by S. and H. Lämmle. Stuttgart: Spectrum, 1966. Pp. 144.

German translation of *Alice in Wonderland*.

**A66:20]**   Montemagno, Vito, trans. *Le avventure di Alice al di là dello specchio*. Illustrations by Red B. Stimson. Bologna: Capitol, 1966. Pp. 145, color illustrations.

New edition. Italian translation of *Through the Looking-Glass and what Alice found there*. Translation first appeared in 1955. Reprinted in 1967, 1975.

**A66:21]**   Oechsli, Kelley, illus. *The Hunting of the Snark: an Agony in Eight fits*. New York: Pantheon Books, 1966. Pp. 48, part color illustrations.

**A66:22]**   Patankar, Raghuneth, G., trans. *Alice in Wonderland*. Balgaon, Pakistan: Abhinav Prakashan, [1966?]. Pp. 80, illustrations, paperback.

Title and text in Marathi.

**A66:23]**   Rackham, Arthur, illus. *Alice's Adventures in Wonderland:* With a proem by Austin Dobson. London: Heinemann; New York: F. Watts, 1966. Pp. 161, part color illustrations.

First appeared in 1907.

**A66:24]**   Reichert, Klaus, trans. *Briefe an kleine Mädchen*. Frankfurt am Main: Insel, 1966. Pp. 109, illustrations.

German translation of *Letters to His Child-Friends*. Reprinted in 1976 in a revised and expanded paperback edition containing over thirty photographs by Carroll and many sketches; pp. 169.

**A66:25]**   Runnquist, Åke, trans. *Alice i underlandet*. Illustrations by Tove Jansson. Afterword by Åke Runnquist. Stockholm: Albert Bonniers, 1966. Pp. 112, part color illustrations.

Swedish translation of *Alice in Wonderland*.

**A66:26]**   Schrey, Kurt, trans. *Alice im Wunderland*. Illustrations by John Tenniel. Munich: Goldmann [1966]. Pp. [ix] + 201, paperback.

German translation of *Alice in Wonderland*. English / German parallel text. Translation first appeared in 1950.

**A66:27]**   Semenović, Luka, trans. *Alisa u zemlji čuda*. Sarajevo: Svjetlost, 1966. Pp. 119.

Serbian translation of *Alice in Wonderland*. Translation appeared in 1959.

**A66:28]**   Vos, Peter, illus. *The Hunting of the Snark*. Utrecht: De Roos, 1966. pp. 39.

## 1967

**A67:1]**   *Alice for the Very Young*. Illustrations by John Tenniel. New York: The Grolier Society, 1967. Pp. 64, paperback, color illustrations.

A reprint of *The Nursery "Alice,"* in a reduced size.

**A67:2]**   *Alice nel paese delle meraviglie*. Bologna: Capitol, 1967. Pp. 123, illustrations.

New edition. Italian translation of *Alice in Wonderland*.

**A67:3]**   *Alice's Adventures in Wonderland* and *Through the Looking-Glass.* 3 vols. Louisville, Kentucky: American Printing House for the Blind, 1967. Vol. I—84 sheets; vol. II—44 sheets; vol. III—58 sheets.

Reimbossing of 1953 edition.

**A67:4]**   *Le avventure di Alice nel paese delle meraviglie / Dietro lo specchio.* Preface by André Maurois. Illustrations by John Tenniel. Milan: Sugar, 1967. Pp. 297.

Italian translation of *Alice's Adventures in Wonderland* and *Through the Looking-Glass.*

**A67:5]**   *Sylvie and Bruno.* Illustrations by Harry Furniss. (A Legacy library facsimile.) Ann Arbor: University Microfilms, 1967. Pp. xxiv + 400, brown-and-white illustrations.

Facsimile reprint of 1890 *Sylvie and Bruno* only.

**A67:6]**   *Through the Looking-Glass.* Illustrations by John Tenniel. London: Macmillan, 1967. Pp. 208.

The People's Edition, first published in 1887, and frequently reprinted since.

**A67:7]**   Atsuhide, Iijima, trans. *Fushiga no kuni no Arisu.* Tokyo: Kôdansha, 1967, pp. 7–124, color illustrations.

Japanese translation of *Alice in Wonderland,* Volume (pp. 292) also includes Wilde's *The Happy Prince,* Topelius' *Pinsessan Lindagum,* and Burton's *My Friend Mr. Leakey.*

**A67:8]**   Bay, André, trans. *Alice au pays des merveilles.* Illustrations by Lewis Carroll. Preface by André Bay. Paris: le Club français du livre, 1967. Pp. 254 + xxvi.

French translation of *Alice in Wonderland.* Translation first appeared in 1948.

**A67:9]**   Bossi, Elda, trans. *Alice nel paese delle meraviglie.* 3rd ed. Florence: Giunti Bemporad Marzocco, 1967. Pp. 124.

Italian translation of *Alice in Wonderland.*

**A67:10]**   Carano, Ranier, trans. *Alice nel paese delle meraviglie.* Illustrations by Ralph Steadman. Introduction by Oreste del Buono. Milan: Milano Libri Edizioni, 1967. Pp. 108.

Italian translation of *Alice in Wonderland.*

**A67:11]**   Demurova, Nina, trans. *Alisa v strane čudes / Skvoz zerkalo i cto tam uvidela Alisa.* Poetry translations by Samual Marsak and Dina Orlovskaja. Illustrations by P. Chuklev. Introduction by Nina Demurova. Sofia, Bulgaria: Foreign Language Publishing House, 1967. Pp. 226.

A Russian translation of the *Alice* books published in Bulgaria to be sold in the USSR. Introduction in Russian. An attempt at nonliteral translation, using as the original for the parodies some of Marshak's well-known Russian translations of nursery rhymes.

Reviewed by: Kornei Chukovsky, *Literaturnaya Russia,* 20 September 1968, p. 22 (rpt. in English in *Soviet Literature,* 9 [1969], 167–70); Sinovii Kanevsky, *Soviet Woman* (English edition), No. 9 (1968), p. 23; Vladimir Kharitonov, *Novyi Mir,* No. 1 (1969), 224–27.

**A67:12]**   Enzensberger, Christian, trans. *Alice im Wunderland.* Illustrations by Lewis Carroll. Frankfurt am Main: Insel, 1967. Pp. 126.

German translation of *Alice in Wonderland.* Translation first appeared in 1963. Reprinted in 1970.

**A67:13]**   Galasso, Alfonso, and Tommaso Kemeni, trans. *Le avventure di Alice nel paese delle meraviglie / Dietro lo specchio.* Milan: Sugar, 1967. Pp. 298, illustrations.

Italian translation of *Alice's Adventures in Wonderland* and *Through the Looking-Glass.*

**A67:14]**   Kölling, Fritz, trans. *Alice im Wunderland.* Stuttgart and Hamburg: Dt. Bücherbund, 1967. Pp. 158, illustrations.

German translation of *Alice in Wonderland.*

**A67:15]**   Llobet, Juan José, trans. *Alicia en el país del espejo.* Illustrations by Aurelia Cuschie. Buenos Aires: Acmé, 1967. Pp. [ii]

+ 218, illustrations in rose-red.

Spanish translation of *Through the Looking-Glass*. Sixth edition in 1971.

**A67:16]**   Morrison, Sean, illus. *The Mad Gardener's Song*. Indianapolis: Bobbs-Merrill, 1967. Pp. [40].

**A67:17]**   Nowell-Smith, Simon, ed. *Letters to Macmillan*. London: Macmillan; New York: St. Martin's, 1967.

Exchange of letters between Carroll and his publisher, pages 71–77.

**A67:18]**   Remané, Lieselotte and Martin, trans. *Alice im Wunderland*. Illustrations by Frans Haacken. Berlin (East): Alfred Holz, 1967. Pp. 194, color illustrations.

German translation of *Alice in Wonderland*. Reprinted: Recklinghausen, West Germany: Paulus, 1968; Zurich: Buchclub Ex Libris, 1969; Recklinghausen: Bitter, 1971; Munich: Deutscher Taschenbuch, 1973, pp. 201, paperback.
   Reviewed by Hildegard Krahé, *Die Zeit*, 29 March 1968; see also D68:2.

**A67:19]**   Rouillard, Henriette, trans. *Alice au pays des merveilles*. Illustrations by A. Pécoud. Paris: Delagrave, 1967. Pp. 94.

French translation of *Alice in Wonderland*. Translation first appeared in 1935.

**A67:20]**   Shukaev, E., illus. *Alice's Adventures in Wonderland*. Introduction by D. Urnov. Commentary by L. Golovchinskaya. Moscow: Progress Publishers, 1967. Pp. 235, part color illustrations.

English edition with introduction and commentary in Russian. Includes Russian versions of "Jabberwocky" and "The Walrus and the Carpenter."

**A67:21]**   Soares, Maria Merces Mendonsa, trans. *Alice no país do espelho*. Illustrations by John Tenniel. Lisbon: Verbo, 1967. Pp. 175.

Portuguese translation of *Through the Looking-Glass*.

**A67:22]**   Steadman, Ralph, illus. *Alice in Wonderland*. London: Dobson, 1967; New York: Potter, 1973. Pp. 108, hardcover (both), paperback (Potter).

Potter edition reprinted in 1974.
    Reviewed by: *JJLCS,* No. 5 (Autumn 1970), pp. 2–3; Corrine Robbins, *New York Times Book Review,* 6 January 1974, pp. 2, 3; Lavinia Marina Learmont, *Books and Bookmen,* May 1974, pp. 95–96; J. R. Christopher, *Mythprint,* 12, No. 2 (August 1975), 6–7.

**A68:1]**  *Alice au pays des merveilles / Ce qu'Alice trouva de l'autre côté du miroir.* Paris: Selection of Reader's Digest, 1968. Pp. 576, illustrations.

French translation of *Alice in Wonderland* and *Through the Looking-Glass and what Alice found there.*
    Volume also includes Cooper's *Le Dernier des Mohicans (The Last of the Mohicans)* and Hilton's *Horizons perdus (Lost Horizons).*

**A68:2]**  *Alice in Wonderland.* Illustrations by John Tenniel. London: R. Watts, 1968. Pp. 192.

Large type edition.

**A68:3]**  *Alice's Adventures in Wonderland & Through the Looking-Glass.* Illustrations by John Tenniel. (Magnum Easy Eye Books.) New York: Lancer Books, 1968. Pp. 288, paperback.

Reprinted in 1972, 1975, 1976.

**A68:4]**  *Selections from Alice's Adventures in Wonderland.* New York: Pyramid Books, 1968. Pp. 62, paperback.

**A68:5]**  Accornero, V., illus. *Alice in Wonderland.* London: Murray's Sales & Service, 1968. Pp. 78.

The text is *The Nursery "Alice."*

**A68:6]**  Andreaus, Hans, trans. *Alice in Wonderland en sprookjes van Andersen.* Illustrations by Janet and Anne Grahame Johnstone. Rome: Fratelli Spada Ciampino, 1968. Pp. 121.

Dutch translation of *Alice in Wonderland;* see A68:21.

**A68:7]**  Bernhard, Alfred, ed. *Alice in Wonderland.* Illustrations by John Tenniel. Munich: Max Hueber Verlag, 1968. Paperback.

English text with notes in German. Copyright 1953.

**A68:8]**   Bosch, Cora, trans. *Alicia tras el espejo*. Buenos Aires: Atlántida, 1968. Pp. 148, illustrations.

Spanish translation of *Through the Looking-Glass*.

**A68:9]**   Brink, André P., trans. *Alice deur die spieël*. Illustrations by John Tenniel. Introduction by Die Vertaler. Capetown: Human & Rousseau, 1968. Pp. 139.

Afrikaans translation of *Through the Looking-Glass*.

**A68:10]**   Çavuşef, Ismail A., trans. *Alis hârikalar ülkesinde*. Introduction by Stefan Geçef. Sofia: Narodna prosvesta, 1968. Pp. 125, illustrations.

Turkish translation of *Alice in Wonderland*.

**A68:11]**   Chakravasti, Anilendo, trans. *Ainar deshe ela*. Calcutta: Bengal Publishers, 1968. Pp. 92, illustrations.

Hindi translation of *Through the Looking-Glass*.

**A68:12]**   Chambers, Dave, Gwen Gordon, and John Spencer, illus. *Alice in Wonderland*. New York: Graphics International, 1968. Pp. 24.

An adaptation by Albert G. Miller, designed by Paul Taylor. A Pop-up edition.

**A68:13]**   Durane, Françoise, trans. *Alice au pays des merveilles*. Illustrations by Guy Doré. Paris: Deux coqs d'or, 1968. Pp. 240, part color illustrations.

French translation of *Alice in Wonderland*. Reprinted in 1970.

**A68:14]**   Ernst, Max, illus. *The Hunting of the Snark: an Agony in Eight fits / Die Jagd nach dem Schnark; Agonie in acht Krämpfen*. [Stuttgart]: Manus Presse, 1968. Pp. 100, part color illustrations.

English / German parallel text.
   Limited edition of 130 copies numbered and signed by Ernst; issued in portfolio.

**A68:15]**  Fietta, Maria Voghera, trans. *Alice nel paese delle meraviglie*. Milan: Mondadori, 1968. Pp. 246, illustrations.

Italian translation of *Alice in Wonderland*.

**A68:16]**  Gallo, Elías, trans. *Adventuras de Alicia en el país de las maravillas*. Illustrations by John Tenniel. Buenos Aires: Brújula, 1968. Pp. 202 + vi, notes, paperback.

Spanish translation of *Alice's Adventures in Wonderland*.

**A68:17]**  ———, trans. *A través del espejo y lo que encontró Alicia allí*. Illustrations by John Tenniel. Buenos Aires: Brújula, 1968. Pp. 226 + vi, notes, paperback.

Spanish translation of *Through the Looking-Glass and what Alice found there*.

**A68:18]**  Gien, Yu Mi, trans. *Alice in Wonderland*. Taipei: Eastern Publisher, 1968. Pp. 40, illustrations.

Title and text in Chinese. The title, *Alice Man Yu Cgi Ching*, translates to *Alice Wandering in Wonder Land*.

**A68:19]**  González de León, Ulalume. "Con motivo del no-aniversario de Lewis Carroll." *Revista de la UNAM,* December 1968, pp. 18–24.

Contains an essay on Carroll's games and puzzles, a Spanish translation of some "Doublets," and an annotated Spanish translation of "Jabberwocky."

**A68:20]**  Iskimži, Nina, and Vitalie Filip, trans. *Alis yn cara minunilor*. Kišinev, Moldavia: Lumina, 1968. Pp. 130, illustrations.

Moldavian translation of *Alice in Wonderland*.

**A68:21]**  Johnstone, Janet, and Anne Grahame Johnstone, illus. *Alice in Wonderland*. Manchester: World Distributors, 1968. Pp. 61, color illustrations.

Reprinted in 1973.

**A68:22]**  Maroule, Theodorou N., trans. *E Alike stē chōra ton thaumatōn*. Illustrations by John Tenniel. Athens: Ekdotikos, 1968. Pp. 119.

Greek translation of *Alice in Wonderland*.

**A68:23]** Newell, Peter, illus. *Alice's Adventures in Wonderland / Through the Looking-Glass and what Alice found there.* Rutland, Vermont: C. E. Tuttle Co., 1968. Pp. 529.

Combined volume of editions originally published by Harper & Brothers in New York in 1901 and 1902 respectively.

**A68:24]** Parisot, Henri, trans. *Les Aventures d'Alice au pays des merveilles.* (Collection L'Age d'Or.) Paris: Flammarion, 1968. Pp. 189 + vii, paperback.

French translation of *Alice's Adventures in Wonderland*. Reprinted with corrections in 1970, 1972, and 1975. Cover illustration by Max Ernst.

**A68:25]** Reichert, Klaus, trans. *Die Jagd nach dem Schnark.* Illustrations by Henry Holiday. Afterword by Klaus Reichert. Frankfurt am Main: Insel, 1968. Pp. 95.

German translation of *The Hunting of the Snark*. English / German parallel text.

**A68:26]** Rodoreda, M. V., trans. *Alicia en el país de las maravillas.* Barcelona: Bruguera, 1968. Pp. 223, illustrations.

Spanish translation of *Alice in Wonderland*.

**A68:27]** Rose, Gerald, illus. *Jabberwocky and Other Poems by Lewis Carroll.* London: Faber and Faber, 1968. Pp. [32], color illustrations.

Eleven nonsense poems selected from the *Alices* and the *Sylvie and Bruno* books.
   Also published as *The Walrus and the Carpenter and Other Poems by Lewis Carroll*. New York: Dutton, 1969.

**A68:28]** Scudder, Elisha. *The Game of Croquet.* Edited and augmented by Paul Seabury. Foreword by Rex Stout. New York: Abercrombie and Fitch, 1968.

Contains "Castle Croquet," pages 45–52.

**A68:29]** Zuberi, Saieda, trans. *Ilyas "Aenabee dunixa maign."* Illustrations by A. Karina. Lahore: West Pakistan Publishing Co., 1968. Pp. 180, paperback.

Urdu translation of *Alice's Adventures in Wonderland*. First printed in 1954 in an edition of 200 copies, not for sale.

# 1969

**A69:1]**   *Alice in Wonderland*. Illustrations by John Tenniel. (Armada Paperback.) London: May Fair, 1969. Pp. 128, paperback.

Stated to be a reprint of 1954 edition by William Collins Sons (U.K.), but differs considerably.

**A69:2]**   *Alice in Wonderland*. Illustrations by John Tenniel. (Mayflower Paperback.) London: Mayflower, 1969. Pp. 126, paperback.

Companion volume of A69:4.

**A69:3]**   *A Tangled Tale*. Illustrations by Arthur B. Frost. London: Rex Collings, 1969. Pp. [x] + 67.

Abbreviated version.
   Reprinted: New York: Third Press; New York: Joseph Okpaku Publishing Company, 1974.

**A69:4]**   *Through the Looking-Glass and what Alice found there*. Illustrations by John Tenniel. (Mayflower Paperback.) London: Mayflower, 1969. Pp. 126, paperback.

Companion volume of A69:2.

**A69:5]**   *Through the Looking-Glass*. (A Bancroft Classic.) London: Bancroft & Co., 1969. Pp. 112.

Frequently reprinted, including in 1970 and 1972.

**A69:6]**   Aalbees, Ankie, trans. *Alice in Wonderland*. (wonderserie.) Netherlands: Uitgeverig Geka B.V. 1969. Pp. 94.

Dutch translation of *Alice in Wonderland*. Reprinted in 1976.

**A69:7]** Benedetti, Lúcia, trans. *Alice no país das maravilhas.* Rio de Janeiro: Ouro, 1969. Pp. 96, illustrations.

Portuguese translation of *Alice in Wonderland.*

**A69:8]** Byran, Brigitte, illus. *Alice in Wonderland / Through the Looking-Glass.* Chicago: Children's Press, 1969. Pp. 192.

**A69:9]** Chao, Yuen Ren, trans. *Through the Looking-Glass.* (Readings in Sayable Chinese, Vol. 2.) San Francisco: Asian Language Publications, Inc., 1969, © 1968. Pp. 285.

Chinese translation (Mandarin) with "sayable" transliteration on facing pages.

**A69:10]** Dali, Salvador, illus. *Alice's Adventures in Wonderland.* New York: Random House / Maecenas Press, 1969. Pp. 150, issued in portfolio, color illustrations.

Twelve woodcuts superimposed on heliogravure color illustrations, and one etching. Issued in a limited edition of 2700 portfolios, 2500 on Mandeure paper, 200 numbered I–CC on Rives paper, with the etching signed in pencil, and including a double suite of the twelve illustrations on Japon Nacre.
  Discussed by: Raymond A. Sokolov, "Dali in Moneyland." *Newsweek*, 74 (10 November 1969), 120–22; Ian Ball, *Daily Telegraph Magazine*, 268 (28 November 1969), 36–43.

**A69:11]** Gamkrelidze, A., trans. *Alisa v strane čudes.* Illustrations by Z. Nizharadze. Tbilisi, Georgia: Nakaduli, 1969. Pp. 137, paperback.

Georgian translation of *Alice in Wonderland.*

**A69:12]** Gernsheim, Helmut. *Lewis Carroll Photographer.* New York: Dover; London: Peter Smith, 1969. Pp. x + 127, paperback.

Third revised edition of book published in 1949 by Parrish in London. Contains sixty-three photographs by Carroll. Extensive introduction and notes by Gernsheim. Revised edition contains a new preface and two different photographs than the 1949 edition.
  Reviewed [by Anne Clark] in *JJLCS*, No. 8 (Autumn 1971), pp. 6–7.

**A69:13]** Honeybourne, Rosemary, illus. *Allice in Wonderland.*

London: Purnell; Toronto: McClelland & Stewart, 1969. Pp. [50], part color illustrations.

**A69:14]** Jakopin, Gitica, trans. *Alica v čudežni deželi*. Illustrations by Arthur Rackham. Afterword by Gitica Jakopin. Llubljana, Yugoslavia: Mladinska knjiga, 1969. Pp. 109.

Slovenian translation of *Alice in Wonderland*.

**A69:15]** Kuzhiveli, Mathew M., and N. Ramakrishnan, trans. *Atbhuta lokattile Alice*. Trivandrum, India: Balan, 1969. Pp. 90 + vi, illustrations.

Malayalam translation of *Alice in Wonderland*.

**A69:16]** Manent, M., trans. *En el mundo del espejo*. 2nd ed. Illustrations by John Tenniel. Barcelona: Editorial Juventud, 1969. Pp. 152.

Spanish translation of *Through the Looking-Glass*.

**A69:17]** Marianowicz, Antoni, trans. *Alicja w krainie czarów*. Illustrations by Olga Siemaszko. Warsaw: Nasza Ksiegarnia, 1969. Pp. 201.

Polish translation of *Alice in Wonderland*. Translation first appeared in 1955.

**A69:18]** Massa, Clotilde, trans. *Alice nel paese delle meraviglie*. 2nd ed. Illustrations by Lamberto Lombardi. Rome: Edizioni Paoline, 1969. Pp. 119 + [vi].

Italian translation of *Alice in Wonderland*.

**A69:19]** Parisot, Henri, trans. *De l'autre côté du miroir et ce qu'Alice y trouva / La chasse au snark*. Paris: Flammarion, 1969. Pp. 236, illustrations.

French translation of *Through the Looking-Glass* and *The Hunting of the Snark*. Parisot's first translation of *Through the Looking-Glass* (with A. Bay) appeared in 1949. His first *Snark* appeared in 1940.

**A69:20]** ———, ed. *Le rire des poètes*. Paris: Pierre Belfond, 1969.

An anthology of humorous poetry with verses by Carroll translated in French by Parisot on pages 26–76; includes *The Hunting of the Snark.*

**A69:21]** ———, (*Alice*), and Jacques Papy (*Letters*), trans. *Alice racontée aux petits enfants / Poésies pour Alice / Lettres à des petits enfants.* Illustrations by John Tenniel. Paris: Eric Losfeld /Le Terrain Vague, 1969. Pp. 284, paperback.

French translation of *The Nursery "Alice,"* poems from the *Alice* books, and selected letters to children.

**A69:22]** Peake, Mervyn, illus. *The Hunting of the Snark.* London: Chatto & Windus; Toronto: Clarke, Irwin, 1969. Pp. 46.

Fifth impression of an edition published in 1953. Reprinted in 1973.

**A69:23]** Rackin, Donald, ed. *Alice's Adventures in Wonderland: A Critical Handbook.* Belmont, California: Wadsworth, 1969. Pp. vi + 369, paperback.

Contains chronology of Dodgson's life, a reprint of Derek Hudson's "The Creation of Alice's Adventures" (1954), the text of *Alice's Adventures in Wonderland,* fascimile of *Alice's Adventures Under Ground,* study questions, a selected bibliography and reprints of the following articles: Walter de la Mare, "Lewis Caroll's Dream Vision" (1930); Edmund Wilson, "C. L. Dodgson: The Poet Logician" (1932); Henry Seidel Canby, "An Introduction to *Alice's Adventures in Wonderland*" (1932); Harry Morgan Ayres, "Alice's Adventures in Education" (1932, 1936); Virginia Woolf, "Lewis Carroll's Crystallized Childhood" (1939; rpt. C66:21); Elizabeth Sewell, "The Field of Nonsense" (1952); John Hinz, "Alice Meets the Don" (1953); Phyllis Greenacre, "*Alice in Wonderland*: A Psychoanalytic Study of Charles Dodgson" (1955); Roger W. Holmes, "The Philosopher's *Alice in Wonderland*" (1959); Donald Rackin, "Alice's Journey to the End of Night" (C66:16).

  Reviewed by Selwyn Goodacre, *JJLCS,* No. 12 (Autumn 1972), p. 24; Nina Demurova, *Sovremennaya Khudozhestvennaya Literatura za Rubezhon,* No. 1 (1974), pp. 95–98.

**A69:24]** Shtcherbakov, Alexander, trans. *The Looking-Glass.* Illustrations by G. Kovenchuk. *Koster,* Nos. 3–7 (1969).

Title and text in Russian. Published in the Leningrad children's magazine. Translator uses modern colloquial idioms; the poems are translated literally.

**A69:25]**   Simone, O. Aurelio, trans. *Il gioco della logica*. Rome: Astrolabio, 1969. Pp. 106, paperback.

Italian translation of *The Game of Logic.*

**A69:26]**   Uyar, Tomris R., trans. *Alice harikalar ülkesinde*. Illustrations by John Tenniel. Istanbul: Kok Yayinlar, 1969. Pp. 124, paperback.

Turkish translation of *Alice in Wonderland.*

**A69:27]**   Valori, Duccio, trans. *Una storia ingarbugliata*. Rome: Astrolabio, 1969. Pp. 102, paperback.

Italian translation of *A Tangled Tale.*

**A69:28]**   Walt Disney Productions, trans. *Alicia en el país de las maravillas*. Illustrations by Walt Disney Productions. Barcelona: Bruguera, 1969. Pp. 223.

Spanish translation of *Alice in Wonderland.* Second edition 1973.

**A69:29]**   Ziliotto, Donatella, and Antonio Lugli, trans. *Alice nel paese delle meraviglie / Alice nello speccho*. Illustrations by Adriana Mazza Saviozzi. Florence: Valecchi, 1969. Pp. 176.

Italian translation of *Alice in Wonderland* (by Donatella) and *Through the Looking-Glass* (by Lugli).

# 1970

**A70:1]**   *Alice in Wonderland and Through the Looking-Glass*. London: Abbey Classics, 1970.

**A70:2]**   *La caza del snark: un agonía en ocho paroxismos*, 2nd ed. Buenos Aires: Calatayud-Dea, 1970. Pp. 75, illustrations.

Spanish translation of *The Hunting of the Snark.*

**A70:3]**   Bay, André, trans. *Alice au pays des merveilles. De l'autre côté du miroir*. Illustrations by Gilbert Koull and Jean Meuer. Evreux, France: le Cercle du bibliophile, 1970. Pp. 311 + xii.

French translation of *Alice in Wonderland* and *Through the Looking-Glass*. Bay's first translation of *Alice* appeared in 1948, and his first translation of *Through the Looking-Glass* (with H. Parisot) appeared in 1949.

**A70:4]**   Behrend, Katrin, trans. *Alice im Wunderland*. Illustrations by Gustave Doré. Stuttgart and Zurich: Delphin, 1970. Pp. 235, part color illustrations.

German translation of *Alice in Wonderland*.

**A70:5]**   Bossi, Elda, trans. *Alice nel paese delle meraviglie e nello specchio*. Milan: Club degli editori, 1970. Pp. 307, illustrations.

Italian translation of *Alice in Wonderland* and *Through the Looking-Glass*. Translation first appeared in 1963.

**A70:6]**   Buddingh', Cees, trans. *Brieven aan Kinderen*. Amsterdam: Querido, 1970. Pp. 93.

Dutch translation of *Letters to His Child-Friends*; includes sixteen pages of photographs by Carroll.

**A70:7]**   Copeland, Alexandra, illus. *The Walrus and the Carpenter*. Warrandyte, Australia: Pig Publications, 1970. Pp. 12.

**A70:8]**   Doré, Guy, illus. *Alice in Wonderland*. (Gold Star Library.) London: Hamlyn, 1970. Pp. 188 + i, part color illustrations.

**A70:9]**   Ernst, Max, illus. *Lewis Carroll's Wunderhorn*. Stuttgart: Manus Press, 1970. Pp. 78, color illustrations.

A selection of Carroll's logic and letters illustrated with lithographs.

**A70:10]**   Fensch, Thomas, ed. *Alice in Acidland*. Cranbury, New Jersey: A. S. Barnes; London: Yoseloff, 1970. Pp. 146.

Complete text of *Alice's Adventures in Wonderland* with an introduction, annotations, and an appendix that includes a lexicon of psychodelic drug terms. The plot and characters are explained in terms of drug use.

**A70:11]**  Gilliam, Florence, and Guy Levis Mano, trans. *La chasse au snark.* Paris: le Club français du livre, 1970. Pp. 146, illustrations.

French translation of *The Hunting of the Snark.* Translation first appeared in 1948.

**A70:12]**  Johnson, Edna, et al., eds. *Anthology of Children's Literature.* 4th ed. Boston: Houghton Mifflin, 1970.

Contains a selection of primary works and a brief biographical note. Previously published in 1935, 1948, and 1959. Secondary or post-secondary textbook.

**A70:13]**  Kaisaros, Emmanouēl, trans. *Hoi peripeteies tēs Alikēs se mia paramythenia chōra.* (Klassikē bibliothēkē neōn 13.) Athens: M. Pechlibanides, [1970?]. Pp. 280, part color illustrations.

Greek translation of *Alice's Adventures in Wonderland.* Translation first appeared in 1956.

**A70:14]**  Lara, E. F., trans. *Alicia en el país de las maravillas.* Illustrations by Ferroni. Buenos Aires: Editorial difusión, 1970. Pp. 157.

Spanish translation of *Alice in Wonderland.*

**A70:15]**  _____, trans. *Alicia a través del espejo.* Illustrations by Ferroni. Buenos Aires: Difusión, 1970. Pp. 173.

Spanish translation of *Through the Looking-Glass.*

**A70:16]**  Ojeda, Jaime de, trans. *Alicia en el país de las maravillas.* Illustrations by John Tenniel. Prologue by Jaime de Ojeda. Madrid: Alianza, 1970. Pp. 211, paperback.

Spanish translation of *Alice in Wonderland.* Reprinted in 1972 (2nd ed.) and 1973 (3rd ed.).

**A70:17]**  Oxenbury, Helen, illus. *The Hunting of the Snark.* London: Heinemann; New York: Watts, 1970. Pp. 48, part color illustrations.

**A70:18]** Parisot, Henri, trans. *Les aventures d'Alice au pays des merveilles.* Illustrations by Lewis Carroll. Chronology, Preface and Bibliography by Jean Gattégno. Paris: Aubier-Flammarion, 1970. Pp. 319, paperback.

Bilingual edition of *Alice in Wonderland* with English and French on facing pages.
   Reprinted with minor corrections in 1976, 1978.

**A70:19]** Rausch–Hüger, Annegret, trans. *Alice im Wunderland.* Balve / Westfalien: Engelbert, 1970. Pp. 106, illustrations.

German translation of *Alice in Wonderland.*

**A70:20]** Schroeder, Ted, illus. *Alice's Adventures in Wonderland / Through the Looking-Glass.* Racine, Wisconsin: Whitman, 1970. Pp. 212, green–and–white illustrations.

**A70:21]** Skoumalovi, Aloys and Hana, trans. *Alenka v kraji divů a za zrcadlem.* Illustrations by John Tenniel. Prague: Albatros, 1970. Pp. 256.

Czech translation of *Alice in Wonderland* and *Through the Looking-Glass.*

**A70:22]** Suveren, Gülten, trans. *Alice harikalar ülkesinde / Alice aynalar ülkesinde.* [Istanbul?]: Altin Kitaplar Yayinevi, 1970. Pp. 327.

Turkish translation of *Alice in Wonderland* and *Through the Looking-Glass.*

**A70:23]** Tomoko, Nakayama, trans. *Fushigi no kuni no Arisu.* Tokyo: Bunken shuppan, 1970. Pp. 246.

Japanese translation of *Alice in Wonderland.*

**A70:24]** Verachtert, Frans, trans. *Alice in Wonderland.* Illustrations by Rita van Nuffel. Ritie, Belgium: Kempische Boekhandel, 1970. Pp. 158.

Dutch translation of *Alice in Wonderland.*

## 1971

**A71:1]**  *Alice's Adventures in Wonderland.* Illustrations by John Tenniel. Bucharest: Editura didactică și pedagogică, 1971. Pp. 195.

English edition of *Alice* with an introduction by Hermina Jocobsohn and Stefan Stoenescu. Not seen.

**A71:2]**  *The Rectory Umbrella and Mischmasch.* Foreword by Florence Milner. New York: Dover, 1971. Pp. xiii + 193, paperback.

Reprint of 1932 edition published by Cassell & Company, London (*WMG* 308).
    Reviewed in *Times Literary Supplement*, 14 July 1972, p. 812; [ J. R. Christopher] *Choice*, 9, No. 7 (September 1972), 810.

**A71:3]**  *Useful and Instructive Poetry.* Introduction by Derek Hudson. [Folcroft, Pennsylvania]: Folcroft Library Editions, 1971. Pp. 45.

Reprint of the 1954 edition published by G. Bles, London (*WMG* 316).

**A71:4]**  Anglada, Lola, illus. *Alicia en el país de las maravillas.* Barcelona: Juventud, 1971. Pp. 150 + [ii].

Spanish translation of *Alice in Wonderland.* This is the eighth printing.

**A71:5]**  Artiaga, Yolanda, Nina Videira, and Luis Lobo, trans. *Alice de outro lado do espelho.* Lisbon: Estampa, 1971. Pp. 139 + [v], paperback.

Portuguese translation of *Through the Looking-Glass.*

**A71:6]**  Asimgil, Suna, trans. *Alice tuhafliklar ülkesinde.* (Armagan çocuk klasikleri: 24.) Istanbul: Nesriyat Anonim Sirketi, 1971. Pp. [x] + 214, illustrations.

Turkish translation of *Alice in Wonderland.*

**A71:7]**  Benedetti, Lúcia, trans. *Alice na país das maravilhas.* Illustrations by Sergio Leone. Rio de Janeiro: Ouro, 1971. Pp. 140, paperback.

Portuguese translation of *Alice in Wonderland*.

**A71:8]** Bohne, Pall W., illus. *Jabberwocky*. Rosemead, California: Bookhaven Press, 1971. Pp. 42 + [i].

Miniature edition limited to 300 copies. Contains comments and a glossary by Bohne.
 Reviewed by Hilda Bohem, *JJLCS*, No. 7 (July 1971), p. 5.

**A71:9]** D'Amico Masolino, trans. *Le avventure di Alice nel paese delle meraviglie / Attraverso lo specchio e quello che Alice vi trovò*. Illustrations by John Tenniel. Milan: Longanesi, 1971. Pp. 352 + viii.

Italian translation of Martin Gardner's *Annotated Alice* with new translations of *Alice's Adventures in Wonderland* and *Through the Looking-Glass and what Alice found there*. All Gardner's notes are translated with additional commentary by the translator. All poems are presented in English, with the Italian translations given in the notes.

**A71:10]** Devlin, Harry, illus. "Father William," *Children's Digest*, March 1971, pp. 14–17.

**A71:11]** González de León, Ulalume. "Con la venia de Carroll / *La casa del Snark*." *Plural*, No. 2 (November 1971), pp. 21–28.

An essay on and Spanish translation of *The Hunting of the Snark*.

**A71:12]** Gray, Donald, ed. *Alice in Wonderland: Authoritative Texts of Alice's Adventures in Wonderland, Through the Looking-Glass, The Hunting of the Snark / Backgrounds / Essays in Criticism*. (A Norton Critical Edition.) New York: Norton, 1971. Pp. xi + 434, hardcover and paperback.

Contains an introduction, texts of the *Alices* and *The Hunting of the Snark*, a selected bibliography, and a four-part background section. Sections on Carroll's early life and writing and on the writing of the *Alice* books contain letters, excerpts from the Diaries, and other writing as well as biographical accounts by Collingwood and Hudson.

The section on his later life includes the following reprints (extracts): Helmut Gernsheim's "Lewis Carroll—Photographer" (1950), Warren Weaver's "The Mathematical Manuscripts of Lewis Carroll" (1954–55), R. B. Braithwaite's "Lewis Carroll as Logician" (1932), Isa Bowman's "[A Visit to Christ Church]" (1899), as well as pieces by Carroll, Collingwood, and Hudson.

The section on essays in criticism contains the following reprints: Gillian Avery's "Fairy Tales with a Purpose" (C65:1) and "Fairy Tales for Pleasure" (C65:1), Peter Coveney's "Escape" (1957; rpt. C67:5), William Empson's "The Child as Swain" (1935), A. L. Taylor's "[Chess and Theology in the *Alice* Books]" (1952), Elizabeth Sewell's "The Balance of Brillig" (1952), George Pitcher's "Wittgenstein, Nonsense, and Lewis Carroll" (C65:16), Michael Holquist's "What Is a Boojum? Nonsense and Modernism" (C69:16), and Phyllis Greenacre's "Reconstruction and Interpretation of the Development of Charles L. Dodgson and Lewis Carroll."

Reviewed by: John Gardner, *New York Times Book Review*, 30 January 1972, pp. 3, 22; Selwyn Goodacre, *JJLCS*, No. 12 (Autumn 1972), p. 23.

**A71:13]**   Green, Roger Lancelyn, ed. *Alice's Adventures in Wonderland / Through the Looking-Glass and what Alice found there.* Illustrations by John Tenniel. (Oxford English Novels.) London and New York: Oxford Univ. Press, 1971. Pp. xxxiii + 277. bibliography.

Issued in paperback in 1975; paperback reprinted in 1976. Reprinted in London: Book Club Associates, 1973.

Reviewed by: [Anne Clarke] in *JJLCS*, No. 9 (Winter 1971), p. 10; [ J.R. Christopher] *Choice*, 9, No. 4 (June 1972), 504; Selwyn H. Goodacre, *Notes & Queries*, n.s. 20 (July 1973), 279–80.

**A71:14]**   _____, ed. *The Diaries of Lewis Carroll.* Westport, Connecticut: Greenwood Press, 1971. Pp. 604 + xxvi, two volumes.

Reprint of the 1953 edition published by Cassell & Company, London (*WMG* 315).

**A71:15]**   House, Gordon, and Graham Ovenden, illus. 365 + 1 = 364 *or Chapter VI Humpty Dumpty from Through the Looking-Glass and what Alice found there.* London: Ornament Press, 1971. Pp. 20, paperback.

Limited edition of 200 numbered and signed copies. Includes 1893 photograph of Carroll.

Reviewed by Anne Clark, *JJLCS*, No. 10 (Spring 1972), pp. 4–5.

**A71:16]** Hüttenmoser, Anita, trans. *Alice im Wunderland.* Illustrations by Moritz Kennel. Zurich: Silva, 1971. Pp. 128, color illustrations.

German translation of *Alice in Wonderland.* Translation appeared in 1947.

**A71:17]** Ikuno, K. trans. *Fushigi no kuni no Arisu.* Illustrations by John Tenniel. Tokyo: Fukuinkan, 1971. Pp. 180, paperback.

Japanese translation of *Alice's Adventures in Wonderland.*

**A71:18]** Kross, Tolkinud Jaan, trans. *Alice imedemaal.* Illustrations by Vive Tolli. Tallinn, Estonia: Éêsti raamat, 1971. Pp. 104, illustrations in color.

Estonian translation of *Alice in Wonderland.*

**A71:19]** Kuzhantaivelan, N., trans. *Alicin arbhuta ulakam.* Madras: Saivasiddhanta, 1971. Pp. 108.

Abridged Tamil translation of *Alice in Wonderland.* Copyright appears to be 1907.

**A71:20]** Livingston, Myra Cohn, ed. *Speak Roughly to Your Little Boy.* New York: Harcourt Brace Jovanovich, 1971.

"A Collection of Parodies and Burlesques, Together with the Original Poems, Chosen and Annotated for Young People." Carroll is represented by ten poems, one original, nine parodies.

**A71:21]** Papadache, Frida, trans. *Peripetiile Alisei în lumea oglinzii.* Illustrations by Petre Vulcănescu. Bucharest: Ion Creangă, 1971. Pp. 192, part color illustrations.

Rumanian translation of *Through the Looking-Glass (Alice's Adventures in the Looking-Glass).*

**A71:22]** Parisot, Henri, trans. *De l'autre côté du miroir et ce qu'Alice y trouva / La chasse au snark.* Eight *Snark* illustrations by

Max Ernst. Introduction by Hélène Cixous. Chronology and bibliography by Jean Gattégno. Paris: Aubier–Flammarion, 1971. Pp. 318, paperback.

Bilingual edition of *Through the Looking-Glass* and *The Hunting of the Snark* with English and French on facing pages. Reprinted with minor revisions in 1976.

**A71:23]**  Pereira, José Vaz, and Manuel Jõao Gomes, trans. *Adventuras de Alice no país das maravilhas.* Illustrations by John Tenniel. Edited by Fernando Ribeiro de Mello. Introduction and notes by Manuel J. Gomes. Lisbon: Edições Afrodite, 1971. Pp. 276 + [vi], paperback.

Portuguese translation with annotations of *Alice's Adventures in Wonderland.*

**A71:24]**  Peter, Charlotte, trans. *Alice au pays des merveilles.* Illustrations by Moritz Kennel. Zurich: Silva, 1971. Pp. 127, color illustrations.

French translation of *Alice in Wonderland.*

**A71:25]**  Pfister-Cippà, Albina, and Camillo Valsangiacomo, trans. *Alice nel paese delle meraviglie.* Illustrations by Moritz Kennel. Zurich: Silva, 1971. Pp. 127, color illustrations.

Italian translation of *Alice in Wonderland.*

**A71:26]**  Runnquist, Åke, trans. *Alice i underlandet.* Illustrations by John Tenniel. Stockholm: Aldus / Bonniers, 1971. Pp. 128 + [ii], paperback.

Swedish translation of *Alice in Wonderland.*

**A71:27]**  Seferjan, S., and G. Bandurjan, trans. *Alisa v strane cudes. Skvoz' zerkalo i cto tam uvidela Alisa.* Erevan, Armenia: Ajastan, 1971. Pp. 224, illustrations.

Armenian translation of *Alice in Wonderland* and *Through the Looking-Glass and what Alice found there.*

**A71:28]**  Semenović, Luka, trans. *Alisa u zemlji čuda.* Belgrade: Beogradski izdavačko-grafički zavod; Provesta, 1971. Pp. 160.

Serbian translation of *Alice's Adventures in Wonderland*. Translation appeared in 1951.

**A71:29]** _____, trans. *Alisa u zemlji čuda*. Sarajevo, Yugoslavia: Svjetlost, 1971. Pp. 103.

Serbian translation of *Alice in Wonderland*. Translation appeared in 1959 and has been used in several editions.

**A71:30]** Shôno, Kôkichi, trans. *Fushigi no kuni no Arisu*. Illustrations by John Tenniel. Tokyo: Fukuinkan Shoten, 1971. Pp. 180

Japanese translation of *Alice in Wonderland*.

**A71:31]** Soydas, Leylâ, and Bige Atasagun, trans. *Alis harikalar diyarinda*. Istanbul: Itimat Kitabevi, 1971. Pp. 95, illustrations, paperback.

Turkish translation of *Alice in Wonderland*. Translation first appeared in 1960.

**A71:32]** Stilman, Eduardo, trans. *Aventuras de Alicia en el país de las maravillas*. Illustrations by John Tenniel. Buenos Aires: Brújula, 1971. Pp. 202.

Spanish translation of *Alice's Adventures in Wonderland*.

**A71:33]** Tamihei, Iwasaki, trans. *Fushigi no kuni no Arisu*. Tokyo: Kadokawa Shoten, 1971. Pp. 168.

Japanese translation of *Alice in Wonderland*.

**A71:34]** Zakhoder, Boris, trans. *Alice in Wonderland*. Illustrations by V. Chizhikov. *Pioneer*, No. 12 (1971); No. 3 (1972).

Title and text in Russian. A free retelling by a popular children's writer and translator published in the Moscow children's magazine.

## 1972

**A72:1]** *Alice au pays des merveilles.* Paris: Hachette, 1972. Pp. 156, illustrations.

French translation of *Alice in Wonderland.*

**A72:2]** *Alice in Wonderland / Through the Looking-Glass.* (Sugar Puffs Library.) Published in England for Quaker Oats Ltd. by McGraw-Hill, [1972?]. Pp. 189, paperback.

**A72:3]** "Circular Billiards & The Nyctograph." *Juillard* (Leeds), No. 9 (Spring 1972), n.p.

**A72:4]** *Gendai-shi-techo.* Tokyo: Shichosha, 1972. Pp. 324.

Special issue of *Anthology of Modern Poems* devoted to Carroll. Contains Japanese translations of "A Mad Tea-Party," "Jabberwocky," and *The Hunting of the Snark.* Critical articles translated into Japanese include G. K. Chesterton's "A Defense of Nonsense" (1901; rpt. C64:3), William Empson's "Alice in Wonderland: The Child as Swain" (1935), Elizabeth Sewell's "Lewis Carroll and T. S. Eliot as Nonsense Poets" (1958), and Harry Levin's "Wonderland Revisited" (C65:11).

**A72:5]** *La Guida di Braglia: A Ballad Opera for the Marionette Theatre.* [London: privately printed for Denis Crutch, 1972]. Thirty leaves, printed on one side only.

Reprint of the text of the first publication in *Queen* magazine. Edition limited to twenty photocopies.

**A72:6]** Acerte, Julio C., trans. *Alicia en el país de las maravillas / Detrás del espejo.* Barcelona: Bruguera, 1972. Pp. 332 + [iv].

Spanish translation of *Alice in Wonderland* and *Through the Looking-Glass.*

**A72:7]** Amir, Aharon, trans. *Alisa b'erez ha-pelaot.* Illustrations by John Tenniel. Tel-Aviv: A Levin Epstein, 1972. Pp. 111 + [iv].

Hebrew translation of *Alice in Wonderland.*

**A72:8]** Bué, Henri, trans. *Aventures d'Alice au pays des merveilles.* Illustrations by John Tenniel. Introduction by Morton N. Cohen. New York: Dover; London: Constable, 1972. Pp. xiii + 196. paperback.

Reprint of 1869 French translation of *Alice in Wonderland* published by Macmillan, London (*WMG* 73). New introduction.
   Reviewed by A. Leonard, *JJLCS*, 2, No. 1 (Spring 1973), 18–19.

**A72:9]** Clark, Anne. "Carroll Drawings." *JJLCS*, No. 11 (Summer 1972), pp. 26–27.

First publication of a drawing by Carroll of a cat. Announcement of a proposed collected edition of Carroll's drawings. For a discussion of the drawing see Philip S. Benham's letter in *JJLCS*, 3, No. 1 (Winter 1973), 24–26.

**A72:10]** Darrell, Margery, ed. *Once Upon A Time: The Fairy-Tale World of Arthur Rackham.* Illustrations by Arthur Rackham. Introduction by Margery Darrell. London: Heinemann, 1972. Pp. 296, part color illustrations

A collection of children's stories illustrated by Rackham including *Alice's Adventures in Wonderland*, pages 71–138. Reprinted in 1974.

**A72:11]** De Alba, Adolfo, trans. *Alicia en el país de las maravillas / Al otro lado del espejo.* Illustrations by John Tenniel. Prologue by Sergio Pitol. Mexico City: Porrúa, 1972. Pp. xvi + 166 + [xiv], paperback.

Spanish translation of *Alice in Wonderland* and *Through the Looking-Glass*. Limited to five thousand numbered copies.

**A72:12]** De Zeeuw, P., trans. *Alice in Wonderland.* 6th ed. Illustrations by John Tenniel. The Hague: Van Goor, 1972. Pp. 120.

In Dutch. Reprinted in 1972 (7th ed.), 1978. See A62:13; same except for translator's name.

**A72:13]** Deaño, Alfredo, trans. *El juego de la lógica y otros escritos.* Madrid: Alianza, 1972. Pp. 175.

Spanish translation of *The Game of Logic* and other writings. Second edition 1976.

**A72:14]** Deleuze, Fanny, trans. *Sylvie et Bruno / Sylvie et Bruno suite et fin.* Illustrations by Harry Furniss. Preface by Jean Gattégno. Paris: Seuil, 1972. Pp. 468 + [x], paperback.

French translation of *Sylvie and Bruno* and *Sylvie and Bruno Concluded.*
    Reviewed by André Bay, *Les Nouvelles Littéraires,* 17–23 July 1972; Hélène Toubeau, *Critique,* 29, No. 309 (February 1973), 131–35.

**A72:15]** Escalas, R. Ballester, trans. *Alicia en el país de las maravillas.* Barcelona: Mateu, [1972?]. Pp. 218 + [v].

Spanish translation of *Alice in Wonderland.*

**A72:16]** Hansen, Eva Hammer, trans. *Alice i eventyrland.* Copenhagen: Lademann, 1972. Pp. 59, illustrations.

Danish translation of *Alice in Wonderland.*

**A72:17]** Hassan, Honarmandi E., trans. *Alis dar sarzamin-e ajâyeb.* 2nd ed. Teheran: Zavâr, 1972. Pp. 186, illustrations.

Farsi translation of *Alice in Wonderland.*

**A72:18]** Krüss, James, ed. *Seifenblasen zu verkaufen: Das grosse Nonsens-Buch mit Versen aus aller Welt.* Illustrations by Eberhard and Elfriede Binder-Stassfurt. Gütersloh: Bertelsman Jugendbuch-verlag, 1972.

An anthology of nonsense poems from around the world which includes six poems from the *Alice* books, four translated by Christian Enzensberger and two presumably by the editor, Krüss.

**A72:19]** Kunnas, Kirsi, and Eeva-Liisa Manner, trans. *Liisan seikkailut ihmemaassa.* Illustrations by John Tenniel. Jyväskylä, Finland: Gummerus, [1972]. Pp. 138.

Finnish translation of *Alice in Wonderland.* Reprinted in a slightly revised format in 1975, pp. 127.
    Reviewed by Timo Haajanen, *Aika,* (1972), pp. 332–33.

**A72:20]** Lobato, Monteiro, trans. *Alice no país das maravilhas / Alice no país do espelho.* Illustrations by Lila Figueiredo. São Paulo: Brasiliense, 1972. Pp. 182.

Portuguese translation of *Alice in Wonderland* and *Through the Looking-Glass.*

**A72:21]** Ovenden, Graham. *Pre-Raphaelite Photography.* London: Academy Editions; New York: St. Martin's Press, 1972.

Contains twenty-six photographs by Lewis Carroll.

**A72:22]** ———, and Robert Melville. *Victorian Children.* London: Academy Editions; New York: St. Martin's Press, 1972. Pp. [131].

Contains eleven identified, and probably two additional, photographs by Carroll, several previously unpublished, and a passing mention in the introduction.

**A72:23]** Parisot, Henri, trans. *Les aventures d'Alice au pays des merveilles.* Illustrations by John Tenniel. Paris: Flammarion, 1972. Pp. 175, color illustrations.

French translation of *Alice in Wonderland.*

**A72:24]** [Rouillard, Henriette, trans.] *Alice au pays des merveilles.* Illustrations by Daniel Dupuy. Paris: Delagrave, 1972. Pp. 125, illustrations in black and white with orange wash.

French translation of *Alice in Wonderland.*

**A72:25]** Runn, Chao Yuen, trans. *Alice in Wonderland.* Taipei: Good Literature Publishing Company, 1972.

Chinese translation with parallel English text.

**A72:26]** Saracchi, Emma, trans. *Alice nel paese delle meraviglie.* Illustrations by Maraja. Milan: Fabbri, 1972. Pp. 117 + [iii].

Italian translation of *Alice in Wonderland.*
  Reprint of 1954 edition.

**A72:27]** Shôno, Kôkichi, trans. *Kagami no kuni no Arisu.* Illustrations by John Tenniel. Tokyo: Fukuinkan shoten, 1972. Pp. 223.

Japanese translation of *Through the Looking-Glass.* Reprinted in 1973.

**A72:28]** Słomczyński, Maciej, trans. *O tym, co Alicja odkryła po drugiej stronie lustra.* Illustrations by John Tenniel. Warsaw: Czytelnik, 1972. Pp. 151, paperback.

Polish translation of *Through the Looking–Glass and what Alice found there.*

**A72:29]** _____, trans. *Przygody Alicji w krainie czarów.* Illustrations by John Tenniel. Warsaw: Czytelnik, 1972. Pp. 136, paperback.

Polish translation of *Alice's Adventures in Wonderland.*

**A72:30]** Steadman, Ralph, illus. *Through the Looking-Glass and what Alice found there.* London: MacGibbon & Kee, 1972; New York: Potter, 1973. Pp. 144, hardcover (both), paperback (Potter).

Reviewed by: *Times Literary Supplement,* 15 December 1972, p. 1525; *Economist,* 245 (1973), 45; *Newsweek,* 26 February 1973, p. 87A; Joseph Kanon, *Saturday Review of the Arts,* 3 February 1973, p. 68; Corrine Robins, *New York Times Book Review,* 6 January 1974, pp. 2–3; Lavinia Marina Learmont, *Books and Bookmen,* 19, No. 8 (May 1976), 95–96.

**A72:31]** Takasugi, Ichiro, trans. *Fushigi no kuni no Arisu.* Illustrations by John Tenniel. Tokyo: Kodansha, 1972. Pp. 225, part color illustrations.

Japanese translation of *Alice's Adventures in Wonderland.* "World Children's Literature Series No. 4." Contains twenty pages of notes.

## 1973

**A73:1]** *Alice's Adventures in Wonderland.* Illustrations by John Tenniel. New York: Avenel Books, [1973]. Pp. [xvii] + 192.

**A73:2]**  *Alice's Adventures in Wonderland*. London: Pan Books, 1973. Pp. 124 + [iv], color illustrations.

Illustrated with 22 color plates from the 1972 Josef Shaftel film.

**A73:3]**  *Euclid and his Modern Rivals*. Introduction by H.S.M. Coxeter. New York: Dover, 1973. Pp. xxxi + 275, paperback.

Modern reprint of the 1885 second edition of the work published by Macmillan and Company in London (*WMG* 175). New introduction.

**A73:4]**  *Feeding the Mind*. Prefatory note by William H. Draper. [Folcroft, Pennsylvania]: Folcroft Library Editions, 1973. Pp. 30.

Modern reprint of the 1907 edition published by Chatto & Windus, London (*WMG* 290–1).

**A73:5]**  *Novelty and Romancement: A Story by Lewis Carroll*. Introduction by Randolph Edgar. [Folcroft, Pennsylvania]: Folcroft Library Editions, 1973.

Reprint of the 1925 edition published by B. J. Brimmer, Boston (*WMG* 297).

**A73:6]**  *Through the Looking-Glass and what Alice found there*. Illustrations by John Tenniel. New York: Avenel Books, [1973]. Pp. [xv] + 224.

**A73:7]**  Arancibia, José Martin, trans. *Silvia y Bruno*. Madrid: Mauricio D'Ors, 1973. Pp. 312.

Spanish translation of *Sylvie and Bruno*.

**A73:8]**  Asimgil, Suna, trans. *Tilsimli ayna*. Istanbul: Nesriyat Anonim Sirketi, 1973. Pp. 238.

Turkish translation of *Alice in Wonderland*. Possibly a reprint of A71:6.

**A73:9]**  Bennett, Arlene, illus. *The Hunting of the Snark*. [Normal, Illinois: Arlene Bennett, 1973]. N.p.

**A73:10]**  Colom, Maricel Lagresa, trans. *Alicia en el país de las maravillas*. Illustrations by Trini Tintoré. Barcelona: Bruguera,

1973; Mexico City: Bruguera, 1974. Pp. 122 + [ii], color cartoon illustrations.

Spanish translation of *Alice in Wonderland*.

**A73:11]**  Danilov, Yu. A., trans. *A Tangled Tale*. Introduction by Ya. A. Smorodinsky. Illustrations by Yu. A. Vashcshenko. Moscow: Mir, 1973. Pp. 407.

Title and Text in Russian. Also includes *Pillow Problems, Symbolic Logic,* and miscellaneous works.

**A73:12]**  Dumpty, Humpty, trans. *Alicia en el país de las maravillas*. Illustrations by Arthur Rackham. Barcelona: Bibliotheca de Bolsillo Junior, 1973. Pp. 174 + [ii], paperback.

Spanish translation of *Alice in Wonderland*.

**A73:13]**  Enzensberger, Christian, trans. *Alice im Wunderland*. Illustrations by John Tenniel. Afterword by Christian Enzensberger. Frankfurt am Main: Insel, 1973. Pp. 139, paperback.

German translation of *Alice in Wonderland*. Translation first copyrighted in 1962. Reprinted in 1974, 1975.

**A73:14]**  Fisher, John, ed. *The Magic of Lewis Carroll*. London: Nelson; New York: Simon & Schuster, 1973. Pp. 288.

A comprehensive collection of Carroll's games and puzzles with other contemporary tricks and games which may have influenced Carroll. Introduction, afterword, and bibliography.

Reprinted in paperback: Harmondsworth: Penguin Books, 1975; and reprinted in hardcover in New York: Bramhall House, 1976.

Reviewed by: *Library Journal*, 98 (1973), 3560; [Anne Clark] *JJLCS*, 2, No. 2 (Summer 1973), 21–22; Martin Gardner, *Book Week*, 14 October 1973, p. 4; Peter Conrad, *New Statesman*, 86, No. 2231 (21 December 1973), 946; Roger Lancelyn Green, *Sunday Telegraph*, 23 December 1973; C. C. Barfoot, *English Studies,* 55 (1974), 383; Benny Green, *Spectator*, 232, No. 7499 (16 February 1974), 207; [ J. R. Christopher] *Choice*, 11, No. 1 (March 1974), 87–88.

**A73:15]**  Hatch, Evelyn M., ed. *A Selection from the Letters of Lewis Carroll (The Rev. Charles Lutwidge Dodgson) to His Child-Friends Together with 'Eight or Nine Wise Words About Letter-Writ-*

*ing.'* Introduction and Notes by Evelyn Hatch. [Folcroft, Pennsylvania]: Folcroft Library Editions, 1973.

Reprint of the 1933 edition published by Macmillan and Co., London (*WMG* 311).

**A73:16]** Holmes, Edward, ed. *Verses from Wonderland.* Illustrations by John Tenniel, tinted by Kira Henken. London: Thomas Nelson, 1973. Pp. 45

Verses selected for children from *Alice in Wonderland* and *Through the Looking-Glass.*

**A73:17]** Jenkins-Jones, Aneurin, trans. *Alys yn nhir swyn.* [Illustrations by Hutchings.] Llandysul, Wales: [Gwasg Gomer, 1973?]. Pp. [16], color illustrations, paperback.

Welsh translation of abridged *Alice in Wonderland.* See *JJLCS,* 3, No. 2 (Autumn 1974), 7, for a discussion of the illustrations by Brian Sibley.

**A73:18]** Kahmen, Volker. *Fotografie als Kunst.* Tubingen: Ernst Wasmuth, 1973.

Contains six Carroll photographs.
Published in the U.S. as *Art History of Photography.* Translated by Brian Tubb. New York: Viking, 1974. Published in England as *Photography as Art.*

**A73:19]** Koumantarea, Menē, trans. *I peripeteies tes Alikēs stē chōra ton thaumatōn.* Athens: Ermeias, 1973. Pp. 160.

Greek translation of French translation of *Alice's Adventures in Wonderland.*

**A73:20]** Livingston, Myra Cohn, ed. *Poems of Lewis Carroll.* New York: Thomas Y. Crowell, 1973. Pp. 149.

Selected poems with their original illustrations by Tenniel and others. Contains an introduction and notes designed for young readers.
Reviewed by K. Narayan Kutty, *Children's Literature,* 5 (1976), 286–87.

**A73:21]** Lobato, Monteiro, trans. *Alice no país do espelho.* 4th ed. São Paulo: Brasiliense, 1973. Pp. 86, illustrations, paperback.

Portuguese translation of *Through the Looking-Glass.*

**A73:22]**   Minnion, John, illus. *Jabberwocky*. Wood Green, England: Aloes Books, 1973. Pp. [12].

Limited edition of one thousand numbered copies.
  Reprinted in a slightly revised unlimited edition in 1975.
  Reviewed by Selwyn H. Goodacre, *JJLCS,* 3, No. 1 (Winter 1973), 29.

**A73:23]**   Ojeda, Jaime de, trans. *Alicia a través del espejo, y lo que Alicia encontró al otro lado*. Illustrations by John Tenniel. Prologue by Jaime de Ojeda. Madrid: Alianza, 1973. Pp. 223, paperback.

Spanish translation of *Through the Looking-Glass and what Alice found there*.

**A73:24]**   Opie, Peter and Iona, eds. *The Oxford Book of Children's Verse*. New York and Oxford: Oxford Univ. Press, 1973.

Contains eight poems by Carroll and a brief biographical note.
  Reviewed in an article by Janet Adam Smith, "Proper Cautions," *New Statesman,* 25 May 1973, pp. 776–77. Until the nineteenth century the prevailing modes in children's verse were exhortation and instruction, but then the instructors became jollier and the moral story was turned inside out by the revolutionaries, Lear, Carroll, and Belloc.

**A73:25]**   Ovenden, Graham. *A Liddell Family Album*. Uxbridge: Hillingdon Press, 1973. Pp. 22.

Contains photographs by Lewis Carroll. Edition limited to three hundred copies.

**A73:26]**   Schonfield, Hugh, J., ed. *For the Train: Five Poems and a Tale by Lewis Carroll. Being Contributions to the 'The Train,' 1856–1857, With the original illustrations by C. H. Bennett and W. McConnell; together with some Carolean* [sic] *Episodes concerning Trains*. Preface by Hugh J. Schonfield. [Folcroft, Pennsylvania]; Folcroft Library Editions, 1973; Philadelphia: R. West, 1976.

Reprints of the 1932 edition published by Denis Archer, London (*WMG* 307).

**A73:27]**   Stiller, Robert, trans. *Wyprawa na Żmireacza: Męka w Ośmiu Konwulsjach*. In *Literatura na Świecie,* No. 5 (1973), pp. 290–307.

Polish translation of *The Hunting of the Snark*.

**A73:28]**   Stilman, Eduardo, trans. *Aventuras de Alicia en el país de las maravillas* y *A través del espejo y lo que Alicia encontré alli.* Illustrations by Lewis Carroll and John Tenniel. Buenos Aires: Corregidor, 1973. Pp. 316 + [iv], paperback.

Spanish translation of *Alice's Adventures in Wonderland* and *Through the Looking-Glass.*

**A73:29]**   Winkfield, Trevor, ed. *The Lewis Carroll Circular No. 1.* Leeds, England: privately printed, 1973.

". . . hitherto scarce, unpublished or 'lost' Carrolliana . . . contains: 'The Ligniad'; 'The Christ-Church Commoner'; 'Railway Rules'; ' "Love's" Railway Guide'; 'Atlanta in Camden Town' (original version); Letter from Mabel; 'The Farewell'; 'Castle Croquet' (2nd edition); 'The Shepherd of Salisbury Plain'; Sequel to 'The Shepherd of Salisbury Plain'; 'Enigma'; Explication of the 'Enigma'; 'Two Circulars About Shakespeare'; 'Telegraph Cipher'; 'American Telegrams'; Photographs (1860); Photograph of Carroll's Miniature Tool-set; 'To Find The Day Of The Week For Any Given Month'; 'Reasonings on Rubbish'; 'Thoughts on Thistles'; 'Things in General'; 'Tears'; 'Rust'; 'Terrors'; 'But'; 'Yang-Ki-Ling'; 'Musings on Milk'; 'Screams'; 'Ideas upon Ink'; 'Twaddle on Telescopes'; 'Cogitations on Conclusions.' " Notes. Edition of sixty numbered and signed copies.

Reviewed by Anne Clark, *JJLCS,* 2, No. 2 (Summer 1973), 3–4.

## 1974

**A74:1]**   *Alice in Wonderland.* Illustrations by John Tenniel. (Tempo.) New York: Grosset & Dunlap, [1974]. Pp. 149, paperback.

**A74:2]**   *Alice's Adventures in Wonderland / Through the Looking-Glass.* (A Young Person's Classic.) London: Heron Books, [1974?]. Pp. 246, illustrations.

**A74:3]**   Almansi, Guido, ed. *Le bambine di Carroll: foto e lettere di Lewis Carroll a Mary, Alice, Irene, Agnese.* Introduction by Guido

Almansi. Biographical notes by Christina Bertea. Afterwords by Helmut Gernsheim and Brassaï. Parma, Italy: Franco Maria Ricci, 1974. Pp. 189.

Deluxe edition of tipped-in photographs of children taken by Carroll accompanied by a series of letters to various child friends translated into Italian. The photographs are drawn primarily from the Gernsheim Collection with a few from the Parrish Collection. The commentaries, translated into Italian, are not new. Limited to three thousand copies.

Appeared in French with a new introduction as: *Lewis Carroll: Photos et lettres aux petites filles*. Preface by Jean Gattégno. Afterwords by Brassaï and Helmut Gernsheim. Translation by Henri Parisot. Parma: Franco Maria Ricci, 1975. Pp. 192. Limited to three thousand copies.

Reviewed by José Pierre, *La Quinzaine Littéraire*, No. 224 (16 March 1976), pp. 14–15.

Appeared in English as *Lewis Carroll: Photos and Letters to His Child Friends*. Edited by Guido Almansi. Notes by Brassaï and Helmut Gernsheim. Translated by William Weaver. Parma: Franco Maria Ricci, 1975. Distributed by Rizzoli International Publications. Pp. 213. Limited to three thousand copies.

Reviewed by John Russell, *New York Times Book Review*, 18 July 1976, p. 6.

**A74:4]**   Angeli, Natalina, trans. *Alice nel paese delle meraviglie / Alice nello specchio*. Novara, Italy: Edipem, 1974. Pp. 93 + [iv].

Italian translation of the *Alice* books illustrated with color photographs from the Radio-television Italian production *Nel mondo di Alice* starring Milena Vukotic.

**A74:5]**   Bartley, W. W., III, "Through the Logical Microscope on the Far Side of the Looking-Glass: Lewis Carroll's Logical Problems." *Antaeus*, 13 / 14 (Spring / Summer 1974), 400–407.

Contains "some teasing fragments and puzzles" from the "lost" Part II of *Symbolic Logic,* illustrated by Edward Gorey and with commentary by Mr. Bartley.

**A74:6]**   Belmas, Jean, trans. *Une histoire embrouillée*. Paris: Belibaste, 1974. Pp. 117 + [iii], paperback.

French translation of *A Tangled Tale*.

**A74:7]**   Cattaneo, Tony, illus. *The Walrus and The Carpenter*.

(Stuff and Nonsense Books.) London & New York: Warne, 1974. Pp. 24.

**A74:8]**   Crespi, Adriana, trans. *Alice nel paese delle meraviglie / Attraverso lo specchio*. Milan: Bietti, 1974. Pp. 199 + [v].

Italian translation of *Alice in Wonderland* and *Through the Looking-Glass*.

**A74:9]**   Ford, Colin, ed. *Lewis Carroll at Christ Church*. London: The National Portrait Gallery, 1974. Pp. 32.

"Twenty-eight portraits by Lewis Carroll together with 'Hiawatha's Photographing' and an Introduction by Morton N. Cohen." Catalogue of an exhibition at the National Portrait Gallery, 17 January to 24 February 1974. In his introduction Cohen offers a biographical account of Carroll's interest in photography.

**A74:10]**   Frontin, J. L. Gimenez, and Marta Pessarrodona, trans. *Niñas*. Barcelona: Lumen, 1974. Pp. 76 + [iv], paperback.

Spanish translation of selected letters by Carroll to his child friends, with twenty-three photographs by Carroll.

**A74:11]**   Goodacre, Selwyn H. "The Stranger Circular." *JJLCS*, 3, No. 4 (Autumn 1974), 11–12.

Reprints the two variant versions of the famous circular (*WMG* 220) in which Dodgson "acknowledges no connection whatever with any 'pseudonym.' "

**A74:12]**   Guarnieri, Rossana Valeri, trans. *Alice nel paese delle meraviglie*. Illustrations by Lima and Sani. Milan: Fabbri, 1974. Pp. 111, color illustrations.

Italian translation of *Alice in Wonderland*.

**A74:13]**   Heath, Peter, ed. *The Philosopher's Alice: Alice's Adventures in Wonderland & Through the Looking-Glass*. Illustrations by John Tenniel. Introduction and notes by Peter Heath. New York: St. Martin's; London: Academy, 1974. Pp. 249.

Annotated edition from a philosophical perspective. Bibliography.

Reviewed by: *Kirkus Reviews,* 15 May 1974, pp. 562–63. Hunter, *Library Journal,* 99 (1 June 1974), 1818; *New Republic,* 15 June 1974; Stan Kurman, *Los Angeles Times,* 11 August 1974; E.H., *Psychology Today,* 8 (November 1974), 28, 30; Brian Sibley, *JJLCS,* 3, No. 4 (Autumn 1974), 13–16; Anthony Quinton, *Times Literay Supplement,* 20 December 1974, p. 1436; Penelope Palmer, *Philosophical Quarterly,* 25, No. 99 (April 1975), 172–73; Edward Guiliano, *Children's Literature,* 4 (1975), 186–91.

**A74:14]**  Jacques, Robin, illus. *Tweedledum and Tweedledee.* London: Warren Editions, 1974. Pp. 10.

Miniature edition limited to 250 copies.

**A74:15]**  Kaufman, Lisa, illus. *Three poems by Lewis Carroll.* [Northampton, Mass.: Smith College Student Printing Office, 1974].

"Jabberwocky," "Turtle soup," and "The mad hatter's song" illustrated with woodcuts. Broadsides, issued in portfolio. Limited edition of fifteen portfolios.

**A74:16]**  Kölling, Fritz, trans. *Alice im Wunderland.* Illustrations by Anjella Schreiber. Stuttgart: Spectrum, 1974. Pp. 144.

German translation of *Alice in Wonderland.*

**A74:17]**  Kosztolányi, Dezsö, trans. and Tibor Szobotka, reviser. *Alice csodaországban.* 2nd ed. Illustrations by Tamás Szeckskó. Budapest: Móra Ferenc Könyvkiadó, 1974. Pp. 97 + [viii].

New edition of 1958 Kosztolányi / Szobotka Hungarian edition of *Alice in Wonderland* published in Hungary and Czechoslovakia (pp. 109). No textual changes. The Kosztolányi Hungarian translation first appeared in 1936.

**A74:18]**  Kuniyoshi, Kaneko, illus. *Alice's Adventures in Wonderland.* Milan: Olivetti, 1974. Pp. 119 + [3].

**A74:19]**  Lobato, Monteiro, trans. *Alice no país das maravilhas.* São Paulo: Brasiliense, 1974. Pp. 77, illustrations, paperback.

Portuguese translation of *Alice in Wonderland.* Translation first appeared in 1931.

**A74:20]**  Parisot, Henri, trans. *Les aventures d'Alice au pays des* *merveilles*. Illustrations by Nicole Claveloux. Paris: Grasset-Jeunesse, 1974. Pp. 96, most illustrations in color.

Deluxe edition of *Alice in Wonderland* in French.
  Reviewed by Brian Sibley, *JJLCS*, 4, No. 2 (Spring 1975), 37–38.

**A74:21]**  Rhys, Ernest, ed. *A Book of Nonsense.* London: J. M. Dent, 1974. Pp. 206.

Reprint of 1927 edition with a new introduction by Roger Lancelyn Green. See table of contents for Carroll entries.

**A74:22]**  Rochlitz, Christiane, trans. *Alice im Wunderland.* Illustrations by Ingeborg Haun. Göttingen, West Germany: W. Fischer, 1974. Pp. 130.

German translation of *Alice in Wonderland.*

**A74:23]**  Serrano, Miguel, trans. *Alice no país das maravilhas.* Illustrations by Maria Barrera. [Amadora?]: Livrariz Bertrand, 1974. Pp. 255.

Portuguese translation / adaptation of *Alice in Wonderland* including scenes from *Through the Looking-Glass.* Based on A63:25.

**A74:24]**  Sewell, Byron, illus. *The Hunting of the Snark.* Introduction by Martin Gardner. London: Catalpa Press, 1974.

Illustrations include a series of special effects. Limited edition of 250 numbered and signed by illustrator.
  Reviewed by Anne Clark, *JJLCS*, 4, No. 2 (Spring 1975), 39–40.

**A74:25]**  Tillier, Rina, and Italo Grange, trans. *Alice nel paese delle meraviglie.* Illustrations by Carla Ruffinelli. [Rome?]: Paoline, 1974. Pp. 77 + [iii].

Italian translation of *Alice in Wonderland.*

**A74:26]**  Uliet, Veronica Van, trans. *Alice in Wonderland.* Illustrations by John Tenniel. The Hague: Van Goor Zonen, 1974. Pp. 120.

Dutch translation of *Alice in Wonderland.*

**A74:27]**   Winkfield, Trevor, ed. *The Lewis Carroll Circular No. 2.* New York: privately printed, 1974. Pp. 74.

Contains "hitherto scarce, unpublished or 'lost' items of Carrolliana": "Mister Fox," "Charade," "My First has no beard," "Dedicated to a tea-tea," "Star Dial," "Dress," "Marriage Service," "A 'ot cup of tea when I wake," "Square Poem," "Near Albury, so runs my lay," "Dedicated to the Muse of History," "Alice dear, will you join me in hunting the Snark?" "I have wandered," "Three Couplets for Postcards," "What hand may wreathe thy natal crown," "Life of Richard Hakluyt," "Word-Links," "Lanrick," "Three Puzzles," "2 Puzzles," "Two Brothers Problem," "Number-Guessing," "Rule for Finding the Quotient & Remainder produced by Dividing a Given Number by 9," "A Mysterious Number," "Problem," "Memoria Technica: Dates," "Memoria Technica: Couplets," "Memoria Technica: Specific Gravity of Metals, &c," "Memoria Technica: Logs of Nos. from 101 to 109, and from 1001 to 1009," "Registration of Parcels," "Circular About Appointments (1)," "Circular About Appointments (2)," "Second-Hand Books," "Letter to the Dramatic Profession," and a reprint of Chap. 11 of *The Lost Plum-Cake.* Edition of sixty numbered and signed copies.

Reviewed by Selwyn Goodacre, *JJLCS,* 3, No. 4 (Autumn 1974), 16–19.

**A74:28]**   Zimmermann, Antonie, trans. *Alice's Abenteuer im Wunderland.* New York: Dover, 1974. Pp. 178, paperback.

Reprint of 1869 German translation of *Alice's Adventures in Wonderland* published by Hartknoch, Leipzig (*WMG* 72).

═══════════════  **1975**  ═══════════════

**A75:1]**   *Alice's Adventures in Wonderland.* Illustrations by John Tenniel. Franklin Center, Pa.: The Franklin Mint. Pp. x + 161.

A leather-bound limited edition in a series "The 100 Greatest Books of All Time."

**A75:2]**   *Alice's Adventures in Wonderland / Through the Looking-Glass.* Illustrations by John Tenniel. Introduction by May Lamberton Becker. (Rainbow classics.) Cleveland: Collins-World, 1975, © 1974. Pp. 315.

**A75:3]**   *The Golden Treasury of Stories for Boys and Girls.* London: Gollancz, 1975.

Revised and reprinted edition of a book which appeared in 1959. Contains complete text of *Alice's Adventures in Wonderland.*

**A75:4]**   *Jabberwocky as explained to Alice.* Easthampton, Massachusetts: Chamberlain Press, 1975. Pp. [27].

Contains "Jabberwocky," Humpty Dumpty's explanation from *Through the Looking-Glass,* and illustrations. Limited to seventy-five copies signed by Sharah Chamberlain.

**A75:5]**   *The Rectory Magazine.* Introduction by Jerome Bump. Austin: Univ. of Texas Press, 1975. Pp. [xxvi] + 117.

Facsimile of Carroll's family magazine (1845; 5th ed. 1850). First publication.

One hundred copies in wrappers printed in 1975 for Friends of the Harry Ransom Humanities Research Center. A hardcover trade edition was issued in 1976 (with an errata slip).

Reviewed by: Doris Grumbach, *New York Times Book Review,* 24 April 1977, p. 8; Peter Heath, *Virginia Quarterly Review,* 53, No. 2 (Summer 1977), 534–40; Edward Guiliano, *Phaedrus,* 4 (Fall 1977), 46–47; Derek Hudson, *JJLCS,* 6, No. 2 (Spring 1977), 45–47.

**A75:6]**   Bay, André, trans. *Alice au pays des merveilles / De l'autre côté du miroir.* Neuilly-sur-Seine, France: Saint-Clar; Paris: F. Beauval, 1975. Pp. 247.

French translation of *Alice in Wonderland* and *Through the Looking-Glass.* Translation first appeared in 1948.

**A75:7]**   Beaton, Cecil, and Gail Buckland. *The Magic Image: The Genius of Photography from 1839 to the Present Day.* Boston: Little, Brown and Company, 1975.

Contains two paragraphs of commentary / biography treating Carroll on page 54. "The Elopement" is reproduced.

**A75:8]**   Colles, Dorothy, illus. *Alice's Adventures in Wonderland / Through the Looking-Glass and Other Writings.* Introduction by Robin Deniston. London: Heron Books, [1975?]. Pp. 311.

Also contains *The Hunting of the Snark* and selected verses. The illustrations are Tenniel redrawings. Reprint of 1954 Collins edition in a larger, slightly altered format.

**A75:9]**  Enzensberger, Christian, trans. *Alice hinter den Spiegeln.* Illustrations by John Tenniel. Frankfurt am Main: Insel, 1975. Pp. 145 + xv, paperback.

German translation of *Through the Looking-Glass.* Translation first appeared in 1963.

**A75:10]**  Fukushima, Masami, trans. *Fushigi no kuni no Arisu.* Illustrations by Makoto Wada. Tokyo: Kadokawa-shoten, 1975. Pp. 183, paperback.

Japanese translation of *Alice in Wonderland.*

**A75:11]**  Galasso, Alfonso, and Tommaso Kemeni, trans. *Alice nel paese delle meraviglie / Dietro lo specchio.* Milan: Garzanti, 1975. Pp. 286, paperback.

Italian translation of *Alice in Wonderland* and *Through the Looking-Glass* (see A67:13).

Introduction includes biographical sketch and reprint of D'Amico's translation of Martin Gardner's introduction to *The Annotated Alice* (A71:9).

**A75:12]**  Grashoff, Cof, trans. *Alice in Wonderland.* Illustrations by Pax Steen. Alkmaar, Netherlands: Uitgeverij Kluitman, [1975]. Pp. 160, paperback.

Dutch translation of *Alice in Wonderland.* Reprinted in 1976.

**A75:13]**  Jones, Harold, illus. *The Hunting of the Snark: an Agony, in Eight fits.* Andoversford, England: Whittington Press, 1975. Pp. 47.

Deluxe limited edition of 750 numbered copies signed by the illustrator. Slipcase. Thirty copies bound in leather.

Reviewed by Selwyn Goodacre. *JJLCS,* 5, No. 2 (Spring 1976), 57–58.

**A75:14]**  Kennel, Moritz, illus. *Alice's Adventures in Wonderland.*

London: Elsevier Phaidon; New York: Crowell, 1975. Pp. 136, color illustrations.

See A71:16.

**A75:15]** Lubin, Leonard B., illus. *The Pig-Tale*. Boston: Little, Brown and Company, 1975. Pp. 32, brown-and-white illustrations.

Some of the stanzas of the tale taken from *Sylvie and Bruno* appeared with Lubin's illustrations in *Cricket: The Magazine for Children*, 2, No. 8 (April 1975), 31–35.

Reviewed by A. Boch, *New York Times Book Review*, 4 May 1975, p. 42.

**A75:16]** Lucie-Smith, Edward. *The Invented Eye: Masterpieces of Photography 1839–1914*. New York: Paddington Press, 1975.

Carroll is discussed in the introduction, and four well-known Carroll photographs are reproduced.

**A75:17]** Melbarzde, Elfrīda, trans. *Alises piedzīvojumi brīnumzemē*. Introduction by E. Melbarzde. Illustrations by V. Vokers. Rīga, Latvia: Izdevniecība "Liesma," 1975. Pp. 128, paperback.

Lettish translation of *Alice in Wonderland*.

**A75:18]** Mitry, John. *Schriftsteller als Photographen 1860–1910*. Luzern and Frankfurt: Bucher, 1975.

Contains nineteen Carroll photographs and a two-page discussion of Carroll in the introduction.

**A75:19]** Oven-van Doorn, M. C. van, trans. *Alice in Wonderland*. Illustrations by Rie Cramer. The Hague: Van Goor Zonen, 1975. Pp. 150, part color illustrations.

In Dutch. Translation first appeared in 1952.

**A75:20]** Papy, Jacques, trans. *Alice au pays des merveilles*. Illustrations by John Tenniel. (Collection 1000 soleils.) Paris: Gallimard, 1975. Pp. 183 + [vii], hardcover and paperback.

French translation of *Alice in Wonderland*. Translation previously appeared in 1961.

**A75:21]**   Parisot, Henri, trans. *De l'autre côté du miroir et ce qu'Alice y trouva.* Illustrations by Jocelyne Pache. Paris: Flammarion, 1975. Pp. 134, part color illustrations.

New illustrated edition of Parisot's French translation of *Through the Looking-Glass.*

**A75:22]**   ———, trans. *Lettres adressées à des petites filles; (suivi de) Alice racontée aux petits enfants; (et de) trois poèmes sans queue ni tête.* (Collection L'Age d'Or.) Paris: Flammarion, 1975. Pp. 250 + [iv] paperback.

French translation of letters to his child friends, *The Nursery "Alice,"* and three nonsense poems.

**A75:23]**   ———, trans. *De l'autre côté du miroir et ce qu'Alice y trouva / La chasse au Snark.* Eight illustrations to the *Snark* by Max Ernst (Collection L'Age d'Or.) Paris: Flammarion, 1975.

French translation of *Through the Looking-Glass* and *The Hunting of the Snark.*

**A75:24]**   Rackham, Arthur, illus. *Alice's Adventures in Wonderland.* Proem by Austin Dobson. New York: Viking, 1975. Pp. [xii] + 162, part color illustrations.

Illustrations first appeared in 1907. See A66:23.

**A75:25]**   Reichert, Klaus, trans. "Acht oder neun weise Worte übers Briefeschreiben." In *Das sehr nützliche Merk-Buch für Geburtstage.* Frankfurt am Main: Insel, 1975, pp. 129–35.

German translation of "Eight or Nine Wise Words about Letter-writing." See also pp. 43, 44, 57, and 94 for quotations from Carroll.
   Reprinted in 1977.

**A75:26]**   Resines, Antonia, trans. *Silvia y Bruno.* Illustrations by Harry Furniss. Madrid: Felmar, 1975. Two volumes.

Spanish translation of *Sylvie and Bruno* and, presumably, *Sylvie and Bruno Concluded.* Not seen.

**A75:27]**   Sheppard, Nancy, trans. *Alitjinya ngura tjukurt-jar-angka / Alitji in the Dreamtime*. Illustrations by Byron W. Sewell. Introduction and editing by Barbara Ker Wilson. Adelaide, Australia: Department of Adult Education in University of Adelaide, 1975. Pp. xiv + 104, hardcover and paperback.

Pitjantjatjara (dialect of Aborigine) translation of *Alice in Wonderland*. Translation has a parallel translation of Pitjantjatjara back into English on facing pages. The illustrations are brown-and-white and are based on Aborigine bark paintings.
   Reviewed by Roy Shackelford, *Australia Now*, 6, No. 2 (December 1976), 10–13.


**A75:28]**   Steadman, Ralph, illus. *The Hunting of the Snark*. London: Michael Demsey, 1975; New York: Potter, 1976. Pp. 71, hardcover (Demsey), paperback (both).

Reviewed by John Minnion, *JJLCS*, 5, No. 1 (Winter 1976), 30–31.


**A75:29]**   Tada, Kōzo, trans. *Fushigi no kuni no Arisu*. Illustrations by John Tenniel. Tokyo: Obunsha, 1975. Pp. 204.

Japanese translation of *Alice in Wonderland;* also contains a brief biography of Carroll.


**A75:30]**   _____, trans. *Kagami no kuni no Arisu*. Illustrations by John Tenniel. Tokyo: Obunsha, 1975. Pp. 218, paperback.

Japanese translation of *Through the Looking-Glass.*


**A75:31]**   Thorne, Jenny, illus. *Alice's Adventures in Wonderland / Through the Looking-Glass*. Introduction by Jane Carruth. London: Purnell, 1975. Pp. 224, part color illustrations.


**A75:32]**   Zakhoder, Boris, trans. *Alice's Adventures in Wonderland*. Illustrations by G. Kalinovskaya. Moscow: Detskaya literatura, 1975. Pp. 157.

Title and text in Russian.
   Slight revision of a translation which first appeared in a magazine (A71:34). Introduction by the translator.

## 1976

**A76:1]**  *Alice in Wonderland.* Illustrations by John Tenniel. London: Academy; New York: St. Martin's, 1976. Pp. 80, paperback.

"Giant Illustrated Edition" with greatly enlarged Tenniel illustrations and double-columned text. Companion volume of A77:3.

**A76:2]**  "Examination Report." *JJLCS,* 5, No. 1 (Winter 1976), 28–29.

A reprint from *Ad Lucem* [Oxford High School Magazine], July 1887, of an unrecorded report of the results of an examination on the "Game of Logic" administered and scored by Charles L. Dodgson.

**A76:3]**  *Lewis Carroll: Three Letters on Anti-Vaccination.* London: The Lewis Carroll Society. Foreword by Denis Crutch. Pp. [16].

Limited edition of 150 copies of three 1877 letters written to the *Eastbourne Chronicle* against the argument put forward by the "Anti-Vaccination League."

**A76:4]**  *Rhyme? and Reason?* Sixty-five illustrations by Arthur B. Frost and nine by Henry Holiday. Preface by K. Naryan Kutty. Bibliographical note by Susan M. Kenney. New York and London: Garland, 1976. Pp. xiv + 214 + [2].

Modern reprint, with a new preface and bibliographical note, of 1883 edition published by Macmillan and Co., London (*WMG* 160).

**A76:5]**  *Sylvie and Bruno.* Illustrations by Harry Furniss. Preface by Edwin J. Kenney, Jr. New York and London: Garland, 1976. Pp. xii + xi + 400 + [3].

Modern reprint, with a new preface, of 1889 edition published by Macmillan and Co., London (*WMG* 217).

**A76:6]**  Andriesse-van de Zande, Gonne, trans. *De Avonturen van Alice in Wonderland.* Illustrations by Arthur Rackham. Proem by Austin Dobson. Baarn, Netherlands: Hollandia, 1976. Pp. 126, part color illustrations.

Dutch translation of *Alice's Adventures in Wonderland.*

**A76:7]**   Barras, Henri, trans. *Les aventures d'Alice au pays des merveilles*. Illustrations by Reynald Connolly. Montreal: Gilles Corbeil, 1976. Issued in portfolio, color illustrations.

French translation of *Alice's Adventures in Wonderland*. Limited edition of seventy-five folios.
   Reviewed in *Perspectives*, 26 June 1976, pp. 1, 10–11.

**A76:8]**   Behre, Ingallit, trans. *Alice i underlandet*. Illustrations by Wench Holistad. [Stockholm]: J. A. Lindblads, 1976. Pp. 156.

Swedish translation of *Alice in Wonderland*.

**A76:9]**   Blake, Quentin, illus. *The Hunting of the Snark*. London: The Folio Society, 1976. Pp. [50], slipcased.

Reviewed by J.N.S. Davis, *JJLCS*, 5, No. 4 (Autumn 1976), 129.

**A76:10]**   Bouman, Lenny, ed. *Alice's Adventures in Wonderland*. Illustrations by John Tenniel. (Bulkbock No. 4.) Utrecht: Knippenberg, 1976. Pp. 28.

English edition in a newspaper format used in Dutch schools. Also contains selections from Martin Gardner's *Annotated Alice*.

**A76:11]**   Boyden, John, illus. *Jabberwocky*. Hove, England: Farthing Press, 1976. Pp. 20.

Limited to ninety-five numbered copies on Arnold Signature and ten numbered copies on Tosa Butten—each has extra illustrations (on japon) signed by the artist.

**A76:12]**   Day, Gene, illus. *Dreaming as the Summers Die*. Gananogue, Ontario: Shadow Press, 1976. Pp. 24.

Eleven poems from *Alice* with illustrations based on Tenniel's original drawings.

**A76:13]**   Dessauer, Maria, trans. *Die Geschichte vom Schwein*. Illustrations by Leonard B. Lubin. Frankfurt am Main: Insel, 1976. Pp. 31.

German translation of "The Pig Tale" from *Sylvie and Bruno*. See A75:10.

**A76:14]** Fisher, John, ed. *Further Magic of Lewis Carroll*. [London?]: privately printed, 1976.

Strictly limited portfolio containing "9 pieces" which Fisher has noted since the publication of *The Magic of Lewis Carroll* (A73:14).

**A76:15]** González de León, Ulalume. " 'Jabberwocky,' el nonsense y algunas conclusiones sobre la lectura de poesia / Antologia de nonsense y canciones." *Plural,* No. 57 (June 1976), pp. 31-42.

Contains an essay on "Jabberwocky" nonsense and the reading of poetry, selected translations of Carroll's nonsense and songs including an annotated translation of "Jabberwocky" and a paraphrase of "Anglo-saxon stanza" with the Carroll's explanations, and a translation of a Philip de Remy "nonsense."

**A76:16]** Minnion, John, illus. *The Hunting of the Snark: an Agony in Eight fits*. London: privately printed, 1976. Pp. 39, paperback.

Reviewed by Brian Sibley, *JJLCS,* 5, No. 4 (Autumn 1976), 127–28.

**A76:17]** Parisot, Henri, trans. *Lettres adressées à Alice et à quelques autres / Alice à la scène / Fantasmagorie*. (Collection L'Age d'Or.) Paris: Flammarion, 1976. Pp. 187, paperback.

French translation of selected letters to Alice and others, highlights by Carroll on how he came to write the *Alices* (spontaneity), and *Phantasmagoria*.

**A76:18]** Schiaffonati, Alessandro, trans. *Le aventure di Alice nel paise delle meraviglie e Attraverso lo specchio*. Illustrations by Sergio Rizzato. Milan: Edizione Accademia, 1976. Pp. 247 + [ix].

Italian translation of *Alice's Adventures in Wonderland* and *Through the Looking-Glass*.

**A76:19]** Sigman, Joseph, and Richard Slobodin. "Stammering in the Dodgson Family; An Unpublished Letter by 'Lewis Carroll.' " *Victorian Newsletter,* No. 49 (Spring 1976), pp. 26-27.

First publication of a letter from Carroll to the Reverend Henry F. Rivers, dated February 2, 1884, detailing the varying degrees to which his sisters stammered—six to some degree, and one not at all.

**A76:20]**  Sirin, V. [Vladimir Nabokov], trans. *Anya v stranye chudes*. Illustrations by S. Zalshupin. New York: Dover, 1976. Pp. 114, paperback.

Unabridged republication of Russian translation originally published by Izdatel'stvo Gamayun, Berlin, 1932.
   Reviewed by B. Lyon Clark, *JJLCS*, 6, No. 3 (Summer 1977), 83–84.

**A76:21]**  Swan, D. K., ed. *Alice in Wonderland*. Illustrations by Carol Tarrant. London: Longman, 1976. Pp. 60, paperback.

"Simplified and brought within the vocabulary of the New Method Supplementary Readers, stage 1."

**A76:22]**  Weöres, Sándor, trans. "Vilmos apó" and "Szajkóhukky." In *Egybegyüjtött müforditasok*. Budapest: Magvetö Könyvkiadó, 1976, II, pp. 841–42.

Hungarian translation of two poems by Carroll, the latter is seemingly "Jabberwocky."

**A76:23]**  Yanase, Naoki, trans. *Siruvi to Bruno*. Illustrations by Harry Furniss. Tokyo: Renga-shobo, 1976. Pp. 320.

Japanese translation of *Sylvie and Bruno*.


=============================  **1977**  =============================


**A77:1]**  *Alice's Adventures in Wonderland*. Cover by Peter Richardson. London and Sidney: Pan Books, 1977. Pp. 124, paperback.

**A77:2]**  *Alice's Adventures in Wonderland*. Illustrations by John Tenniel; frontispiece by James Lewicki. Introduction by John T. Winterich. (Collector's Edition.) Norwalk, Connecticut: Easton Press, 1977. Pp. xiv + 172.

**A77:3]**  *Alice Through the Looking-Glass*. Illustrations by John Tenniel. London: Academy, New York: St. Martin's, 1976. Pp. 96, paperback.

"Giant Illustrated Edition" with greatly enlarged Tenniel illustrations and double-columned text. Companion volume of A76:1.

**A77:4]**   *A Day of Sea Air.* Foreword by Denis Crutch. London: Lewis Carroll Society, 1977. Pp. [xvi].

Contains "Syzygies as a Game for Two Players," facsimile Carroll letter, "A Sea Dirge," and notes and an afterword.

**A77:5]**   Bartley, William Warren, III, ed. *Lewis Carroll's Symbolic Logic.* Pt. 1: *Elementary,* 1896. 5th ed. Pt. 2: *Advanced, Never Previously Published.* New York: Potter / Crown, 1976. Pp. 496.

Reviewed by: Charles Bishop, *Library Journal,* 102 (1977), 1384; *Choice,* 14 (1977), 1074; W. V. Quine, *Times Literary Supplement,* 26 August 1977, pp. 1018–19 (see also letter by W. W. Bartley, 7 October 1977, p. 1149); Edward Guiliano, *Phaedrus,* 4 (Fall 1977), 45–46; Edward Wakeling, *JJLCS,* 6, No. 4 (Autumn 1977), 113–16; Peter Alexander, *Philosophical Quarterly,* 28 (1978), 348–50; James R. Kincaid, *Nineteenth-Century Fiction,* 33 (1978), 272–76, P. T. Geach, *Philosophy,* 53 (1978), 123–25.

**A77:6]**   Cattaneo, Tony, illus. *The Lobster Quadrille.* London and New York: Warne, 1977. Pp. [xxiv].

**A77:7]**   Croft, Richard, adaptor. *Alice's Adventures in Wonderland.* Illustrations by Carol Owen. (Oxford Progressive English Readers.) Oxford: Oxford Univ. Press, 1977. Pp. [viii] + 70, paperback.

Second impression.
   A version simplified according to the language grading scheme compiled by D. H. Howe.

**A77:8]**   Crutch, Denis. "Shakespeare for Girls: An Unrecorded Letter." *JJLCS,* 6, No. 4 (Autumn 1977), 112.

Reprints Carroll's request—for lists of plays by Shakespeare suitable for girls—from the April and May 1882 issues of *Aunt Judy's Magazine.*

**A77:9]**   Gardner, Martin, ed. *The Wasp in a Wig: A "Suppressed" Episode of Through the Looking-Glass and what Alice found there.* Preface, introduction and notes by Martin Gardner. (*Carroll*

*Studies* No. 2.) New York: Lewis Carroll Society of North America, 1977. Pp. xiv + 21 + [14], paperback.

First publication. Includes fold-out facsimile of galley proofs of episode.

Other English editions, all of which reprint the text, notes, and figures from the above-cited edition, are: New York: Lewis Carroll Society of North America, 1977. Pp. xiv + 21 + [14] deluxe limited edition of 750 numbered copies; London: Macmillan, 1977. Pp. 37 + [3], with a frontispiece by Ken Leeder; New York: Potter / Crown, 1978. Pp. xiv + 21 + [18], with a frontispiece by Ralph Steadman.

The galley proofs are reproduced in the *Telegraph Sunday Magazine,* 4 September 1977, pp. 12–21, with an afterword by Morton N. Cohen and color illustrations by Peter Blake, Sir Hugh Casson, Patrick Procktor, and Ralph Steadman. The illustrations and the galleys were reprinted in the *Montreal Star,* 18 September 1977, A1, H3, A4; *The Globe and Mail* (Toronto), 17 September 1977, pp. 1, 10; and in "A Suppressed Adventure of 'Alice' Surfaces After 107 Years." *Smithsonian,* 8 December 1977, pp. 50–57 (includes above illustrations and Carroll's drawing of Alice for the *Under Ground* manuscript).

The following news reports on the existence of the "Wasp" episode appeared: Jennifer Dunning, *New York Times,* 29 May 1977, pp. 1, 30; Fred Emery, *The Times* (London), 30 May 1977, p. 1; *Horizon,* 19 No. 4 (July 1977), 26; Françoise Wagener, *Le Monde,* 23 September 1977.

Reviewed by: Stefan Kanfer, *Time,* 2 June 1977, pp. 73–74; John Rowe Townsend, *Guardian* (Manchester), 17 November 1977, p. 13; Gerard Turner, *Oxford Times,* 25 November 1977, p. 16; George Barker, *Listener;* 99 (1978), 29; Benny Green, *Spectator,* 7 (1978), 21–22; S. Pickering, *Saturday Review,* 86 (1978), lxxxvi; Joseph McLellan, *Washington Post Book World,* 16 March 1978, D19; Donald Rackin, *Analytical and Enumerative Bibliography,* 2, No. 2 (April 1978), 124–32.

**A77:10]**  Gerardts, Evert, trans. and illus. *Da Jacht Op De Strok.* Amsterdam: Drukwerk, 1977. Pp. 100.

Dutch translation of *The Hunting of the Snark.*

**A77:11]**  González de León, Ulalume. "Reaparece el episodio perdido de Alicia / La Avispa con peluca." *Vuelta,* No. 1 (December 1977), pp. 5–11.

An essay on and Spanish translation of "The Wasp in a Wig."

**A77:12]**  Hoog, Else, trans. "De wesp in de pruik / Het ontbrekende hoofdstuk vit Alice." Illustrations by Ralph Steadman.

*Un Vrij Nederland,* 22 October 1977, pp. 4–6.

Dutch translation of "The Wasp in a Wig." Also see Carel Peeters's background essay "Het grote gelijk van de witte Koningin," pages 7–9.

**A77:13]**  Jansson, Tove, illus. *Alice's Adventures in Wonderland.* (A Merloyd Lawrence Book.) New York: Delacorte Press / Seymour Lawrence, 1977. Pp. [vii] + 120.

**A77:14]**  McDermott, John Francis, ed. *The Russian Journal and Other Selections from the Works of Lewis Carroll.* New York: Dover, 1977. Pp. 252, paperback.

Reprint of the 1935 edition published by E. P. Dutton, New York (*WMG* 312).

**A77:15]**  Parisot, Henri, trans. *Lettres à ses amies-enfants / Fantasmagorie et autres poèmes.* Chronology, introduction and bibliography by Jean-Jacques Mayoux. Paris: Aubier-Flammarion, 1977. Pp. 377, paperback.

French translations of selected letters to Carroll's child friends, "Phantasmagoria," and other poems. English / French parallel text.

**A77:16]**  Reedijk, Lenie, trans. *Alice in Wonderland: Opnieuw verteld voor de kleintjes.* Illustrations by John Tenniel. Postscript by W. E. Richartz. Utrecht and Antwerpen: A. W. Bruna & Zoon, 1977. Pp. 72, color illustrations, paperback.

Dutch translation of *The Nursery "Alice."*

**A77:17]**  Richartz, W. E., trans. *Die kleine Alice.* Illustrations by John Tenniel. Postscript by W. E. Richartz. Zurich: Diogenes, 1977. Pp. 72, color illustrations, paperback.

German translation of *The Nursery "Alice."*

**A77:18]**  Spits, Erdwin, trans. *De Jacht op de Trek.* Illustrations by Inge Vogel. The Hague: Vitgeverij J. Couvreur, 1977. Pp. 44.

Dutch translation of *the Hunting of the Snark.*

**A77:19]**   Takashashi, Yasunari, ed. and trans. *Kyaroru in wandarando.* Tokyo: Shishokan, 1977. Pp. 143.

Japanese anthology, entitled *Carroll in Wonderland,* contains photographs of and by Carroll, and translations of verses, puzzles, *The Rectory Umbrella* and selected letters by Carroll.

**A77:20]**   ———, and Jun-Nosuke Sawazaki, eds. and trans. *Riusu kyaroru shishu.* Tokyo: Chikumashobo, 1977. Pp. 386.

*The Collected Verse of Lewis Carroll.* Japanese translations include *The Hunting of the Snark,* early verse, "Phantasmagoria," "Three Sunsets," acrostics and verses from *Alice in Wonderland* and *Through the Looking-Glass.* Contains illustrations by Carroll, Tenniel, Holiday, and Furniss.

Some of Takahasi's translations previously appeared in the Lewis Carroll special issue of the poetry magazine *Gendaishi-techō,* June 1972. See A72:4.

**A77:21]**   ——— and Takahashi, M., trans. *Kodono-beya no Arisu.* Illustrations by John Tenniel. Tokyo: Shinshokam, 1977. Pp. 78, illustrations in color.

Japanese translation of *The Nursery "Alice."*

**A77:22]**   Yanese, Naoki, ed. and trans. *Fushigi no kuni no ronrigaku.* Tokyo: Asahi-shuppansha, 1977. Pp. 222.

Japanese anthology entitled *Logic in Wonderland.* Contents include puzzles from *Wonderland,* acrostics, doublets, and excerpts from the *Game of Logic* and *Euclid and his Modern Rivals.*

**A77:23]**   ———. *Motsureppanashi.* Illustrations by A. B. Frost. Tokyo: Renga-shobo, 1977. Pp. 206.

Japanese translation of *A Tangled Tale.*

**A77:24]**   Zalben, Jane Breskin, illus. *Jabberwocky.* Annotations by Humpty Dumpty. London and New York: Warne, 1977. Pp. [xxxii].

**A77:25]**   Zimmer, Dieter E. "Der Wesp mit der Perücke," *Die Zeit,* 23 December 1977, "Modernes Leben" section p. 48.

German translation of "The Wasp in a Wig."

# Section B. *Reference and Bibliographical Works and Exhibitions*

## 1960

**B60:1]** Shaw, John Mackay. *The Parodies of Lewis Carroll and Their Originals.* [Tallahassee]: Florida State University Library, 1960. Pp. 14 leaves printed on one side.

Catalogue of an exhibition; notes.

## 1962

**B62:1]** Green, Roger Lancelyn. "Bibliographer in Wonderland." *The Private Library,* 4, No. 4 (October 1962), 62–65.

An account of the compilation of the revision to the *Lewis Carroll Handbook.*

**B62:2]** Williams, Sidney Herbert, Falconer Madan, and Roger Lancelyn Green. *The Lewis Carroll Handbook: Being a New Version of A Handbook of the Literature of C. L. Dodgson by Sidney Herbert Williams and Falconer Madan First published in 1931 Now Revised, Augmented and brought up to 1960 by Roger Lancelyn Green.* London: Oxford Univ. Press, 1962. Pp. 307.

Reviewed by: John Hayward in *Book Collector,* 11 (August 1962), 372, 375–76; *Times Literary Supplement,* 17 July 1962, p. 516 (letter by Green, 20 July 1962, p. 525); Stanley Godman, *Notes & Queries,* n.s. 11, No. 3 (December 1963), 476–78; W. H. Bond, *Journal of English and Germanic Philology,* 42 (1963), 411–12.

Slightly revised reprint issued in 1970 by Dawsons, London and Folkestone.

## 1963

**B63:1]**   Montgomery, Lall F. "The Eastern Alice." *Literature East & West,* 7, No. 1 (Spring 1963), 3–9.

Surveys Eastern and Middle-Eastern translations of *Alice.*

**B63:2]**   Weaver, Warren, and Alfred C. Berol. *The India Alice: the story of a recently discovered copy of the genuine first edition, 1865, of Alice's Adventures in Wonderland.* Privately printed [Marchbanks Press], 1963. Pp. 15, paperback.

Limited to sixty-six copies prepared in connection with a dinner at the Grolier Club, New York, on 19 December 1963.

A revision of the text (without census) appears in *The Private Library,* 6, No. 1 (January 1965), 1–7.

## 1964

**B64:1]**   Hiscock, W. G. "The Lost Christ Church 'Alice.' " *Times Literary Supplement,* 7 May 1964, p. 402.

Concerns the copy of the suppressed 1865 *Alice* which was either lost or stolen from the Christ Church Senior Common Room before 1928.

**B64:2]**   Weaver, Warren. *Alice in Many Tongues: The Translations of Alice in Wonderland.* Madison: Univ. of Wisconsin Press, 1964. Pp. 147.

Contains histories, discussions, and extensive listings of translations of the *Alices.*

Reviewed by: Alan Pryce-Jones, *Herald Tribune Book Week,* 2 August 1964, p. 2; Derek Hudson, *Notes & Queries,* n.s. 13 (1965), 80; Roger Lancelyn Green, *Private Library* (January 1965); Edward Basset, *Modern Philology,* 63 (1965), 171–75; Danielle Chavy Cooper, *Books Abroad,* 39 (1965), 348–49; Leon Carnovsky, *Library Quarterly,* 36, No. 1 (January 1966), 50; Christian Enzenberger, *Anglia,* 84 (1966), 247–48.

## 1966

**B66:1]**   Smith, R. D. Hilton, compiler. *Alice One Hundred: Being a Catalogue in Celebration of the 100th Birthday of Alice's Adventures in Wonderland.* Victoria, British Columbia: Adelphi Book Shop, 1966. Pp. 77.

Comprehensive catalogue of 450 items of Carrolliana, from first editions to critical works. The collection is now housed at the University Library, University of British Columbia. Limited edition of 600 copies—500 hardcover, 100 paperback.

## 1967

**B67:1]**   Crutch, Denis. *A Century of Annotations to The Lewis Carroll Handbook.* [London]: Yellowhammer Press, 1967. Pp. 16, paperback.

One hundred corrections and additions to *The Lewis Carroll Handbook* (B62:2).

**B67:2]**   *The Houghton Library 1942–1967: A Selection of Books and Manuscripts in Harvard Collections.*

A note on Carroll holdings with facsimile reproductions of items, pages 76–78. Lewis Carroll is among Houghton's specialties.

**B67:3]**   *Notable Acquisitions 1965–1966.* Philadelphia: The Philip H. & A. S. W. Rosenbach Foundation, [1967?]. Pp. 28.

Carroll acquisitions—books, photographs, autograph letters—cited on pages 6–10.

**B67:4]**   Smith, M. A. "Autograph Letters." *Manchester Review,* 2 (Spring / Summer 1967), 97–120.

Description of letter holdings in the Manchester Central Library. A "handful" of letters to Alice Crompton from Carroll are mentioned and a few extracts are given on page 105.

========================    **1968**    ========================

**B68:1]**  Clarke, Alexander P. "Belles Lettres." *Manuscripts,* 20 (Winter 1968), 41–44.

Proofs of eight different title pages of *Through the Looking-Glass* were part of an exhibition of authors' corrected proofs held at the Grolier Club in New York City from 18 October to 10 December 1967.

**B68:2]**  Cohen, Morton N., and Roger Lancelyn Green. "The Search for Lewis Carroll's letters." *Manuscripts,* 20 (Spring 1968), 4–15.

The two editors of Carroll's letters recount their steps since 1961, when they decided to collect Carroll's correspondence with a view to editing for publication. Several unusual letters are reproduced in facsimile. [Two volumes of these edited letters appeared in 1979.]

========================    **1969**    ========================

**B69:1]**  G[reen], R[oger] [Lancelyn]. "Lewis Carroll." *The New Cambridge Bibliography of English Literature.* Vol. 3: 1800–1900. Ed. George Watson. Cambridge: Cambridge Univ. Press, 1969, 977–80.

**B69:2]**  Marx, Stan. "Extending the Lewis Carroll Bibliography." *Journal of the Long Island Book Collectors,* [1] (1969), pp. 21–22.

Four editions not listed in *WMG.* Reprinted in *JJLCS,* No. 3 (March 1970), pp. 12–13. For descriptions of two bibliographical variants see Selwyn H. Goodacre's note in *Knight Letter,* No. 5 (August 1976), pp. 1–2.

# 1970

**B70:1]** Berol, Alfred. *"Alice in Wonderland* in Russia, 1879." *Book Collector,* 19, No. 4 (Winter 1970), 526–27.

Bibliographical description of the 1879 Russian translation of *Alice in Wonderland.*

**B70:2]** B[ohem], H[ilda]. "Lewis Carroll." *UCLA Librarian,* March 1970, p. 15.

A brief description of the Carroll holdings in the UCLA Library's Special Collections. A holograph letter to Lady Waldgrave dated June 13, 1892, is reproduced.
  Reprinted in slightly altered form, and without reproduction, in *JJLCS,* No. 4 (Summer 1970), pp. 13–14.

**B70:3]** Goodacre, Selwyn. " 'Alice' Exhibition—Waddington Galleries—December 1970." *JJLCS,* No. 6 (Winter 1970), pp. 24–25.

Review of a general Carroll exhibition which featured illustrations by Graham Ovenden and Peter Blake.

**B70:4]** _____. "A Short Note on the Salvador Dali *Alice.*" *JJLCS,* No. 4 (Summer 1970), p. 9.

Bibliographical description.

**B70:5]** Weaver, Warren. "The Parrish Collection of Carrolliana." *JJLCS,* No. 5 (Autumn 1970), pp. 3–9.

Weaver's description of the Carroll holdings in the Parrish Collection at Princeton first published in the *Princeton University Library Chronicle,* 17 (1956), 85–91, is reprinted and brought up to 1970 with an addenda.

**B70:6]** _____. "In Pursuit of Lewis Carroll." *Library Chronicle—University of Texas,* No. 2 n.s. (November 1970), pp. 38–45.

Weaver discusses his interests and adventures in collecting Carrolliana, and surveys his collection housed in the Library at the University of Texas at Austin.

## 1971

**B71:1]**  Beale, Tony. "Circular About Books to Give Away." *JJLCS,* No. 9 (Winter 1971), 8–10.

Reports that Lewis Carroll's announcement about books to give away, previously thought not to have survived, appears with the advertisements in a copy of *A Fascinating Mental Recreation.* It is reprinted in the article.

**B71:2]**  Goodacre, Selwyn. "My Lewis Carroll Collection." *JJLCS,* No. 9 (Winter 1971), pp. 25–26.

Specializes in English editions of the *Alices* and magazine articles.

**B71:3]**  Tanselle, G. T. "Book-Jackets, Blurbs, and Bibliographers," *The Library,* 27, No. 2 (June 1971).

Includes description of the 1876 dust-wrapper for *The Hunting of the Snark.*

**B71:4]**  Weaver, Warren. "The First Edition of *Alice's Adventures in Wonderland:* A Census." *The Papers of the Bibliographical Society of America,* 65, No. 1 (January / March 1971), 1–40.

A history of the publication of the 1865 *Alice* and a history and description of each of the nineteen known, extant copies.

## 1972

**B72:1]**  "*Alice in Wonderland* Parodies and Imitations and Related Matters, Listed from the Collection of Dr. Lall Montgomery." *JJLCS,* No. 12 (Autumn 1972), pp. 13–17.

Seventy items listed. See *JJLCS,* No. 13 (Winter 1972), pp. 17–19, and *JJLCS,* 2, No. 1 (Winter 1972), 21–22, for additions and emendations.

**B72:2]**  Goodacre, Selwyn. "Bibliographic Notes on 'Christmas Greetings.' " *JJLCS,* No. 11 (Summer 1972), pp. 21–23.

Record of six printings in Carroll's lifetime, and textual variants. For additional discussion see letter by R. Shaberman, *JJLCS*, No. 12 (Autumn 1972), p. 29, and Goodacre's reply *JJLCS*, No. 13 (Winter 1972), p. 18.

**B72:3]** _____. "The 1866 Second Edition of *Alice's Adventures in Wonderland.*" *JJLCS*, No. 13 (Winter 1972), pp. 8–9.

Argues that there are two variants of the 1866 2nd edition, and that a total of four thousand copies were printed—in two impressions of two thousand.

**B72:4]** _____. "Lewis Carroll's 'Easter Greeting.' " *Notes & Queries*, 19 (July 1972), 264–65.

Textual discussion of the ten issues of *An Easter Greeting to Every Child who Loves "Alice"* with corrections to the *Handbook* description, and a listing of textual revisions.

**B72:5]** _____. "The Mouse's Tail." *JJLCS*, No. 11 (Summer 1972), pp. 9–12.

Graphic and bibliographic résumé of nine printed versions of "The Mouse's Tail" approved by Lewis Carroll. See *JJLCS*, No. 12 (Autumn 1972), pp. 27–28; *JJLCS*, No. 13 (Winter 1972), p. 18; and *JJLCS*, 2, No. 1 (Autumn 1972), p. 23, for additions and emendations.

**B72:6]** \_ \_\_\_\_. "The Text for the Steadman *Through the Looking-Glass.*" *JJLCS*, No. 13 (Winter 1972), pp. 15–16.

Concerns corrections made towards a definitive text. See B73:3.

## 1973

**B73:1]** *Alice.* Sheffield, England: Sheffield City Art Galleries, 1973.

A folder containing a catalogue of the December 1973 to January 1974 "Alice" exhibition based upon the "Alice at Longleat" exhibition (see B73:2). Includes a brief account of the Goodacre collection, which supplied all of the books and some of the exhibits.

**B73:2]**   *Companion-Guide to the Exhibition "Alice at Longleat" 2nd
April-30th September 1973.* Longleat, Warminster: The Lewis
Carroll Society (England), 1973. Pp. 14.

Also in C73:32.

**B73:3]**   Goodacre, Selwyn H. "Lewis Carroll's 1887 Corrections to *Alice.*" *The Library,* 5th ser. 28, No. 2 (June 1973),
131–46.

It has not been noted that Carroll made major alterations to the *Alice* books for
the 1887 People's Editions—different alterations from those made for the 1897
edition, since Carroll had apparently forgotten about his previous revisions.
These revisions must be taken into account in any future editions of his works.
Textual variants are recorded.
   For emendations see Goodacre's letter in *JJLCS,* 3, No. 4 (Autumn 1974),
23–24.

**B73:4]**   _____. "The Textual Alterations to *Alice's Adventures in
Wonderland* 1865–1866." *JJLCS,* 3, No. 1 (Winter 1973), 17–20.

Records eighty-nine points of difference between the 1865 and 1866 editions of
*Alice;* also records which revisions were retained in later editions.
   See letter by Jeffrey Stern, *JJLCS,* 7, No. 1 (Winter 1977 / 78), 28.

**B73:5]**   Jaques, Philip Dodgson. "Lewis Carroll's Last Pocket
Notebook." *JJLCS,* 2, No. 1 (Spring 1973), 1.

Description of unrecorded pocket notebook Carroll kept in 1897.

**B73:6]**   Leonard, A. "Esperanto *Alice.*" *JJLCS,* 3, No. 1 (Winter 1973), 4–5.

Description of a copy of the 1910 translation of *Alice* into Esperanto.

**B73:7]**   Sibley, Brian, ed. *Bandersnatch: The Lewis Carroll Society*
[England] *Newsletter.* No. 1 (December 1973).

"A light-hearted newsletter [which] keeps members informed with details of
Society activities, and news of books, plays, films and Carrollian ephemera."
Includes brief reviews of virtually all new British play productions and
publications.

# 1974

**B74:1]**   Brabant, Joseph A. "Correspondence." *JJLCS*, 3, No. 3 (Summer 1974), 20.

Notes interesting features of the sixty-first thousand copies of *Through the Looking-Glass* (1897) containing Carroll's final corrections.

**B74:2]**   "Childhood in Poetry Collections." *JJLCS*, 3, No. 2 (Spring 1974), 28.

Announcement of an exhibit at the John Mackay Shaw Collection of Childhood in Poetry at Florida State University's Robert Manning Strozier Library focusing on written imitations of *Alice in Wonderland* from 1871 to 1959.

**B74:3]**   Coleman, A. D. "They Liked Their Subjects." *New York Times Arts & Leisure Section,* 25 August 1974, p. 24.

Report on an exhibition of Lewis Carroll and Julia Margaret Cameron photographs at the Scott Eliot Gallery in New York City. A Carroll portrait of Virginia Dalrymple is reproduced.

**B74:4]**   Crutch, Denis. *A Handlist of Editions of "Alice" Published in Great Britain During the Two Years After Expiry of Copyright.* London: privately printed, 1974. Pp. 11.

**B74:5]**   Goodacre, Selwyn H. "Correspondence." *JJLCS*, 3, No. 2 (Spring 1974), 28.

In response to a remark made by Brian Sibley in his review of *Mr. Dodgson: Nine Lewis Carroll Studies, JJLCS*, 3, No. 1 (Winter 1973), 4, Goodacre affirms that all copies of *The Nursery "Alice"* "with the 1889 date are either copies individually prepared for gifts, or as samples for possible sale of the rejected printing abroad, or are copies of the People's Edition (issued in 1891) or the reduced price copies of 1896–7."

**B74:6]**   ———. *The Listing of the Snark.* Burton-on-Trent, England: privately printed, 1974. Pp. 9 + i.

". . . a listing of editions and issues of Lewis Carroll's *The Hunting of the Snark* from its inspiration on July 18, 1874 to July 18, 1974." Limited edition of eighty numbered and signed copies.

A two-page addendum was issued by Goodacre in March 1975.
Reviewed by Denis Crutch, *JJLCS,* 3, No. 4 (Autumn 1974), 19–20.

**B74:7]** _____, and Denis Crutch. *Lewis Carroll: an exhibition.*
London: The Lewis Carroll Society, 1974. Pp. 27.

Blackheath Exhibition Catalogue, designed and illustrated by John Minnion.
Includes a revision of an essay by Selwyn Goodacre, "Lewis Carroll the Creative Writer," which was first published in *Mr. Dodgson* (C73:32). Mentions that
the probable "original" looking-glass still exists—at Charlton Kings.

The exhibition, when mounted at the Ranger's House, was reviewed in *The
Times* (London), 7 March 1974, p. 16D.

**B74:8]** _____, C. Brown, and J. Davis. "The Early *Alice*
Translations—Binding Variants." *JJLCS,* 3, No. 4 (Autumn
1974), 9–10.

For additional information about bindings of early *Alice* translations see letters
by Denis Crutch and R. B. Shaberman, *JJLCS,* 4, No. 2 (Spring 1975), 41–42;
and G. P. Franks, *JJLCS,* 5, No. 2 (Spring 1976), 62.

**B74:9]** Marx, Stan, ed. *Knight Letter,* No. 1 (August 1974).

The newsletter of the Lewis Carroll Society of North America. Prints news of
the Society, brief notes and queries, notices and brief reviews of plays, movies,
and publications; and notes Carroll ephemera of interest to the Society's
members.

**B74:10]** _____. *The Many Faces of Lewis Carroll.* Hewlett, New
York: privately printed, 1974. Pp. [4], paperback.

An introduction to an April 1974 Lewis Carroll exhibit at the Hewlett-Wood-
mere Public Library. Carroll's diverse published achievements are discussed.

**B74:11]** Sibley Brian, ed. *Bandersnatch: The Lewis Carroll Society*
[England] *Newsletter.* Nos. 2–7 (February, April, June, August,
October, December 1974).

See B73:7.

**B74:12]** Williams, Sidney Herbert. *A Bibliography of the Writings
of Lewis Carroll.* [Folcroft, Pennsylvania]: Folcroft Library Edi-

tions; [Belfast, Maine]: Porter; [Philadelphia]: R. West, 1974. Pp. 142 + xiii.

Modern reprint of the 1924 edition published by *The Bookman's Journal*, London (*WMG* V; 1979 ed., 505).

# 1975

**B75:1]** "Alice at the Bobst." *Bulletin of the Society for Libraries of New York University*, No. 82 (Spring 1975), p. 4.

An announcement of the acquisition by the Bobst Library of the Carroll collection previously owned by Alfred Berol. Some of the highlights of the collection are mentioned.

**B75:2]** Breasted, Mary. "Memorabilia of Lewis Carroll Moves on to N.Y.U. Library." *The New York Times*, 19 March 1975, pp. 49, col. 1, 67.

Discusses the Alfred C. Berol Collection donated to N.Y.U. The bulk of the collection is devoted to Lewis Carroll.

**B75:3]** Crutch, Denis N. "Alice in Paperback." *JJLCS*, 4, No. 2 (Spring 1975), 23–26.

A listing of all paperback editions of the two *Alice* books (both separate and combined) published in Great Britain.
    For additions see *JJLCS*, 5, No. 4 (Autumn 1976), 130.
    Also appeared in a slightly earlier version in the *Newsletter of the Penguin Collectors' Society*, 1, No. 3 (January 1975), 36–40.

**B75:4]** ———. "A Note on Editions of *Alice* in the Readers Library Series." *JJLCS*, 4, No. 2 (Spring 1975), 31–32.

Bibliographic descriptions of the four Readers Library editions of *Alice in Wonderland* (1924, 1926, 1932, 1932). Supercedes *Handbook* entries.
    For discussion and additions see letters by John N. S. Davis and Selwyn Goodacre in *JJLCS*, 4, No. 4 (Autumn 1975), 122.

**B75:5]**   Goodacre, Selwyn H. "Bibliographical Notes on *A Tangled Tale.*" *JJLCS*, 4, No. 1 (Winter 1975), 7–9.

Corrections and notes to be added to the *Handbook* description of the variants of *A Tangled Tale*. Also includes supplementary notes on the display logos (4) Macmillan & Co. used within the pages of Lewis Carroll's works. For a discussion and emendations see the letter by Denis Crutch and Goodacre's reply in *JJLCS*, 4, No. 3 (Summer 1975), 82–83; and letter from Crutch, *JJLCS*, 7, No. 1 (Winter 1977 / 78), 27.

**B75:6]**   _____. "A Bibliography of *Sylvie and Bruno.*" *JJLCS*, 4, No. 3 (Summer 1975), 66–67.

Supercedes bibliographic listings and descriptions in the *Handbook* for "Bruno's Revenge," *Sylvie and Bruno* and *Sylvie and Bruno Concluded.*

For corrections, additions, and comments prepared by Denis Crutch see *JJLCS*, 4, No. 4 (Autumn 1975), 124. Further emendations by Goodacre appear in *JJLCS*, 6, No. 1 (Winter 1977), 32; and *JJLCS*, 7, No. 2 (Spring 1978), 51.

**B75:7]**   _____. "The First Separate Edition of "Jabberwocky." *JJLCS*, 4, No. 2 (Spring 1975), 33–36.

Recently uncovered March 1872 printing of Vansittart's translation of the poem into Latin elegiacs. English version is printed on a separate sheet.

**B75:8]**   _____. "Lewis Carroll's Rejection of the 60th Thousand of *Through the Looking-Glass.*" *Book Collector*, 24, No. 2 (Summer 1975), 251–56.

Carroll had the entire printing of the 60th thousand cancelled. Goodacre asserts that the differences between the illustrations in the 59th and the 60th thousand are more acute than those between the 1865 and 1866 editions of *Alice in Wonderland.*

**B75:9]**   _____. "*The Nursery 'Alice'*—A Bibliographical Essay." *JJLCS*, 4, No. 4 (Autumn 1975), 100–120.

The publication history of *The Nursery 'Alice'* including a listing of bibliographic variants.

See *JJLCS*, 5, No. 2 (Spring 1976), 63–64 for corrections and emendations.

**B75:10]** ———. "An Unrecorded Carroll Advertisement." *JJLCS,* 4, No. 1 (Winter 1975), 10.

A slip advertising *Phantasmagoria* can be found in certain copies of *Alice.*

**B75:11]** Guiliano, Edward. *Lewis Carroll: An Annotated Bibliography for 1974.* (Carroll Studies No. 1.) New York: The Lewis Carroll Society of North America, 1975. Pp. 16 + [2].

Treats: A. Primary Works; B. Reference and Bibliographical Works and Exhibition; C. Biography and Criticism; D. Miscellaneous—Including Dramatic and Pictorial Adaptations. Introduction.

**B75:12]** Howard, Philip. "The riddle of Lewis Carroll gets curiouser and curiouser. . . ." *Times* (London), 25 March 1975, p. 19.

An account of the opening of the "Lewis Carroll and Hatfield House" exhibition. See B75:13.

**B75:13]** *Lewis Carroll and Hatfield House: A Companion to The Exhibition in The Old Riding School, 25th March—7th October 1975.* [London] The Lewis Carroll Society, 1975. Pp. 25 + [3] + [4] of plates.

**B75:14]** *Lewis Carroll, An Un-Birthday Celebration: A Hand-List of the Exhibits Lent by the Rare Book Department Univ. of Virginia Library and Professor Peter Heath, Department of Philosophy.* Charlottesville: Alderman Library of the Univ. of Virginia, March 1975. Pp. [9].

Catalogue of an exhibition in the Alderman Library of the University of Virginia selected and arranged by Angelika Powell and Peter Heath.

**B75:15]** Marx, Stan, ed. *Knight Letter,* Nos. 2, 3 (February, August 1975).

See B74:9.

**B75:16]** Sibley, Brian, ed. *Bandersnatch: The Lewis Carroll Soci-*

*ety* [England] *Newsletter*. Nos. 8–12 (February, April, June, August, October 1975).

See B73:7.

**B75:17]** ——. "Correspondence." *JJLCS*, 4, No. 1 (Winter 1975), 19.

Concerns Carroll's contribution to Daniel's *Garland of Rachel*.

**B75:18]** Weaver, Warren. "Ink (and Pen) Used by Lewis Carroll." *JJLCS*, 4, No. 1 (Winter 1975), 3–4.

"Roughly speaking, Carroll used black ink (often faded to brownish) until and including October 10, 1870: then purple ink until about the end of 1890: and then black again until his death."

**B75:19]** *Lewis Carroll Exhibition*. Oxford: Christ Church, 1975. Pp. 4.

Catalogue of exhibits displayed at Christ Church. Editions in English, French, and German.

**B75:20]** ——. "The Shorthand Editions of *Alice*." *JJLCS*, 4, No. 1 (Winter 1975), 5–6.

See *JJLCS*, 5, No. 2 (Spring 1976), 64, for corrections and emendations.

# 1976

**B76:1]** *Childhood in Poetry: A Catalogue, with Biographical and Critical Annotations, of the Books of English and American Poets Comprising the Shaw Childhood in Poetry Collection, Library of the Florida State University, with Lists of poems that relate to childhood, notes, and index by John Mackay Shaw*. Second supplement. Detroit: Gale, 1976. Two volumes.

Collection includes Carroll volumes. See index.

**B76:2]**   Dakin, D. Martin. "Variant Readings." *JJLCS*, 5, No. 3 (Summer 1976), 89–92.

The poem "The Dear Gazelle" (1855) also appears with alterations as "Tema con Variazioni" and "Theme with Variations." Presents the poem's history of publication and contains a record of textual changes.

**B76:3]**   Dreyfus, Catherine. "Les soeurs d'Alice: Les photos ambiguës d'un pasteur respectable et timide, Lewis Carroll." *Nouvel Observateur*, 10–24 October 1976, p. 88.

Review of an exhibition of Carroll photographs held in Paris at the Contre-Jour gallery. The photographs were drawn from A74:3.

**B76:4]**   Goodacre, Selwyn. "Bibliographical Note on *The Hunting of the Snark* illustrated by Mervyn Peake." *The Mervyn Peake Society Newsletter*, No. 2 (Spring 1976), 22–24.

**B76:5]**   _____. "Correspondence." *JJLCS*, 5, No. 2 (Spring 1976), 62–63.

Argues that the plates in the 1911 Macmillan combined volume of the *Alice* books were not colored by Tenniel.

**B76:6]**   _____. "*The Hunting of the Snark*—A History of the Publication." *JJLCS*, 5, No. 4 (Autumn 1976), 110–18.

Traces the *Snark's* first trip into print and discusses its subsequent publication history during Carroll's lifetime. The article also contains two endnotes: one concerns the "Baker for Banker" misprint and the other treats the poem's revisions and lists changes.

For corrections and emendations see *JJLCS*, 6, No. 1 (Winter 1977), 31–32.

**B76:7]**   _____. "An Unrecorded Early American *Alice's Adventures in Wonderland*." *Knight Letter*, No. 4 (February 1976), pp. 1–2.

Bibliographic description of unrecorded Lee and Shephard edition dated 1872.

**B76:8]**   Marx, Stan, ed. *Knight Letter*, Nos. 4, 5 (February, August 1976).

See B74:9.

**B76:9]**  Sewell, Byron W., ed. *Lewis Carroll in the Popular Culture: A Continuing List.* New York: Lewis Carroll Society of North America, 1976.

The first issue of a loose sheet document containing records and descriptions of "minor Carrolliana." Categories of items recorded are: A. Reprints, Excerpts and Abbreviated Versions of Works by Lewis Carroll; B. Anthologies and School Texts; C. Parodies, Imitations and Cartoons; D. Biographical, Bibliographical, Critical Essays, Book Reviews, Exhibitions, and Collections; E. Carroll Works Set to Music and on the Screen; F. Photographs, Posters, Prints, Original Art, and Carroll's Illustrators; G. Advertisement, Editorial and Book Cover Art; H. Toys and Games; I. Stationery, Bookplates, and Miscellaneous Paper Items; J. Erotica; K. Oblique References to Lewis Carroll; L. Miscellanea. Periodic additions.

**B76:10]**  Sibley, Brian, ed. *Bandersnatch: The Lewis Carroll Society* [England] *Newsletter.* Nos. 13–16 (January, April, July, October 1976).

See B73:7.

=========================  **1977**  =========================

**B77:1]**  Crutch, Denis. "Correspondence." *JJLCS,* 6, No. 1 (Winter 1977), 30.

Records a minor textual alteration in the early 1897 printing of *The Hunting of The Snark.*

**B77:2]**  Goodacre, Selwyn H. "A Hand-List of Printed Works of Charles Dodgson, M.A. Archdeacon of Richmond." *JJLCS,* 6, No. 2 (Spring 1977), 35.

Twenty-four printed works by Carroll's father are identified. Locations of extant copies are given.

**B77:3]**  _____. "Rhyme? and Reason?—An Annotated Hand-List." *JJLCS,* 6, No. 4 (Autumn 1977), 107–11.

A bibliographical history of editions of *Rhyme? and Reason?* published during Carroll's lifetime. Includes a record of textual changes.

**B77:4]**   Heath, Peter, ed. *Knight Letter,* No. 8 (November 1977).

See B74:9.

**B77:5]**   Marx, Stan, ed. *Knight Letter,* Nos. 6, 7 (January, June 1977).

See B74:9.

**B77:6]**   Sibley, Brian, ed. *Bandersnatch: The Lewis Carroll Society England Newsletter.* Nos. 17–21 (January, April, July, October, Christmas 1977).

See B73:7.

**B77:7]**   Zerkow, Syma. *Lewis Carroll: an Exhibition at the Houston Public Library.* Cover illustration by Byron Sewell. Houston: Houston Public Library, 1977. Pp. [20], paperback.

Catalogue of a Carroll exhibition of primary and secondary materials and ephemera on loan from Byron and Susan Sewell.

# Section C.  *Biography and Criticism*

## 1960

**C60:1]**  Atherton, James S. *The Books at the Wake: A Study of Literary Allusions in James Joyce's "Finnegans Wake."* New York: Viking, 1960.

See pages 124–36 for a treatment of Carroll and *Finnegans Wake*.

**C60:2]**  Butor, Michel. "Esquisse D'un Seuil Pour Finnegan." In *Répertoire*. Paris: Éditions de Minuit, 1960, pp. 219–33.

A reprint of a 1957 essay which contains a comparison of Carroll's use of language with Joyce's (pp. 221–22). In French.

**C60:3]**  Firman, Catharine. "Lewis Carroll, Oxford Satirist." *Claremont Quarterly*, 8, No. 1 (1960), 69–72.

Brief background and summary of *Facts, Figures, and Fancies* and *The New Belfry of Christ Church, Oxford*, on the occasion of the addition of these two pamphlets to the William W. Clary Oxford Collection at the Honnold Library.

**C60:4]**  Gardner, Martin. "Mathematical Games: The Games and Puzzles of Lewis Carroll." *Scientific American*, 202, No. 3 (March 1960), 172–76.

A consideration of Carroll's "more obscure excursions into the game and puzzle field." Several of Carroll puzzles are presented, and their answers are given in the April issue.

Reprinted in Martin Gardner's *New Mathematical Diversions from Scientific American*. New York: Simon & Schuster, 1966, pp. 47–47; London: George Allen & Urwin, 1969; 1975 (paperback), pp. 45–57.

**C60:5]**  Green, R. Lancelyn. *Lewis Carroll*. London: Bodley Head, 1960 (paperback); New York: Walck, 1962. Pp. 83.

In 1968 this biography (*WMG* XXIV; 1979 ed., 529), slightly revised and totally reset, appeared in a hardcover volume with two other biographies as *Three Bodley Head Monographs.*

Reviewed by L. C. Bonnerot in *Etudes Anglaises,* 14 (1960), 382.

**C60:6]**   Lee, Kenneth. "The Most Curious Thing I Ever Saw in All My Life." *Cheshire Life,* 26 (June 1960), 52–53.

Searching around Cheshire for a "glimpse of the original Cheshire Cat." The discussion begins with the Carroll / *Alice* connection.

**C60:7]**   Miller, Margaret J. *Seven Men of Wit.* London: Hutchinson, 1960.

Chapter 2, pages 37–62, is a biography of Lewis Carroll.

**C60:8]**   Morton, Richard. *"Alice's Adventures in Wonderland and Through the Looking-Glass." Elementary English,* 38, No. 8 (December 1960), 509–13.

Carroll has little concern with connecting links in the *Alices,* books which have a literary relationship to the Renaissance quest. "The quest here is molded to fit the adventures of a child in an adult world." The impact for the young reader is more powerful because "there is a sudden moment of glory, unprepared for an unexpected, a successful revolt in the very citadels of adult life, the law court, and the dinner table."

**C60:9]**   Stafford, Jean. "The Jabberwock Anatomized." *The Griffen,* 9, No. 6 (June 1960), 2–11.

Extended review article on *The Annotated Alice.*

**C60:10]**   Thomson, J. F. "What Achilles Should Have Said to the Tortoise," *Ratio,* 3 (1960), 95–105.

A contribution to the controversy over inference initiated by Carroll. Argues that Achilles should have refused to fall into the infinite-regress trap. See C62:3 and C74:31.

## 1961

**C61:1]**  Dams, Reverend Victor, and Reverend Dyott W. Darwall. *Lewis Carroll and his Birth-Place Daresbury.* [Chester, England: privately printed by S. G. Mason], 1961.

Illustrated guide first published in 1937. Reprinted in 1961, 1964, 1966, and 1967. Reprinted in 1973 with emendations and additions, pp. 18 + [1], paperback.

**C61:2]**  Fisher, Margery. *Intent upon Reading: Critical Appraisal of Modern Fiction for Children.* Leicester: Brockhampton Press, 1961.

See pages 162–67 for a critical discussion of the *Alices,* especially their humor; also see index.

**C61:3]**  Lee, Harold Newton. *Symbolic Logic.* New York: Random House, 1961.

See index for brief references to Carroll, his *Symbolic Logic,* and his work on infinite regress.

**C61:4]**  Sewell, Elizabeth. "Dreams and Law Courts." In *The Logic of Personal Knowledge: Essays Presented to Michael Polanyi on his Seventieth Birthday.* London: Routledge & Kegan Paul, 1961, pp. 171–88.

Discusses the "trials" in the *Alices* and in *The Hunting of the Snark* within the framework of dream. See C71:23 for a French translation which contains revisions by the author. See C76:18 for a refinement of some of the ideas expressed in this article.

**C61:5]**  Spacks, Patricia Meyer. "Logic and Language in *Through the Looking-Glass.*" *ETC.: A Review of General Semantics,* 18, No. 1 (1961), 91–100.

The rigid conformity to the logical demands of language in *Through the Looking-Glass* suggests a sense of insanity in the ordinary world. The looking-glass world is one of truth and order where what seems disorderly "is a condemnation of the ordinary sloppy thinking of the reader and the sloppy traditions of his language." Language is a theme underlying virtually all of the book's episodes.

Reprinted in C71:24.

# 1962

**C62:1]**  Aivaz, David George. "A Study of Correspondences in the Writings of Walter Pater and Lewis Carroll." Dissertation Harvard University 1962.

Although Carroll and Pater differ widely in subjects, genres, purposes, and audience, several notions and motifs in Carroll's writing are strikingly similar to notions and motifs in Pater's writing. "These notions and motifs derive from the writers' basic assumptions about nature, the inner nature of man and animals, and the force of 'passion' which, in their view, inexorably drives all living things" (Introduction). Argues that Pater's and Carroll's own sense of terror at their view of the natural world and the natural man underlies everything they wrote.

**C62:2]**  Auden, W. H. "Today's 'Wonder-World' Needs Alice." *New York Times Magazine,* 1 July 1962, pp. 5, 16, 17, 19.

*Alice in Wonderland's* genesis and history are recalled on the occasion of the one-hundredth anniversary of the famous boat ride up the Thames when Alice's story was first told. Auden also analyzes the *Alices* and looks at the American reader's response to the stories.

Reprinted in C71:24.

**C62:3]**  Bartley, W. W., III. "Achilles, the Tortoise, and Explanation in Science and History." *British Journal for the Philosophy of Science,* 13 (May 1962), 15–33.

Concerns Karl R. Popper's schema of causal explanation and includes a discussion of "an important error about inference which seems to lie at the root of much of the controversy: the interpretation Gilbert Ryle and others give to Lewis Carroll's story about Achilles and the Tortoise."

**C62:4]**  Boulby, Mark. "Zum Begriff des Nonsense in der englischen Kinderliteratur." *Studien zur Jugendliteratur,* (1962), pp. 801–8.

Carroll is among the writers mentioned in this consideration of the similarities and differences between tales and nonsense poetry. Notes that practically all English nonsense poets also have drawn caricatures of the world. In German.

**C62:5]**  Buchalter, Barbara Elpern. "Logic of Nonsense." *Mathematics Teacher,* May 1962, pp. 459–64.

Demonstrates the mathematician at work in the *Alices.* Cites Carroll ability to use the fallacy, to reduce logic to the absurd, to create the syllogism which is logical to its conclusion but fallacious in its premise.

**C62:6]**  Durre, Clement V. *Readable Relativity.* London: G. Bell, 1962.

Chapter 2, pages 11–21, entitled "Alice Through the Looking-Glass" is a discussion of Garnett's May 1918 article in the *Mathematical Gazette.*

**C62:7]**  Graham, David. "The Centenary of 'Alice.'" *Coming Events in Britain,* July 1962, pp. 32–33, 57.

An illustrated account of the famous boat trip.

**C62:8]**  Green, Roger Lancelyn. "One immortal fine day." *The Sunday Telegraph,* 10 June 1962, p. 12.

An account of the famous boat trip when Alice's story was first told.

**C62:9]**  _____. "Picnic on Wonderland." *The Junior Bookshelf,* 26, No. 3 (July 1962), 110–14.

An account of the famous boat trip and subsequent events.

**C62:10]**  _____. *The Story of Lewis Carroll.* London: Methuen & Co. Ltd, 1962.

Second reprint of the biography, written for children, first published in 1949. Contains slightly updated reading list, as published in the 1954 reprint.

**C62:11]**  Hildebrandt, Rolf. "Nonsense-Aspekte de englischen Kinderliteratur." Dissertation Hamburg 1962.

See C70:18.

**C62:12]** Hugh-Jones, Siriol. "A new review of 'Alice.' " *Punch,* 243, No. 6372 (24 October 1962), pp. 596–98.

In a series entitled "Children's Classics Revisited," *Alice* is reviewed as if the book had only just been published.

**C62:13]** Karilas, Tauno. "Lewis Carroll, matemaatikko ja sadunkertoja." *In Robinsonista Muumipeikkoon.* Helsinki: Werner Söderstöm, 1962, pp. 92–95.

Brief biography of "Lewis Carroll, a mathematician and storyteller." In Finnish.

**C62:14]** Kenner, Hugh. "Art in a Closed Field." *Virginia Quarterly Review,* 38, No. 4 (Autumn 1962), 597–605.

Elizabeth Sewell's notion of Carroll's nonsense existing in a closed field (first discussed in her *The Field of Nonsense*) is endorsed in a study of the principle of the closed field in the imaginative literature of the past one hundred years.

**C62:15]** Kirk, Daniel F. *Charles Dodgson, Semeiotician.* (Humanities Monographs Series No. 11.) Gainesville: Univ. of Florida Press, 1962. Pp. 78.

Reviewed by: P. T. Geach in *Notes & Queries,* n.s. 10 (1963), 473; Robert D. Sutherland, *Philological Quarterly,* 43 (1964), 429–31.

**C62:16]** Kneale, William and Martha. *The Development of Logic.* Oxford: Clarendon Press, 1962.

See index for brief references to Carroll, his *Symbolic Logic* and his work on inference. Reprinted in 1964.

**C62:17]** La Cour, Tage. "Alice i vidunderlandet." *Aftenposten* (Norway), 5 July 1962.

The one-hundredth anniversary of the famous boat trip up the Thames during which *Alice's Adventures* was first told is celebrated with a discussion of the genesis and history of *Alice.* In Norwegian by a Danish author.

**C62:18]** Lennon, Florence Becker. *The Life of Lewis Carroll.* New York: Collier, 1962.

Revised edition of *Victoria through the Looking-Glass* published in 1945 by Simon and Schuster, New York.

A second revision—the third edition—containing a new preface was published as: *The Life of Lewis Carroll: Victoria through the Looking-Glass*. New York: Dover; London: Constable, 1972.

**C62:19]**  Mathews, Dorothy Elaine. "The Literary Reputation of Lewis Carroll in England and America in the Nineteenth Century." Dissertation Case Western Reserve University 1962.

A study of the state of children's literature prior to Carroll, the facts of publication of *Alice in Wonderland* and its sequel, the subsequent history of *Alice* and its reputation among English and American critics, the publication and reception of Carroll's subsequent works, and the Lewis Carroll legend at the time of his death.

Carroll is the writer most responsible for turning the tide toward lesson-free imaginative literature for children in the twentieth century. *Alice* received little critical attention when it was first published, but it was lavishly praised upon the publication of *Through the Looking-Glass*. Thereafter, Carroll maintains an extraordinary high place in public esteem throughout the century. Contains extensive bibliographical entries.

**C62:20]**  "One Golden Afternoon." *Time*, 80 (6 July 1962), pp. 66–67.

Recalls, on its one-hundredth anniversary, the famous boat trip up the Thames during which Alice's adventures were first told.

**C62:21]**  Potter, Stephen. "Alice from Underground." *The Guardian*, No. 36079, 4 July 1962.

A review of *Alice*, as if it had just been published from a hitherto undiscovered manuscript.

**C62:22]**  Reardon, Margaret. "A Present for Alice." *Horn Book*, 38 (June 1962), 243–47.

The famous boat trip up the Thames during which Alice's adventures first took shape is recalled and discussed on the occasion of its one-hundredth anniversary.

Reprinted in *Horn Book Reflections*. Ed. E. W. Field. Boston: Horn Book, 1969, pp. 286–90.

**C62:23]**   Sewell, Elizabeth. "Lewis Carroll and T. S. Eliot as Nonsense Poets." In *T. S. Eliot: Twentieth Century Views.* Ed. Hugh Kenner. Englewood Cliffs, New Jersey: Prentice-Hall, 1962, pp. 65–72.

Reprint of 1958 essay; also reprinted in C71:24.

**C62:24]**   Sichelschmidt, Gustav. "Die hundertjährige Alice." *Jugendliteratur,* 8, No. 12 (1962), 529–32.

Centenary account on *Alice in Wonderland.* In German.

**C62:25]**   Steen, Marguerite. *A Pride of Terrys: Family Saga.* London: Longmans, 1962.

Carroll's friendship with the Terry family is discussed on pages 105–7.

# 1963

**C63:1]**   Beaslai, Piaras. "Was Joyce Inspired by Lewis Carroll?" *Irish Digest,* 78, No. 1 (1963), 35–38.

Not seen.

**C63:2]**   Burke, Kenneth. "The Thinking of the Body: Comments on the Imagery of Catharsis in Literature." *Psychoanalytic Review,* 50, No. 3 (1963), 25–67 [375–417 in annual numbering].

Considers, on pages 25–28, the "ways in which the functions of bodily excretion attain expression" in *Alice in Wonderland.* Looks at the "sneezing" in the "Pig and Pepper" chapter, for example, and finds the whole kitchen scene "a dizzy transcendence by concealment through nonsense, so that food could perversely stand for its opposite, offal." Burke finds the anal-oral reversibility continued in the scene of The Mad Tea Party.

　　The article is reprinted as chapter 2 in Burke's *Language as Symbolic Action* (Berkeley and Los Angeles: Univ. of California Press, 1966), pp. 308–43.

　　Reprinted in C71:24.

**C63:3]**   Earnest, Ernest. "The Walrus and the Carpenter." *CEA Critic*, 26, No. 3 (December 1963), 1, 6–7.

An analysis of "The Walrus and the Carpenter" which reveals archetypal elements with Freudian implications. Notes parallels between Carroll's poem and Eliot's *The Waste Land.*

**C63:4]**   Green, Roger Lancelyn. *Authors & Places: A Literary Pilgrimage.* New York: G.P. Putnam's Sons, 1963.

Carroll and Oxford are discussed on pages 150–57, et passim.

**C63:5]**   ———. "My name is Alice. . ." *The Sunday Times Colour Magazine,* 7 April 1963.

An account of the genesis of the *Alice* books, with emphasis on the origins of *Through the Looking-Glass* at Charlton Kings, April 1873.

**C63:6]**   Lennon, Florence Becker. "Author in Wonderland." *Author's Guild Children's Book Committee Newsletter,* 4, No. 1 (Spring 1963).

An account of Carroll's most satisfactory relationship with Macmillan & Co., his lifelong publisher.
     Reprinted in *JJLCS,* No. 8 (Autumn 1971), pp. 3–4.

**C63:7]**   Liede, Alfred. *Dichtung als Spiel: Studien zur Unsinnspoesie an der Grenze der Sprache.* Berlin and New York: Walter de Gruyter & Co., 1963. Vol. I.

Title translates as *Poetry as Game: Studies in Nonsense Poetry at the Limits of Language.* Carroll is discussed primarily on pages 172–204. In German.

**C63:8]**   O'Brien, Hugh. "*Alice in Wonderland:* The French Lesson-Book." *Notes & Queries,* n.s. 10 (December 1963), 461.

Alice's French lesson-book referred to in chapter II of *Alice in Wonderland* was *La Bagatelle,* first published in London in 1804.

**C63:9]**   ———."Où est ma chatte?" *Irish Times,* 5 April 1963, p. 10.

*La Bagatelle,* a French lesson-book, played an important part in the genesis of *Alice in Wonderland.*

**C63:10]**   Richardson, Joanna. *The Young Lewis Carroll.* Illustrations by Susan E. Sims. New York: Roy, 1963; London: Parrish, 1964. Pp. 134.

Biography focusing on the years 1837–50. Intended for sixth-grade readers and up.

**C63:11]**   Taylor, Alexander L. *The White Knight: A Study of C. L. Dodgson (Lewis Carroll).* Chester Springs, Pennsylvania: Dufour, 1963.

Reprint of the 1952 edition published by Oliver & Boyd, Edinburgh (*WMG* XXIII; 1979 ed., 528).
   Reprinted: [Folcroft, Pennsylvania]: Folcroft Library Editions, 1974.

**C63:12]**   Thwaite, M. F. *From Primer to Pleasure.* London: The Library Association, 1963.

See "An Introduction to the History of Children's Books in England from the Invention of Printing to 1900," pages 114–17, and index.

**C63:13]**   "What Happened to the Nonsense?" *The Times,* 2 January 1963.

On the difficulties of translating Carroll's works.

## 1964

**C64:1]**   Benét, Laura. *Famous Poets for Young People.* New York: Dodd, Mead & Co., 1964.

Carroll's life and work are presented to young readers (age 9 and up?) on pages 49–57.

**C64:2]**   Boynton, Mary Fuertes. "An Oxford Don Quixote." *Hispania,* 48 (1964), 738–50.

On *Don Quixote* and *Alice in Wonderland.* "To read one of these books with the other in mind is to turn up analogues almost constantly."

**C64:3]**   Chesterton, G. K. *The Spice of Life and Other Essays.* Beaconsfield: Darween Finlayson, 1964.

Contains a reprint of Chesterton's essay "Both sides of the Looking-Glass," pages 66–70.

**C64:4]**   Collingwood, Frances. "The Carroll-Tenniel Partnership." *Books* (November / December 1964), pp. 232–35.

Discusses Carroll's *Alice* drawings and his relationship with Tenniel.

P. H. Muir offers corrections and further discussion in a letter, "Carroll and Tenniel," in *Books* (January / February 1965), pp. 30–31; also see letters from Joseph E. Beckett, p. 31, and Edward Carter, p. 32.

**C64:5]**   Gaál, Gábor. "A százéves Lewis Carroll." Volume I of *Valogatbtt irások.* Bucharest: Trodalmi Könyvkiadó, 1964, pp. 445–46.

A reprint of Gaál's 1932 article written for the centennial of Carroll's birth and first published in *Korunk,* 7, No. 3 (1932), 222–23. The reprint appears in a three-volume set of Gaál's collected writings that was published in Rumania but is in Hungarian.

Lewis Carroll was practically unknown to the wider public in Hungary in the 1930s. He wrote his works for children, but it was the grown-ups who adored them. In an age when children read thrillers and books praising racial discrimination and when writing children's literature became a profitable enterprise, Carroll's works helps us to understand the true function of children's literature.

**C64:6]**   Jung, Carl G. "Approaches to the Unconscious." In *Man and His Symbols.* London: Aldus Books; Garden City, New York: Doubleday, 1964, pp. 53–54.

Notes that *Alice in Wonderland* contains a famous example of a typical infantile motif: the dream of growing infinitely small or infinitely big, or being transformed from one to the other.

**C64:7]**   Leach, Elsie. " 'Alice in Wonderland' in Perspective." *Victorian Newsletter,* No. 25 (Spring 1964), pp. 9–11.

Discussion of the *Alice* books as mid-nineteenth-century children's literature. Dodgson rejected the rational approach of earlier children's writers. "One of the most striking features of the book, especially if one reviews what was the

standard fare for the children of the time, is the strong reaction *against* didacti-
cism which so many of the episodes illustrate. . . . The character of Alice herself is a bit puzzling, even to the modern child, because it does not fit a
stereotype."
   Reprinted in C71:24.

**C64:8]**   Niskanen, Juhani. "Lapsenmielisten valtakunta." *Helsin-
gin Sanomat,* 5 May 1964.

A newspaper article in which Carroll's Nonsense is briefly surveyed, analyzed,
and compared with Edward Lear's. In Finnish.

**C64:9]**   Rackin, Donald. "The Critical Interpretations of *Alice in
Wonderland:* A Survey and Suggested Reading." *Dissertation Abstracts,* 25 (1964), 1217 (University of Illinois).

"A survey of previous critical approaches to *Alice in Wonderland* reveals the
need for a thorough interpretation of the book as an organic aesthetic whole.
Although there have been many serious and perceptive studies of *Alice* in the
past thirty years, almost all of them interpret the work in very specialized
modes—modes inaccessible to the majority of readers and, moreover, modes
that by nature fail to investigate the books as a complete, autonomous work of
art."
   Includes a short biography of Carroll, an exhaustive survey and evaluation
of previous readings of *Alice,* and "an attempt at a complete and unspecialized
exegesis of *Alice in Wonderland* as a separate, organic, self-sufficient, and aes-
thetically satisfying piece of prose fiction. The latter, in revised form, was published as an article; see C66:16.

**C64:10]**   Schöne, Annemarie. "Englische Wort- und Sprach-
spiele im Wandel der Jahrhunderte." *Jahrbuch für Äesthetik und all-
gemeine Kunstwissenschaft,* 9 (1964), 57–81.

Carroll is discussed in a historical survey of British literary wordplayers. In
German.

**C64:11]**   Skinner, John. "Lewis Carroll's Adventures in Wonderland." In *Psychoanalysis and Literature.* Ed. H. M. Ruitenbeek.
New York: Dutton, pp. 218–42.

Reprint of 1947 essay.

**C64:12]**   Straight, Robert L. "Lewis Carroll: Author and Mathematician." *Arithmetic Teacher,* 11 (December 1964), 571–73.

Few people realize the amount of mathematics contained in *Alice in Wonderland,* or do they realize the effect of Carroll's mathematics upon his work. "Of the nearly nine hundred items that were written by Dodgson, only sixteen were books. Ten of these sixteen were books pertaining to mathematics and logic." Surveys Carroll as a mathematician.

**C64:13]** Sutherland, Robert Donald. "Language and Lewis Carroll." *Dissertation Abstracts,* 25 (1964), 2522 (Iowa).

Deals with the three aspects of Carroll's interest in language: as a cultural phenomenon, as an instrument of thought and communication, and as a vehicle for play. Carroll's "studies as amateur philologist and professional logician led him to theoretical conclusions regarding the nature and function of language quite sophisticated for his time and broader in scope than is generally recognized."

Revised and published as a book; see C70:33.

# 1965

**C65:1]** Avery, Gillian. *Nineteenth Century Children: Heroes and Heroines in English Children's Stories 1780–1900.* London: Hodder and Stoughton, 1965.

Carroll and his writings are discussed on pages 128–31 et passim, and imitations on pages 131–34.

**C65:2]** Bossi, Elda. "Alice Centenaria." *La Nazione,* November 1965.

A biographical essay and appreciation of Carroll on *Alice*'s one-hundredth birthday. In Italian.

**C65:3]** "Carroll's Logical Nonsense," *New Knowledge,* 3, No. 10 (1965), 542–44.

A discussion of space and time in the *Alice* books.

**C65:4]** "A Century of Alice." *Newsweek,* 12 July 1965, p. 86.

A look at Carroll and *Alice in Wonderland* on the one-hundredth anniversary of the book's publication.

**C65:5]** Dohm, J[anice] H[ope]. "Alice in America." *Junior Bookshelf,* 29, No. 5 (October 1965), 261–67.

An account of American interest in *Alice in Wonderland,* with a section on the history of the manuscript.

**C65:6]** Gardner, Martin. "A Child's Garden of Bewilderment." *Saturday Review,* 17 July 1965, pp. 18–19.

On the occasion of *Alice*'s one-hundredth birthday, Gardner remarks that "*Alice* is no longer a children's book." Modern adult readers recognize the *Alices* subtle humor, social satire, and philosophical depth. Also contains a comparison of Carroll with L. Frank Baum.

Two follow-up letters on *Alice* and *Oz* appeared on 14 August 1965, p. 26.

**C65:7]** Green, Roger Lancelyn. *Tellers of Tale.* London: Edward Ward, 1965.

Revised edition of the book first published in 1946. Chapter 4, pages 49–62, is on Lewis Carroll.

**C65:8]** Halpern, Sidney. "The Mother-Killer." *Psychoanalytic Review,* 52, No. 2 (Summer 1965), 71–74.

On "Jabberwocky." "The archetypical myth upon which the poem is based, however unconsciously by Carroll, takes us back to Sumerian religious reenactments of the replacement of the matriarchy by filiarchal forces in the form of Enlil (Marduk) slaying the great monster Tiamat."

**C65:9]** Lamey, Annegret. "Alice's Adventures in Wonderland." In *Kindlers Literature Lexicon.* Zurich: Kindler Verlag, 1965, I, pp. 433–34.

Encyclopedia entry on *Alice in Wonderland* with a brief German / English bibliography of primary and secondary works. In German.

**C65:10]** L[ehtonen], P[aavo]. "Salavuotias Liisa." *Uusi Suomi,* 18 July 1965.

A newspaper article on Carroll and "The hundred years old *Alice*." In Finnish.

**C65:11]** Levin, Harry. "Wonderland Revisited." *Kenyon Review*, 27, No. 4 (1965), 591–616.

Readings of the *Alices* and *The Hunting of the Snark*, with passing references to the *Sylvie and Bruno* books, on the one-hundredth anniversary of the publication of *Alice in Wonderland*. Some critical emphasis on the nature of Carroll's nonsense.
Reprinted in C71:24.

**C65:12]** MacNeice, Louis. *Varieties of Parable*. Cambridge: Cambridge Univ. Press, 1965.

See pages 90–94 for a discussion of the allegorical content of the *Alices* et passim for additional references to Carroll and the *Alices*.

**C65:13]** Morris, James. *Oxford*. New York: Harcourt, Brace & World, 1965.

Carroll is discussed on pages 240–43, et passim.
Reprinted: London: Faber and Faber, 1974.

**C65:14]** Parisot, Henri. *Lewis Carroll: Une Etude avec un choix de textes*. (Collection Poètes d'aujourd'hui 29.) Paris: Seghers, 1965.

Revised edition of a French critical biography which includes selections of Carroll's work translated into French. First published in 1952.
Reprinted with slight revisions in 1972.

**C65:15]** Percy, H. R. "100 Years of Alice." *Canadian Author and Bookman* (Editorial), 41, No. 1 (1965), inside cover, p. 2.

Centenary tribute.

**C65:16]** Pitcher, George. "Wittgenstein, Nonsense and Lewis Carroll." *Massachusetts Review*, 6 (1965), 591–611.

Finds affinities between these two logicians, showing that absurdities exposed in the *Tractatus* and *Philosophical Investigations* were exploited by Carroll for comic effect.
Reprinted in A71:12.

**C65:17]** Potter, Greta Largo. "Millions in Wonderland." *Horn Book*, 41 (December 1965), 593–97.

On *Alice*'s one-hundredth birthday, the genesis and history of the manuscript *Alice's Adventures Under Ground* are discussed.

**C65:18]** Schmidtchen, Paul W. "Life: What Is It But a Dream?" *Hobbies,* 70 (October 1965), 106–8.

A brief account of Carroll's life and the publication of the *Alices.*

**C65:19]** Serra, Christóbel. "Dos príncipes del absurdismo inglés: Edward Lear y Lewis Carroll." *Papeles de Son Armadans* (Majorca), 34 (1965), lix–lxiv.

Finds British humor inimitable and cites Shakespeare, Swift, Lear, and Carroll as England's greatest comic geniuses. The humor in the *Alices* is discussed (portmanteau words, comic characters, dream atmosphere), and Carroll is lauded for uniquely creating a dreamworld with logic. Serra comments on the "unforgettable" "Jabberwocky" and the black humor in *The Hunting of the Snark,* a poem which can pass as a tragedy of frustration and fracas. In Spanish.

**C65:20]** Siciliano, Enzo. "Alice Ha Compiuto Cento Anni: Que che può capitare seguendo un coniglio." *Corriere Della Sera,* 11 November 1965.

A biographical essay on Carroll on the occasion of *Alice*'s one-hundredth birthday. In Italian.

**C65:21]** Townsend, John Rowe. *Written for Children: An Outline of English Children's Literature.* New York: Lothrop, Lee & Shepard, 1965.

See chapter 4, especially pages 35–38, for references to Carroll, his work and his influence.

A revised and expanded edition, with the same title, was published in 1974: Harmondsworth: Kestrel Books, 1974; Philadelphia and New York: J. B. Lippincott Company, 1975. See pages 94–101 and index for references to Carroll.

**C65:22]** Vazhdaev, V. "Lewis Carroll and His Fairy Tale." *Inostrannaya Literatura,* No. 7 (1965), pp. 214–19.

A centenary tribute by a specialist in Russian fairy tales. Title and text in Russian.

**C65:23]** White, Alison. "*Alice* After a Hundred Years." *Michigan Quarterly Review,* 4, No. 4 (Fall 1965), 261–64.

A brief survey, on the occasion of *Alice's* centenary, of the diverse critical response that the *Alices* have received. White offers her own comments on the conscious or subconscious treatment of evolution in *Alice in Wonderland* and on the nature of Carroll's drawings for *Alice's Adventures Under Ground.*

**C65:24]**   Williamson, Geoffrey. "Lewis Carroll." In *100 Great Modern Lives.* Ed. John Canning. London: Odhams, 1965; New York: Hawthorn, 1966, pp. 132–37.

Brief biography.
   Reprinted: London, Odhams, 1965, 1967, 1968; New York: Hawthorn, 1974.

# 1966

**C66:1]**   Adrian, Arthur A. *Mark Lemon: First Editor of Punch.* Oxford: Oxford Univ. Press, 1966.

Contains an account of a model for Alice in *Through the Looking-Glass;* see index.

**C66:2]**   Costa, F. "Lewis Carroll parodie Walton: *The Vision of the Three T's.*" *Caliban,* No. 3 (1966), pp. 175–84.

Among the satires Carroll wrote that were inspired by his daily life at Oxford, *The Version of the Three T's* is his longest, most sustained, and most coherent parody. In *The Version of the Three T's* parody became more than an ornament of satire. Contains a comparison and contrast of this pamphlet with the work it parodies, Walton's *The Compleat Angler.* In French.

**C66:3]**   Darton, F. J. Harvey. Children's *Books in England: Five Centuries of Social Life.* Cambridge: Cambridge Univ. Press, 1966.

Carroll and his works, primarily the *Alices,* are discussed with other "children's books" of the period in chapter 14, "The Sixties: *Alice* and After," pages 259–73.
   This book was first published in 1932, was revised in 1958, and was reprinted in 1960.

**C66:4]**   Empson, William. *Some Versions of Pastoral*. Harmondsworth: Penguin Books, 1966.

Reprint of 1935 edition published by Chatto & Windus, London; "Alice in
Wonderland: The Child as Swain" appears on pages 201–33.

**C66:5]**   Ettleson, Abraham. *Lewis Carroll's "Through the Looking-Glass" Decoded*. New York: Philosophical Library, 1966.
Pp. 84.

"Strange as it may seem, the 'Alice' books are written in code, and this book
is a decoding of one of them." Dodgson in *Through the Looking-Glass* is writing
about Judaism. The Jewish allegory is decoded paragraph by paragraph.

**C66:6]**   Gray, Donald J. "The Uses of Victorian Laughter," *Victorian Studies,* 10 (1966), 145–76.

Considers relationships between Carroll's comic writing and other popular
forms of humor in the period.

**C66:7]**   Greenacre, Phyllis. "On Nonsense." In *Psychoanalysis—
A General Psychology: Essays in Honor of Heinze Hartmann*. Eds.
R. M. Lowenstein, L. M. Newman, M. Schur, and A. J. Solnit.
New York: International Univ. Press, 1966, pp. 655–77.

A study of nonsense and its relation to agression and anxiety. The meaning of
nonsense is studied, and Carroll's and Lear's nonsense are analyzed and
compared.
    Reprinted in Phyllis Greenacre, *Emotional Growth*. New York: International
Univ. Press, 1971, II, 592–615.

**C66:8]**   Hudson, Derek. "Lewis Carroll's Father." *Times Literary Supplement,* 26 May 1966, p. 484.

Brief discussion of Carroll's father. Suggests that Canon Dodgson "greatly influenced the Rev. C. L. Dodgson in his outward and 'official' character." Samples of Carroll and his father's handwriting are reproduced.

**C66:9]**   _____. *Lewis Carroll*. (Writers and Their Work 96.) London: Longmans, 1966. Pp. 40.

Reprint of brief biographical study first published in 1958.

**C66:10]** Lehmann, John. "Alice at the Sorbonne." *Listener,* 76 (22 September 1966), 424–25.

Lehmann recounts his lecture tour in 1965 to seven universities in France to discuss the *Alice* books. He discovered, to his surprise, that the centenary was being celebrated enthusiastically in France, where Carroll is a very popular author. He finds "what particularly interests the French intellectual of today in the *Alice* books is, first, the demonstration of Lewis Carroll as one of the most brilliant 'play' logicians who ever existed."
    See also letter by Nina Steane, p. 456.

**C66:11]** _____. "*Alice in Wonderland* and Its Sequel." *Revue des Langues Vivantes* (Brussels), 32 (1966), 115–30.

Publication of a lecture given for the centenary of *Alice*. Lehmann offers a personal reading of the *Alice* books with divers insights and many excerpted passages from the stories.

**C66:12]** *Lewis Carroll and Guildford.* Guildford, England: Guildford Corporation, 1966. Pp. [9], photographs and facsimiles of manuscript material.

An account of Lewis Carroll's association with Guildford, the site of the Dodgson family's home after the death of the elder Dodgson.
    Revised second edition published in 1970.

**C66:13]** Lomer, Gerald R. "Alice One Hundred." *Canadian Library,* 23, No. 2 (September 1966), 80–85.

Discussion of Carroll's life and the *Alice* books on the occasion of the one-hundredth anniversary of the publication of *Alice in Wonderland.*

**C66:14]** MacEachen, Dougald B. "Wilkie Collins' *Heart and Science* and the Vivisection Controversy." *Victorian Newsletter,* No. 29 (Spring 1966), pp. 22–25.

Includes an explanation of Carroll's argument against vivisection in the context of the Victorian anti-vivisectionist movement.

**C66:15]** Martin, Robert. *Nil: Episodes in the Literary Conquest of Void During the Nineteenth Century.* New York: Oxford Univ. Press, 1966.

A critical reading of *The Hunting of the Snark* appears on pages 96–99. In recent years the poem has become "a much more serious piece of humor than it ever was for the Victorians." It "imposes upon the design of the voyage a new and sinister pattern; it presents Nothing, not as an obstacle to be eluded or a test to be passed, but as a predatory potential of the goal itself."

**C66:16]** Rackin, Donald. "Alice's Journey to the End of Night." *Publications of the Modern Language Association,* 81, No. 5 (October 1966), 313–26.

A critical reading of *Alice in Wonderland* as "a self-contained fiction, distinct from *Through the Looking-Glass* and all other imaginative pieces by Carroll. . . . Alice's dogged quest for Wonderland's meaning in terms of her aboveground world is doomed to failure. Her only escape is in flight from Wonderland's complete anarchy . . . [and] is a symbolic rejection of mad sanity in favor of the sane madness of ordinary existence. . . . Her literal quest serves, vicariously, as the reader's metaphorical search for meaning in the lawless haphazard universe of his deepest consciousness. . . . the book is paradoxically both a denial and an affirmation of order.
    Reprinted in A69:23 and C71:24.

**C66:17]** Root, E. Merrill. "Snark Hunting: Lewis Carroll on Collectivism." *American Opinion* 9, No. 4 (April 1966), 73–82.

*The Hunting of the Snark* is the reduction of collectivism to absurdity, a humor-salient critique of this age of ours in so far as it is in the hands of the fanatics of abstract subjective illusion and mania.

**C66:18]** Schrey, Helmut. "Die Englische Nonsense-Dichtung und ihre sprachlichen Voraussetzungen." In *Beiträge zur Fachdidaktik: Eine Aufsatzsammlung.* Ed. J. Heinrich, et. al. Ratingen: A. Henn, 1966, pp. 30–52.

A study of English nonsense poetry through language. Argues that the content and the structure of the English sentence facilitates nonsense; in German the nonsense poets have more difficulties since the position of words is less rigid than in English. The *Alices* are analyzed and used frequently as sources for illustrations. In German.

**C66:19]** Thompson, Malcolm. "Alice's Adventures in Wonderland." In *100 Great Books.* Ed. John Canning. London: Odhams, 1966, pp. 374–80.

History of and commentary on the *Alice* books. Also contains a page of illustrations facing page 353.

Reprinted: London: Souvenir Press, 1974.

**C66:20]** Wood, James, P. *The Snark Was a Boojum: A Life of Lewis Carroll.* Illustrations by David Levine. (A Pantheon Portrait.) New York: Pantheon, 1966.

Biography intended for adolescents.

Reviewed by: R. B. Martin, *Book Week*, 8 May 1966, p. 6; Martha Gould, *Library Journal*, 91 (1 June 1966), 3549; Alice Dalgliesch, *Saturday Review*, 49 (25 June 1966), 61; A. B. Myers, *New York Times Book Review*, 26 June 1966, p. 26; *Horn Book*, 42 (August 1966), 444; *Best Seller*, 26 (1 October 1966), 252; Lucia Johnson, *Christian Science Monitor*, 3 November 1966, p. B10.

**C66:21]** Woolf, Virginia. "Lewis Carroll." In *Collected Essays.* Vol. 1. Ed. Leonard Woolf. London: Hogarth, 1966; New York: Harcourt Brace, 1967, pp. 254–55.

Reprint of 1939 essay on Carroll; also reprinted in C71:24.

# 1967

**C67:1]** Binder, Lucia. "Vorläufer der modernen phantastischen Erzählung." In *Das Irrationale im Jugendbuch.* (Schriften zur Jugendlektüre.) Vienna: [Jugend und Volk?], 1967, pp. 42–55.

The works of Carroll, Cervantes, Swift, Barrie, Tolkien, and others are discussed as precursors of modern fantasies in German for children. In these classic works the real and unreal world often interconnect. There is humor and lack of worry in them, and the irrational is pure vital space. In German.

**C67:2]** Black, Duncan. "The Central Argument in Lewis Carroll's 'The Principles of Parliamentary Representation.' " *Papers on Non-Market Decision Making*, 3 (Fall 1967), 1–17.

A detailed outline of the central argument in Carroll's booklet. For almost a century few have shown any understanding of the booklet. The booklet is a most interesting contribution to political science, "and is one which may yet prove fertile of future developments."

**C67:3]**  Brophy, Brigid, Michael Levey, and Charles Osborne. *Fifty Works of English Literature We Could Do Without.* London: Rapp & Carroll, 1967, pp. 81–82.

*Through the Looking-Glass* is quite amusing, but *Alice* is a comparatively labored affair, the fantasy is anything but free-ranging: it lurches from one labored situation to the next.

**C67:4]**  Collingwood, Stuart Dodgson. *The Life and Letters of Lewis Carroll.* Detroit: Gale; [Philadelphia]: West, 1967.

Modern reprints of 1899 U.S. edition of 1898 edition published by T. Fisher Unwin, London (*WMG* I; 1979 ed., 501).

**C67:5]**  Covey, Peter. *The Image of Childhood.* Harmondsworth: Penguin, 1967.

Revised edition of *Poor Monkey: The Child in Literature*, published in 1957 by Rockliff, London.

   Carroll and his works are discussed in a section treating escape. "The remarkable fact about Dodgson is that by using the very means of his weakness, by succumbing to his dream and fantasy, he should become so intelligently awake." In the *Alices* "one senses the extraordinary power of artistic sublimation that Carroll brought to the achievement of the two books."

**C67:6]**  Gattégno, Jean, and Alain Schifres. "Alice in Analysis." *Réalités,* No. 201 (August 1967), pp. 58–61.

A wide-ranging interview with Jean Gattégno on Carroll. Gattégno's responses are often psychoanalytical. Jonathan Miller's tv / film version of *Alice* is discussed, and the article is illustrated with stills from the screen adaptation.

**C67:7]**  Gordon, Caroline, and Jeanne Richardson. "Flies in Their Eyes? A Note on Joseph Heller's *Catch-22,*" *Southern Review,* n.s. 3 (1967), 96–105.

Compares *Catch-22* with the *Alice* books.

**C67:8]**  Hürlimann, Bettina. *Three Centuries of Children's Books in Europe.* Translated by Brian W. Alderson. Oxford: Oxford

Univ. Press, 1967; New York & Cleveland: World Publishing, 1968.

Chapter 5, "Jabberwocky: A Typical English Element in Children's Literature," contains an extended discussion of Carroll, pages 64–75.

First published as *Europäische Kinderbücher in drei Jahrhunderten.* Zurich and Freiburg: Atlantis Verlag, 1959; reprinted in 1968 by Siebenstern Taschenbuch.

**C67:9]**  Krahé, Hildegarde. "Nonsense-Literature." In *Das Irrationale im Jugendbuch.* Ed. Richard Bamberger. (Schriften zur Jugendlektüre No. 8.) Vienna: [Jugend und Volk?], 1967, pp. 100–112.

Surveys attempts at defining nonsense and argues that the roots of nonsense can be found in nonsensical children's rhymes where the content derives from the use of analogues and is often defined through the rhythm of sounds. Carroll is one of several nonsense poets discussed. In German.

**C67:10]**  O'Brien, Hugh B. "Alice's Journey in 'Through the Looking-Glass.' " *Notes & Queries,* n.s. 14 (October 1967), 380–82.

Suggests that Alice's journey in *Through the Looking-Glass* parallels the rail trip Carroll must have taken from Holyhead to Llandudno Junction when visiting the Liddells at their resort home. Cites parallels.

For a reply by Roger Lancelyn Green see C69:11.

**C67:11]**  Rackin, Donald. "Corrective Laughter: Carroll's *Alice* and Popular Children's Literature of the Nineteenth Century." *Journal of Popular Culture,* 1 (1967), 243–55.

Looks at the prevalent trends in nineteenth-century children's literature and shows how they are a main target of the satire evidenced in *Alice's Adventures in Wonderland.* "Any full-scale analysis must recognize this target because Carroll's hits at it are a significant part of the book's total meaning and success."

**C67:12]**  Reed, Henry M. *The A. B. Frost Book.* Rutland, Vermont: Charles E. Tuttle, 1967.

See index for references to Frost's working relationship with Carroll.

**C67:13]**  Rundus, Raymond J. " 'O Frabjous Day!': Introducing Poetry." *English Journal,* 56, No. 7 (October 1967), 958–63.

"Jabberwocky" offers "a wealth of material to the linguist, the semanticist, and the folklorist. . . ." It also "has specific values which qualify it as a touchstone in a poetry course." Suggests how the poem can be used as an introduction to poetry, and gives two assignments suitable for secondary students.

**C67:14]**   Sacksteder, William. "Looking-Glass: A Treatise on Logic." *Philosophy and Phenomenological Research,* 27 (March 1967), 338–55.

*Through the Looking-Glass* is intimately derived from logic; its organization, direction, and stages are modelled after the verbal and intellectual arts in general, and the result imitates a treatise on logic. "Logicians have overlooked this wider connection with their art, for they often misunderstand predominently literary metaphors and structures." As a logical treatise "*Through the Looking-Glass* predominently hovers between semantics and pragmatics, and suggests a progression from one to the other."

**C67:15]**   Smith, James Steel. *A Critical Approach to Children's Literature.* New York: McGraw-Hill, 1967.

Secondary or postsecondary textbook. See index.

**C67:16]**   Weaver, Warren. *Science and Imagination: Selected Essays of Warren Weaver.* New York and London: Basic Books, 1967.

Chapter 8, pages 234–86, is entitled "Lewis Carroll," and contains parts of five Weaver essays on Carroll in which he discusses Carroll as mathematician, the Indian *Alice,* and collecting Carrolliana.

**C67:17]**   Zukofsky, Louis. "Lewis Carroll." In *Prepositions: The Collected Critical Essays.* London: Rapp & Carroll, 1967; New York: Horizon Press, 1968, pp. 59–60.

Reprint of 1935 essay.

## 1968

**C68:1]**   Chapman, Raymond. *The Victorian Debate: English Literature and Society 1832–1901.* New York: Basic Books, 1968.

In an age where pressures led not to defiance but to retreat, "some, like Lewis Carroll and Edward Lear, created a world of fantasy where fears could be projected into impossible creatures, made safe because they had been formed from imagination." See pages 349, 352, 353, 355 for references to Carroll.

**C68:2]**   Croft-Cooke, Rupert. *Feasting with Panthers: A New Consideration of Some Late Victorian Writers.* New York: Holt, Rinehart & Winston, 1968 © 1967.

See pages 153–59, 242–43, 291–92 for largely biographical references to Carroll.

**C68:3]**   Culler, A. Dwight. "The Darwinian Revolution and Literary Form." In *The Art of Victorian Prose.* Ed. George Levine and William Madden. London / Oxford / New York: Oxford Univ. Press, 1968, pp. 224–46.

Carroll is one of the writers discussed; see pages 239–40. *Alice in Wonderland* is part of the post-Darwinian world, not because "it contains evolutionary materials (as in abundance it does) nor despite the fact that its author is known to have detested Darwin (as he certainly did), rather because, like Darwin, he subjects the rigidities of an ethical, social, and religious world to the fresh natural vision of a child and to the destructive analysis of formal chance."

**C68:4]**   Darling, Richard. *Rise of Children's Book Reviewing in America, 1865–1881.* New York and London: R. R. Bowker, 1968.

See index for numerous references to Carroll's works.

**C68:5]**   Deleuze, Gilles. "Le Schizophrène et le mot." *Critique,* 24, Nos. 255 / 256 (August / September 1968), 731–46.

Although there are similarities between Carroll and Artaud in relation to language, they are essentially dissimilar. Carroll is the master of surfaces, an area to be known and not explored, where the "logique du sens" holds. Artaud is the master of the depths of language. He is still the only one in literature to have explored the "infra-sens." In French.

**C68:6]**   Demurova, Nina. "L'yuis Kerroll i istoriya odnogo piknkia." *Znanie-silia,* 6 (1968), 36–39.

Title translates as "Lewis Carroll and the story of a picnic." Recounts the genesis of *Alice in Wonderland.* Title and text in Russian.

**C68:7]** Doherty, H. B. "The Weather on *Alice in Wonderland* Day." *Weather,* February 1968, pp. 75–78.

The weather on 4 July 1862 was pleasant, indeed a "golden afternoon," and not "cool and rather wet" as meteorological records have suggested. Additional records suggest that it rained during the previous night, but cleared up by lunchtime.

**C68:8]** Doyle, Brian. *The Who's Who of Children's Literature.* London: Evelyn; New York: Schocken, 1968.

Carroll's life and work are discussed briefly on pages 46–49. Six pages of illustrations of various Alices appear between pages 20 and 21. Reprinted in 1971.

**C68:9]** Ellis, Alec. *A History of Children's Reading and Literature.* London: Pergamon, 1968.

Carroll is mentioned in chapter 8, "The Golden Years of Children's Literature, Part I 1869–1890," especially pages 65–69.

**C68:10]** Gaffney, Wilbur G. "Humpty Dumpty and Heresy; or, The Case of the Curate's Egg." *Western Humanities Review,* 22, No. 2 (Spring 1968), 131–41.

"One finds the ghost of Thomas Hobbes wandering, in Cheshire Cat fashion, through both the *Alice* books, in random passages." Records Hobbesian parallels in the Humpty Dumpty chapter of *Through the Looking-Glass.* Speculates on Dodgson's knowledge and appreciation of Hobbes.
     Reprinted in *JJLCS,* No. 6 (Winter 1970), pp. 6–15.

**C68:11]** Gernsheim, Helmut. "Sun Artists: Victorian Photography." *Camera: International Magazine for Photography and Motion Picture,* 47 (December 1968), 4–23, 34-43.

Carroll is among the Victorian photographers discussed. A group of eleven photographs from the Parrish Collection at Princeton, selected and introduced by O. J. Rothrock, Curator of the Graphic Arts Division, is reproduced.

**C68:12]** Ghiehrl, H. E. "Lewis Carroll (1832–1898): Alice im Wunderland." *Pädagogische Warte,* No. 10 (1968), pp. 578–86.

A critical biography of Carroll. Ghiehrl explains how difficult it is for a foreigner to understand the humor and vision of Carroll—the British author who continues to draw the most attention with only the exception of Shakespeare. In German.

**C68:13]** López-Celpecho, Luis. "C. de Carroll y de Cortázar." *Cuadernos Hispanonamericanos* (Madrid), 76 (1968), 663–74.

Compares and contrasts *Historias de cronopios y de famas* with the *Alice* books. Both Carroll and Cortázar treat madness in their works, are fascinated with mirrors, and treat words like a feast. While Carroll introduces Alice, a normal human being, Cortázar introduces inhuman imps with only a semblance of normal human beings.

**C68:14]** Manvell, Roger. *Ellen Terry*. New York: G.P. Putnam's Sons, 1968.

See index for references to Carroll's friendship with Ellen Terry.

**C68:15]** Monfried, Walter. "The Man Who Brought Us Alice." *Modern Maturity*, 11, No. 2 (April / May 1968), 24–26.

Biographical sketch of Tenniel and a discussion of his relationship with Carroll.

**C68:16]** Pillat, Monica. "Ipoteze asupra semnificatiilor operei lui Lewis Carroll." *Viata Româneasca* (Bucharest), 21, No. 6 (1968), 93–99.

Title translates as "Hypotheses on the Significance of Lewis Carroll's Work." Briefly discusses what English-speaking critics Shane, de la Mare, Ayres, Sewell, Greenacre, and Gardner think about Carroll and his work. Pillat next summarizes Carroll's life, and then offers readings of the *Alice* books. Compares Carroll with Kafka and finds in their works the impossibility of escape from the cosmos. In Rumanian.

**C68:17]** Salvadori, Laura Draghi. *Lewis Carroll*. Florence: Le Monnier, 1968. Pp. 137.

Contains a biography of Carroll, a discussion of the *Alices* in Italy, a critical examination of the *Alices*, and extracts from Carroll's writings. In Italian.

**C68:18]** Sokolik, G. "Mir belogo rytsarya." *Znanie-sila,* 6 (1968), 40.

Concerns the mathematical fantasy in Carroll's works. In Russian.

## 1969

**C69:1]**   Binder, Lucia. "Phantastische Erzählungen der Jugend Weltliteratur." In *Trends in der modernen Jugendliteratur*. Vienna: [Jugend und Volk?], 1969, pp. 76–93.

Modern children's literature in German is viewed in the context of European children's literature. *Alice in Wonderland* and other classic European fantasies for children are compared and contrasted. In these works reality becomes the marvelous; the world of the child is contrasted with the world of the adults, which is too rational and therefore dull; there are comic parts; the joy inherent in games is expressed; and there are elements of mystery. In German.

**C69:2]**   Bechtel, Louise Seaman. *Books in Search of Children*. Ed. Virginia Haviland. London: Macmillan, 1969.

Reprints of speeches and essays. See index.

**C69:3]**   Black, Duncan. "Lewis Carroll and the Theory of Games." *American Economic Review*, 59, No. 2 (May 1969), 206–16.

Discusses Carroll's further application of the game theory he postulated in *The Principles of Parliamentary Representation*. Points out that "just as in the two-party contest he makes use of the two-person zero-sum game, so in the non-party or multiparty case Carroll makes use of the basic notions of what we know today as the coalition game with ordinal utilities." Black's presentation appears on pages 206–10 and is followed on pages 211–16 by discussions by Thomas E. Borcherding, A. Alland Schmid, and Benjamin Ward.

**C69:4]**   Cohen, Morton N., and Roger Lancelyn Green. "Lewis Carroll's Loss of Consciousness." *Bulletin of the New York Public Library*, 73, No. 1 (January 1969), 56–64.

Drawing from unpublished material and testimony of medical authorities, Cohen and Green report and discuss the fainting spells Carroll suffered later in life and consider the question of possible epilepsy (probably not).

**C69:5]**   Deleuze, Gilles. *Logique du Sens*. Paris: Editions de Minuit, 1969.

Carroll is discussed at length in this book on the logical, psychoanalytical novel. Deleuze finds Carroll's work to be a game of sense and nonsense, and a depiction of a chaotic universe. It is a work, however, that offers much pleasure to today's readers. Deleuze looks at how Carroll used language and the unconscious through an analysis of a series of paradoxes evidenced in *Alice*. In French.

**C69:6]** Egoff, Sheila, G. T. Stubbs, and L. F. Ashley, eds. *Only Connect: Readings on Children's Literature.* Toronto & New York: Oxford Univ. Press, 1969.

See index.

**C69:7]** Jones, Peter Blundell. "An Examination of 'The Three Voices.' " *JJLCS*, No. 2 (1969), pp. 5–8.

"The Three Voices" is a complex poem in which Carroll seems to have gone further than Kant and suggested that perception is controlled by reason. The poem also shows "a very definite concern with the irrational."

**C69:8]** Fensch, Thomas. "Lewis Carroll: The First Acidhead." In *Story: The Yearbook of Discovery.* New York: Four Winds Press, 1969, pp. 253–56.

" . . . *Alice in Wonderland* echoes the confused, surrealistic world—the world of the LSD trip." Reprinted in C71:24.

**C69:9]** Flescher, Jacqueline. "The Language of Nonsense in *Alice." Yale French Studies*, 43 (1969), 128–44.

An investigation of the interaction of language and reference, order and disorder, in *Alice*. "The backbone of nonsense must be a consciously regulated pattern. It can be the rhythmic structure of verse, the order of legal procedure, or the rules of the chess-game. Implicitly or explicitly, these three variations are all present in Alice. . . . Preoccupation with meaning is constant throughout *Alice,* sometimes to an extreme degree."

The issue of *Yale French Studies* containing Flescher's essay was reprinted as a book: Peter Brooks, ed. *The Child's Part.* Boston: Beacon Press; Toronto: Saunders, 1972.

**C69:10]** Georgiou, Constantine. *Children and Their Literature.* Englewood Cliffs, New Jersey: Prentice-Hall, 1969.

Contains extracts and discussions of Carroll's work. Secondary or postsecondary text. See index.

**C69:11]**   Green, Roger Lancelyn. "Alice's Rail-Journey." *Notes & Queries*, 16, No. 6 ( June 1969), 217–18.

A note written in response to a previous note by Hugh O'Brien; see C67:10. "There is, so far as I know, not a shred of evidence that Dodgson ever travelled by train from Holyhead to Llandudno." Carroll did travel by rail to visit the Liddells at Charlton Kings in April 1863, and it was from this visit that Carroll later developed the Looking-Glass House, the Garden of Live Flowers, and the Red Queen.

**C69:12]**   Gregory, Horace. "On Lewis Carroll's *Alice* and Her White Knight and Wordsworth's 'Ode on Immortality.' " In *The Shield of Achilles: Essays on Beliefs in Poetry*. [Folcroft, Pennsylvania]: Folcroft Library Editions, 1969.

Reprint of 1944 essay and book; also reprinted by Greenwood Press. The essay appears in C71:24 and in Gregory's *Collected Essays*, New York: Grove Press, 1971.

**C69:13]**   Gummere, John F. "Quomodo Quaedam Opera Latine Reddita Sunt." *Classical World*, 62, No. 6 (February 1969), 209.

Briefly notes various attempts at translating light verse into Latin; reprints the opening stanza of a translation of "Jabberwocky" and mentions Clive H. Carruther's translation of the *Alices*.

**C69:14]**   Henkle, Roger Black. "Comedies of Liberation: A Study of Meredith, Carroll, and Butler." *Dissertation Abstracts*, 29 (1969), 3973–74A (Stanford).

"An analysis of the Alice books demonstrates how closely comic rendition of society reflects Carroll's personal impulses. . . . Carroll's writing conforms in tone to the light comedy of the 1850s, and, despite the fact that he is parodying such humor at times, he finds that its melancholy accent expresses his own sadness about growing old and about the limitations of adult life." See C73:21.

**C69:15]**   Hillman, Ellis S. "The World of the Looking-Glass." *JJLCS* [No. 1 (1969) ], pp. 9–12.

On the reversed-image function. In *Through the Looking-Glass* "Lewis Carroll was trying to represent the 'other side of the mirror' as important a breakthrough in concepts of positive, negative and zero as the revolutionary representation of zero and the negative number some hundreds of years ago."

**C69:16]**   Holquist, Michael. "What is a Boojum? Nonsense and Modernism." *Yale French Studies*, 43 (1969), 145–64.

Offers background information on the *Snark*, an outline of the pattern of resistances that exist in the *Snark*, and a conclusion as to the significance of the pattern for readers of experimental modern fiction. Carroll's *Snark* "best dramatized the attempt of an author to insure through the structure of his work that the work could be perceived only as what it was, and not some other thing. . . . "

   Reprinted in A71:12. The issue of *Yale French Studies* containing Holquist's essay was reprinted as a book: Peter Brooks, ed. *The Child's Part*. Boston: Beacon Press; Toronto: Saunders, 1972.

**C69:17]**   Jan, Isabelle. *La Littérature enfantine*. Paris: Les Éditions ouvrières, 1969.

*Alice* is placed within the context of children's literature as a whole. Argues that *Alice* is an expression of the Victorian child's anxiety towards her surroundings.

   Published in English as *On Children's Literature*. Edited with a preface by Catherine Storr. London: Allen Lane, 1973. English translation published with a new preface by Anne Pellowski in New York: Schocken Books, 1974, paperback.

**C69:18]**   Kepes, Ágnes, and Eta Szász. *Uj beszélö Könyvtár / Ifjusági olvasmányok ajánló jegyzéke*. Budapest: Morá Ferenc Konyvkiadó, 1969, p. 81.

*Alice's Adventures in Wonderland* is one of the works listed in this extensive bibliographical compilation of books for young people. *Alice* is summarized and surveyed. According to Kepes and Szasz, the hidden references to Victorian England in the book are hardly understandable to Hungarian children, yet the peculiar English humor and the so-called nonsense poems make this book enjoyable reading. In Hungarian.

**C69:19]**   Leonard, A. "A Lewis Carroll Miscellany." *JJLCS* [No. 1 (1969) ], pp. 5–9.

General introduction to Carroll's life and work.

**C69:20]**   "Lewis Carroll and Guildford." *JJLCS*, No. 2 (1969), p. 4.

Brief account of Carroll's connections with Guildford.

**C69:21]**   Meigs, Cornelia, ed. *A Critical History of Children's Literature*. Rev. ed. London: MacMillan, 1969.

See pages 194–99 and index. Secondary or postsecondary textbook first published in 1953.
  Reviewed in *JJLCS*, No. 7 ( July 1971), p. 11.

**C69:22]**   Pearsall, Ronald. *The Worm in the Bud: The World of Victorian Sexuality*. London: Weidenfeld & Nicolson, 1969.

"Dodgson was only one of many bachelors who sought solace in the companionship of young girls without the evil intent of the licentious virgin takers." See index.
  Published by Pelican Books in 1971 and reprinted as a Penguin Book in 1972.

**C69:23]**   Shibles, Warren. *Wittgenstein, Language and Philosophy*. Dubuque, Iowa: William C. Brown, 1969.

Pages 14-45 are "A Philosophical Commentary on *Alice's Adventures in Wonderland*."

**C69:24]**   "Some details from the Family Tree." *JJLCS*, No. 2 (December 1969), p. 2.

Concerning Amy Menella, third daughter of Hassard Hume Dodgson.

**C69:25]**   Urnov, Dmitrii Mikhailovich. *Kazk voznikla "Strana čudes."* Moscow: Kniga, 1969. Pp. 77, illustrations.

"How 'Alice in Wonderland' originated." Book-length account, in Russian, of *Alice's* genesis and Carroll's biography.

**C69:26]**   Weinfield, Henry. "A Note Towards the Poetics of Lewis Carroll." *Promethean*, 17, No. 1 (1969 / 1970), 36–38.

"There is an extraordinary resonance in the poetry of Lewis Carroll. It is an oral poetry which embraces the celebrated middle voice which, as Plato remarks, is so dear to children. . . . [Carroll] was the last in the glorious tradition of courtly poets, with the minor distinction that by his time not only the court, but the lady herself had disappeared."

## 1970

**C70:1]**  Berol, Alfred C. "Getting The Facts Right." *JJLCS*, No. 4 (Summer 1970), p. 6.

Based on the letters and other material in his collection, Berol offers his opinion on the life of Carroll. "He was an ordinary middle-class Englishman of solid background, shy and bashful because of his speech impediment. . . . He lacked sex appeal and I do not believe that he had strong sexual desires."

**C70:2]**  Bill, E. G. W., and J. F. A. Mason. *Christ Church and Reform: 1850–1867*. Oxford: Claredon Press, 1970.

Contains many references to Carroll.
   Reviewed in *JJLCS*, No. 6 (Winter 1970), 4–5.

**C70:3]**  Black, Duncan. "Evaluating Carroll's Theory of Parliamentary Representation." *JJLCS*, No. 4 (Summer 1970), pp. 19–21.

"The argument throughout Carroll's *The Principles of Parliamentary Representation* is based on the 2-person zero-sum game, and it could have been put into mathematical form only after 1928. . . . In the course of time Carroll's 2-party system will be supplemented by others. . . . None of these subsequent theories of representation, it seems safe to say, will have the elegance of Carroll's."

**C70:4]**  ———. "Lewis Carroll and the Cambridge Mathematical School of P. R.; Arthur Cohen and Edith Denman." *Public Choice*, 8 (Spring 1970), 1–28.

*The Principles of Parliamentary Representation* "is one of the most curious of all Carroll's productions and crazy enough to have a good chance of being correct. It is a quite remarkable contribution to Political Science and . . . the only work in Politics worthy of being placed no more than a single notch below that of Thomas Hobbes." Considers the circumstances in which the book was written—the circumstances which enabled it to be written.

**C70:5]**  Blish, James. "Some Fictional Descendants of Carroll." *JJLCS*, No. 3 (March 1970), pp. 6–8.

Records fiction writers who borrow from or allude to Carroll.

**C70:6]** "A Child Friend of Lewis Carroll." *JJLCS*, No. 4 (Summer 1970), pp. 2–3.

Publication of a brief letter to the Lewis Carroll Society from Mrs. May Hankey, who recalls her personal acquaintance with Lewis Carroll. See also C72:16.

**C70:7]** Cohen, Morton N. "Letters from Wonderland." *New York Times Book Review*, 15 November 1970, pp. 2, 50–52, 54; also published as "Beyond the Looking-Glass." *Daily Telegraph Magazine*, 19 February 1971, pp. 33–36.

Discusses Carroll as a letter writer. Focuses on his letters to his child friends, which taken together are "as exciting as anything Lewis Carroll ever wrote." Contains several previously unpublished letters.

**C70:8]** D'Ambrosio, Michael A. "*Alice* for Adolescents." *English Journal*, 59, No. 8 (November 1970), 1074–75, 1085.

Discusses the relevance of the *Alices* to the lives of twentieth-century adolescents when interpreted as satiric views of adulthood and society.

**C70:9]** "Daresbury." *JJLCS*, No. 5 (Autumn 1970), pp. 25–26.

Daresbury is the town in which Carroll was born. Primarily an account of the Parrish Church and its continuing association with Lewis Carroll.

**C70:10]** Davies, Ivor. "Looking-Glass Chess." *The Anglo-Welsh Review*, 15, No. 43 (Autumn 1970), 189–91.

Considers various rules in chess books owned by Carroll which could account for the seemingly irregular moves in *Through the Looking-Glass*. See C71:10.

**C70:11]** "An Elaborate Hoax." *JJLCS*, No. 4 (Summer 1970), pp. 8–9.

Reprint and discussion of an article that appeared in *Once a Week*, 15 June 1872, which reports the hoax perpetrated by *The Macmillan Magazine* tracing the source of "Jabberwocky" to a German poem. Oliver Wendell Holmes's "Aestivation" is proposed as a true source.

**C70:12]** Ettleson, Abraham. " 'Author's Preface' Decoded." *JJLCS*, No. 3 (March 1970), pp. 6–7.

Argues that in his Preface to *Through the Looking-Glass* Carroll is not talking about chess but is referring to "Sayings of the fathers," which can be found in any complete Jewish Daily Prayer Book.

**C70:13]**   Gattégno, Jean. "D'un Procès à l'Autre, ou de *Pickwick* à *Alice.*" *Etudes Anglaises*, 23 (1970), 208-9.

Shows Dickens' influence on Carroll and compares how justice is rendered in *Pickwick* and *Alice*. In French.

**C70:14]**   ———— . *Lewis Carroll*. Paris: José Corti, 1970.

An attempt at deciphering Carroll's "vision of the world," showing the profound coherence of the Carrollian universe. Gattégno's aim is not to explain Carroll's life and work, but to understand them as they are indissoluably bound by the act of creation. The book is divided into three sections: the first treats Carroll's rejection of the real world; the second, Carroll's links (in art and life) with the world of childhood; and the third, the orientation of Carroll /Dodgson's personality. In French.

**C70:15]**   Goodacre, Selwyn. "Alice and Rip Van Winkle." *JJLCS*, No. 6 (Winter 1970), pp. 23-24.

Suggests Washington Irving's *Rip Van Winkle* as the source for three passages in *Alice in Wonderland*.

**C70:16]**   Harrod, Roy. "Dodgson of Christ Church." *Times Literary Supplement*, 11 December 1970, pp. 1471–72.

An appreciation of Carroll by a Christ Church don. Several Senior Common Room stories are offered to illustrate various aspects of Carroll's personality.
   See follow-up letter by Reginald Pound, 22 January 1971, p. 97.

**C70:17]**   Hector, Josette. "La métaphysiologique de Lewis Carroll." *Synthèses*, 283 / 284 (January / February 1970), 100-101.

Briefly compares and contrasts Mallarmé's, Carroll's, and Artaud's perceptions of time. In French.

**C70:18]**   Hildebrandt, Rolf. *Nonsense-Aspekte der englischen Kinderliteratur*. Weinheim, Berlin and Basel: Julius Beltz, 1970, Pp. 228.

A study of literary nonsense and the world of British children's books. Five

approaches are taken—linguistic, logical, aesthetic, psychological, and literary
historical. Carroll is discussed extensively. In German.
  Reviewed by Reinhold Winkler, *Anglia*, 91 (1973), 142-44.

**C70:19]**  Hillman, Ellis. "Lewis Carroll in London: The Hum-
muns." *JJLCS*, No. 5 (Autumn 1970), pp. 27–28.

Identifications of lodging where Carroll sometimes stayed in London.

**C70:20]**  Horsley, Robert. "How Permissive?" *JJLCS*, No. 5
(Autumn 1970), pp. 28–29.

Recalls briefly Carroll's contacts with Gilbert and Sullivan and his outrage in
1879 at "an outright 'Damme' " in *The Children's Pinafore*.

**C70:21]**  Hudson, Derek. "Lewis Carroll and G. M. Hopkins:
Clergymen on a Victorian See-saw." *Dalhousie Review*, 50,
No. 1 (Spring 1970), 83–87.

Compares and contrasts Carroll with Hopkins. Finds as the most interesting
comparison that "both men welcomed the challenge of the complicated, and
both were absorbed in the study of words."
  Reprinted in *JJLCS*, No. 7 (July 1971), p. 6.

**C70:22]**  Jaques, Irene. "My Uncle, Lewis Carroll, as I Knew
Him." *JJLCS*, No. 3 (March 1970), p. 2.

Very brief reminiscence.

**C70:23]**  Laffay, Albert. *Anatomie de l'humeur et du nonsens*. Paris:
Masson et Cie., 1970.

Contains a section on Lewis Carroll. In French.

**C70:24]**  Matthews, Charles. "Satire in the *Alice* Books." *Criticism*, 21, No. 2 (Spring 1970), 105–19.

One essential characteristic of the carefully structured nonsense in the *Alices* "is
its self-consciousness." Alice learns two principle types of nonsense in her journeys: linguistic and logical.
  "The objects of satire in the books are less clear than we could wish. There
is no apparent political satire in them, except for caricatures of Disraeli which
Tenniel inserted, and—a more significant exception—the trial of the Knave of

Hearts. . . . But what satire the *Alice* books contain is directed less at institutions than at individual human foibles."

**C70:25]** "Member's Query." *JJLCS*, No. 6 (Winter 1970), pp. 3–4.

The background to Tenniel's illustration of "You are old, father William," is given in response to an earlier query.

**C70:26]** Muskat-Tabakowska, E. "General Semantics behind the Looking-Glass." *ETC: A Review of General Semantics*, 27, No. 4 (December 1970), 483–92.

Argues that Carroll had an "amazingly sharp insight into general semantics, a field of knowledge whose laws and principles were scientifically formulated well after his time. Although quite different formally, Korzybski's works on general semantics show some strikingly close relations to certain features in Carroll's books."

**C70:27]** Page, Jane I. "Enduring Alice." *Dissertation Abstracts*, 31 (1970), 3559–60A (Washington).

A survey and classification of the kinds of critical comments on *Alice in Wonderland* and *Through the Looking-Glass* which have appeared in print since the books' publication. Attempts to identify "thematic and stylistic elements which have contributed to the books' enduring appeal, both to the literary critic and to the general reader."

**C70:28]** Reichert, Klaus. "Lewis Carroll: Studien zu einer Theorie des literatischen Unsinns." Dissertation Frankfurt 1970.

See C74:25.

**C70:29]** Salem, Nazira. *História da literatura infantil.* 2nd ed. São Paulo: Mestre Jou, 1970.

Carroll and his work are discussed on pages 39, 176–77. Revised edition of a history of children's literature first published in 1959. In Portuguese.

**C70:30]** Schöne, Annemarie. *Englische Nonsense und Grusel-Balladen.* Göttingen, Germany: Vandenhoeck & Ruprecht, 1970.

After a brief biographical introduction, examples of Carroll's nonsense are cited and discussed on pages 71–81. Sees the kingdom of nonsense as an escape for Carroll, who tries to run away from a world that is too rational and too realistic. In German.

**C70:31]** Seward, Timothy C. "A Literary Analysis of 'The Three Voices.' " *JJLCS*, No. 3 (March 1970), pp. 3–5.

"The Three Voices" is Carroll's longest parody and exhibits an intensity and excitement not present in Tennyson's "Two Voices."

**C70:32]** "Speech Impediments in the Dodgson family." *JJLCS*, No. 3 (March 1970), p. 2.

According to Irene Jaques, among Carroll's brothers and sisters Louisa and Skeffington did not stammer, Wilfred (and Charles) had some hesitation, and Caroline, Mary, Lizzie, Etta, and Maggie all had differing speech defects.

**C70:33]** Sutherland, Robert D. *Language and Lewis Carroll.* The Hague: Moulton, 1970. Pp. 245.

Summarizes Carroll's knowledge of language and explains how he used it in his comic writings. See C64:13.

Reviewed by: *Times Literary Supplement*, 4 December 1970, p. 1415; Anne Falck, *Samlaren,* 91 (1971), 198–99; Martin Gardner, *Semiotica,* 5, No. 1 (1972), 89–92; Nina Demurova, *Sovremennaya Khudozhestvennaya Literatura za Rubezhom* [USSR], No. 6 (1972), pp. 65–68.

**C70:34]** "You May call it Nonsense." *JJLCS*, No. 3 (March 1970), pp. 9–12.

Extract of a talk given to the Lewis Carroll Society (England) by Roger Lancelyn Green on 6 January 1970. "Besides being our greatest nonsense writer, Lewis Carroll demonstrates all the main branches of nonsense literature."

## 1971

**C71:1]** Balotă, Nicolae. "Lewis Carroll." In *Lupta cu absurdul.* Bucharest: Univers, 1971, pp. 78–114.

Translation of the Rumanian title of the book is *The Flight with the Absurd.* Not seen.

**C71:2]**  Blake, Kathleen A. "The Play Theme in the Imaginative Writing of Lewis Carroll." *Dissertation Abstracts*, 32 (1971), 2082A (U. Cal—San Diego).

Blake "establishes the applicability of a play model as psychological incorporation of reality to the ego, in contrast to ego accommodation, using Piaget, Freud, and Erikson," and uses this model to show how games give form and meaning to Carroll's literary works.

Revised and published as a book; see C74:4.

**C71:3]**  Carter, George A. *Warrington and the Mid-Mersey Valley*. Didsbury, Manchester: E. J. Morten, 1971.

Carroll is mentioned on pages 30, 31, and 170 in conjunction with a history and description of the town of Daresbury, his birthplace.

**C71:4]**  Clark, Anne. "Guilty—Or Not Guilty." *JJLCS*, No. 7( July 1971), pp. 18-23.

Since Carroll's personal life has been distorted through popularization and innuendo, the need to look at the facts exists. Evidence regarding Carroll's stammer, his reason for remaining a bachelor, and his relationships with little girls are among the aspects of his life surveyed.

**C71:5]**  Cohen, Eileen S. "Alex in Wonderland, or *Portnoy's Complaint*." *Twentieth Century Literature*, 17, No. 3 (July 1971), 161–68.

*Portnoy's Complaint* has a great deal in common with *Alice in Wonderland*. Alex's literal world is topsy-turvy, and his real world is what other men fantasize. Alex's life is "one in which he can find no truth consistent with the conventions of his particular situation, just as Alice can find no logic in Wonderland in terms of the conventions of the world above ground." Both Alice and Alex "must wonder through their nightmare visions to discover who they are."

**C71:6]**  Cohen, Morton N. "Beyond the Looking-Glass." *The Daily Telegraph Magazine*, No. 330, 19 February 1971, pp. 33-36.

An account of Lewis Carroll's letter writing illustrated with examples from unpublished letters.

**C71:7]**  ———— . "Love and Lewis Carroll." *The Times Saturday Review*, 20 November 1971, p. 6.

Draws from unpublished letters to "dispel a good many myths" about Lewis Carroll and to "sharpen his image." Includes a discussion of Carroll's feelings of love and friendship—especially for his child friends—in the context of the Victorian era.

**C71:8]** _____ . " 'So You Are Another Alice.' " *New York Times Book Review,* 7 November 1971, pp. 2, 19–20.

A centenary essay on *Through the Looking-Glass.* The book's genesis and lasting popularity are discussed, as is Carroll's long friendship with Amy Raikes, the child friend who came up with the notion of the other side of the looking-glass.
   Reprinted in *JJLCS,* No. 12 (Autumn 1972), pp. 5–9.

**C71:9]** Cornforth, Maurice. *Marxism and the Linguistic Philosophy.* New York: International Publishers, 1971.

See index.

**C71:10]** Davies, Ivor. "Looking-Glass Chess." *JJLCS,* No. 8 (Autumn 1971), pp. 11–14.

From the point of view of ordinary chess, there are two things seriously wrong with the sequence of moves in *Through the Looking-Glass.* Citing rules from chess books owned by Dodgson, Davies shows the possible set of circumstances that would allow for the irregular moves.

**C71:11]** De Prez, Edna. "Lewis Carroll—His Birthplace and Childhood." *JJLCS,* No. 7 (July 1971), pp. 12–17.

An account of the Daresbury parish—sites, people, activities, customs—during the Rev. Dodgson's tenure, 1827–43.

**C71:12]** Goodacre, Selwyn. "The Illnesses of Lewis Carroll." *JJLCS,* No. 8 (Autumn 1971), pp. 15–21.

Comprehensive medical history of Lewis Carroll reconstructed from extant documents and interpreted by a British general practitioner. See letter by Goodacre in *JJLCS,* No. 9 (Winter 1971), pp. 26–27, for emendations. See also C72:13, C74:14.

**C71:13]** _____ . "Mrs. Florence Becker Lennon at the Lewis Carroll Society [England]." *JJLCS,* No. 8 (Autumn 1971), pp. 2–3.

Summary of talk principally about the Alices in Carroll's life and the multiple dimensions of Carroll's personality.

**C71:14]** Green, Benny. "Looking through Glasses." *Spectator,* 227 (25 December 1971), 934–44.

A critical appreciation of *Through the Looking-Glass* on the occasion of its centenary. Includes various remarks made by critics over the years.

**C71:15]** Green, Roger Lancelyn. "Looking-Glass Reflections." *JJLCS*, No. 8 (Autumn 1971), pp. 7–11.

Green notes, on the occasion of the centenary of *Through the Looking-Glass*, that "relatively little has been written about the conception of the book. . . . " He offers "reflections" on the book's background details, particularly the associations with Alice Liddell.

**C71:16]** Greenacre, Phyllis. " 'It's My Own Invention': A Special Screen Memory of Mr. Lewis Carroll, Its Form and Its History." In *Emotional Growth*. New York: International Univ. Press, 1971, I, 437–78.

Reprint of 1955 essay. Volume also contains reprint of C66:7.

**C71:17]** Haight, M. R. "Nonsense." *British Journal of Aesthetics,* 11, No. 3 (Summer 1971), 247–56.

Carroll and "Jabberwocky" are discussed at length in this paper on nonsense as literary form. Using "Jabberwocky" as an illustration, Haight demonstrates that nonsense words must belong to some language, and that two aspects of language that nonsense can parody are words and grammar.

**C71:18]** Hillman, Ellis. "Tiny Earthquakes in the Looking-Glass." *JJLCS*, No. 8 (Autumn 1971), pp. 14–15.

Several mild earthquakes that occurred in England during the period when Carroll was writing *Through the Looking-Glass* may account for the mentions of earthquake by the King and Alice. The mention of volcano in the opening chapter may be connected with the Vesuvius eruption of 1868.

**C71:19]** Jones, E. Emrys. "Where Alice Rambled" (letter). *Country Life*, 150 (8 July 1971), 107.

Discussion of Carroll's association with the Welsh town of Llandudno. Photograph of monument to Carroll at Llandudno is reproduced.

**C71:20]**   Kuyk, Dirk A., Jr. "Strategies of Unreason." *Dissertation Abstracts*, 32 (1970), 440A (Brandeis).

In a dissertation on eight non-realistic genres, *Alice in Wonderland* is considered as a work within the genre of nonsense. "Nonsense like Carroll's *Alice in Wonderland* attempts to stifle the non-rational with logic, semantics and mathematics."

**C71:21]**   Muir, Percy. *Victorian Illustrated Books*. London: Batsford, 1971.

See index for references to the Carroll-Tenniel partnership.

**C71:22]**   O'Brien, Hugh. "The Mirror-Image Relationship between *Alice's Adventures in Wonderland* and *Through the Looking-Glass*." *JJLCS,* No. 7 (July 1971), p. 6.

Suggests Carroll incorporated some elaborate mirror-image parallels with *Alice in Wonderland* into *Through the Looking-Glass*. See also C73:14.

**C71:23]**   Parisot, Henri, ed. *Lewis Carroll*. (Cahiers de l'Herne 17.) Paris: Editions de l'Herne, 1971.

Contains the following essays in French (listed in order of appearance): "Au sujet de Humpty Dumpty toujours déjà tombé" by Hélène Cixous (pp. 11–16) looks at Humpty Dumpty's symbolic meanings and the instability of language evidenced in his conversation with Alice; "Jeu de logique, jeu d'univers" by Ernest Coumet (pp. 17–29) investigates the notion in logic of "universe of discourse" appearing in *Symbolic Logic* in an attempt at authenticating the Carroll / Dodgson duality (see C76:18); "Les jeux de langage chez Lewis Carroll" by Luc Etienne (pp. 30–34) investigates the effect of words on Carroll's poetic imagination; "Pour Lewis Carroll" by Jean Gattégno (pp. 35- 40) uses language as a key to decipher and assimilate the diverse views that have been taken of dream and reality in Carroll's works (see C76:18); "Une case en avant, deux cases en arrière" by Jean-Jacques Lecercle (pp. 41–50) analyzes *The Hunting of the Snark;* "Alice chez Polysème" by Jean Paul Martin (pp. 51- 57) argues, in a linguistic analysis and comparison of the *Alice* books, that it is thanks to polysemia that Humpty Dumpty can pretend to improve meaning to words; "Le dialogue d'Alice: confrontation, contestations, humour" by Jean-Jacques Mayoux (pp. 58- 66) analyzes the humor in the conversations in the *Alices*, and demonstrates how Alice, who embodies Carroll's own sense of humor, manages to tolerate the absurd reasoning of various characters she encounters; "Pour franciser les jeux de langage d'Alice" by Henri Parisot (pp. 67–82) talks about the difficulties in translating the *Alices* into French; "De quelques langages animaux imaginaires et notamment du langage chien dans *Sylvie et Bruno*" by Raymond Queneau (pp. 83–86) analyzes the animal language in Chapter XIII of *Sylvie and Bruno*; "Lettre à Alice Liddell" by André Bay (pp. 89–92) recreates the world of Alice Liddell in an imaginary letter from Lewis Carroll to the young Alice; "Tout ce que peint mon imagination" by Robert Benayoun (pp. 93–96) comments on various adaptations of the *Alices* for television and the cinema; "Lewis Carroll photographe ou L'autre côté du miroir" by Brassaï (pp. 99–109) surveys Carroll's interest in photography; "L' immatérialisme berkeleyen dans les deux *Alice*" by Françoise Brocas (pp. 110–17) cites similarities between Berkeley and the Carroll evidenced in the *Alices*— their common preoccupation with language and word problems such as the ambiguity and imperfection of language as a means of expression and the dangers of abstraction; "La certitude cachée" by Pierre Dalle Nogare (pp. 118–19) argues that through Alice Carroll expresses his dissatisfaction with life—the real possibility of vanishing, the immediacy of death—and takes Alice as his double in the dream vision since she is a child who, like the old man, is nearest to the anguish of dying; "Take care of the sense, and the sounds will take care of themselves" by Hubert Juin (pp. 120–27) applauds Carroll's work for continually yielding new riches upon rereadings and offers illustrations; "Du Serquin au cachalot blanc" by Marcel Marnat (pp. 128–32) argues that *The Hunting of the Snark* is an epic poem, a tragedy about frustration and failure, which shares similarities with Melville's *Moby-Dick* and to a lesser extent with works by Coleridge, Defoe, Dickens, and Tennyson; "Alice joue aux échecs" by François Le Lionnais (pp. 133–45) analyzes the moves and positions in the chess game in *Through the Looking-Glass*; "Les marionnettes de *La chasse au Snark*" by Eric Merinat (pp. 146–49) argues that in *The Hunting of the Snark* Carroll attempts to write between the lines through signs (marionettes) and that the non-anecdotal marionette is the only one which can help us come to terms with forgotten myths; "Rencontre imaginaire avec L. C." by Gisèle Prassinos (pp. 150–52) pays an imaginary visit to Lewis Carroll; "Alice a des raisons que la raison connaît" by Claude Roy (pp. 153–58) discusses Carroll's method of teaching logic through the *Alice* books, and cites the applicability of the logic in the books to contemporary politics, economy, war, etc.; "Louisa Caroline" by Pierre Sabourin (pp. 159–69) approaches Carroll through psychoanalytic readings of the language in his works.

Contains translations of the following critical studies that first appeared in English: William Empson, "Alice au pays des merveilles ou La Pastorale de l'enfance" (1935), trans. Jean Gattégno (pp. 173–86); Phyllis Greenacre,

"Charles Lutwidge Dodgson et Lewis Carroll: reconstitution et interprétation d'une évolution" (1955), trans. Isabelle Lamblin (pp. 187–210); Derek Hudson, "Lewis Carroll et G. M. Hopkins: deux prêtres sur une balançoire victorienne" (C70:21), trans. Hélène Seyrès (pp. 211–15); Roger Lancelyn Green, "Lewis Carroll" (A65:16), trans. Jacqueline Michaud (pp. 216–22); Elisabeth Sewell, "Lewis Carroll, poète du Nonsense" (C61:4), trans. Jean Gattégno (pp. 223–31); A. L. Taylor, "Alice et le Professeur" (1952), trans. Hélène Seyrès (pp. 232–38).

Contains translations of the following texts by Carroll: "La canne du destin," trans. André Bay (pp. 241–49); "Le beffroi de Christ Church d'Oxford," trans. J. J. Bison (pp. 250–56); "Un conte embrouillé," (fragment), trans. Jean Gattégno (pp. 257–68); "Des épinards au lard," (extract from *Sylvie and Bruno*), trans. Jean Gattégno (pp. 269–83); "Le don de la fondation Clarendon," trans. Jean Gattégno (pp. 284–85); "La Vision des trois T," trans. Alain Gheerbrandt (pp. 286–97); "Chanson du jardinier fou," trans. Henri Parisot (pp. 298–99); "Limericks," trans. Henri Parisot (p. 300).

Reviewed by: *Times Literary Supplement*, 15 December 1971, p. 1525; Anne Clarke, *JJLCS*, No. 10 (Spring 1972), pp. 15–16.

**C71:24]** Phillips, Robert, ed. *Aspects of Alice: Lewis Carroll's Dreamchild as seen through the Critic's Looking-Glass, 1865–1971.* New York: Vanguard, 1971. Pp. 478.

An anthology of criticism of the *Alices*.

Reprints the following essays (in order of appearance): W. H. Auden, "Today's 'Wonder-World' Needs Alice" (C62:2); Roger Lancelyn Green, "Alice" (C60:5); T. B. Strong, "Lewis Carroll" (1898); Virginia Woolf, "Lewis Carroll" (1939); Alexander Woollcott, "Lewis Carroll's Gay Tapestry" (1939); Walter de la Mare, "On the *Alice* Books" (1932); Florence Becker Lennon, "Escape through the Looking-Glass" (1945); Edward Salmon, "From *Literature For The Little Ones*" (1887); Elsie Leach, "*Alice in Wonderland* in Perspective" (C64:7); Elizabeth Sewell, "Lewis Carroll and T. S. Eliot as Nonsense Poets" (1958); Horace Gregory, "On Lewis Carroll's Alice and Her White Knight and Wordsworth's 'Ode on Immortality' " (1944); George Lanning, "Did Mark Twain Write *Alice's Adventures in Wonderland?*" (1947); John Hinz, "Alice Meets the Don" (1953); Roger W. Holmes, "The Philosopher's *Alice in Wonderland*" (1959); Harry Levin, "Wonderland Revisited" (C65:11); Edmund Wilson, "C. L. Dodgson: The Poet Logician" (1932; revised 1952); Shane Leslie, "Lewis Carroll and the Oxford Movement" (1933); Alexander L. Taylor, "*Through the Looking-Glass*" (1952); Florence Milner, "The Poems in *Alice in Wonderland*" (1903); John Ciardi, "A Burble Through the Tulgey Wood"

(1959); J. B. Priestley, "A Note on Humpty Dumpty" (1921); Patricia Meyer Spacks, "Logic and Language in *Through the Looking-Glass*" (C61:5); A. M. E. Goldschmidt, "*Alice in Wonderland* Psychoanalyzed" (1933); Paul Schilder, "Psychoanalytic Remarks on *Alice in Wonderland* and Lewis Carroll" (1938); John Skinner, "From 'Lewis Carroll's *Adventures in Wonderland*' " (1947); Martin Grotjahn, "About the Symbolization of *Alice's Adventures in Wonderland*" (1947); Phyllis Greenacre, "From 'The Character of Dodgson as Revealed in the Writings of Carroll' " (1955); Géza Róheim, "From 'Further Insights' " (1955); Kenneth Burke, "From 'The Thinking of the Body' " (C63:2); William Empson, "Alice in Wonderland: The Child as Swain" (1935); Donald Rackin, "Alice's Journey to the End of the Night" (C66:16); Thomas Fensch, "Lewis Carroll—the First Acidhead" (C69:8).

The following essays are new: "The *Alice* Books and the Metaphors of Victorian Childhood" by Jan B. Gordon (pp 93–113) looks at the *Alices* in the context of the age in which they are written and argues, among many points, that the "two companion volumes, veritable landmarks of Victorian literary history, are decadent adult literature rather than children's literature; "Alice as Anima: The Image of Woman in Carroll's Classics" by Judith Bloomingdale (pp. 378–90) offers a Jungian reading of the *Alices* and finds that "Circumstances led Carroll to personify his inner image of woman in Alice. . . . She figures in the drama of Wonderland–Looking-Glass as a positive *anima* who moves from innocence to experience, unconsciousness to consciousness."

Reprinted in England with slight modifications and the same title: London: Gollancz, 1972. Reprinted with additions to the notes, corrections, and an updated checklist of criticism: Harmondsworth: Penguin, 1974. Pp. 524, paperback. On the eve of the Penguin edition, Phillips replied to critics in *JJLCS*, 3, No. 1 (Winter 1973), 16–17. Reprinted with the Penguin changes and with the checklist updated to 1976: New York: Vintage, 1977. Pp. 454, paperback.

Reviewed (all editions) by: W. P. Baker, *Library Journal*, 96 (1971), 4095; Christopher Lehmahn-Haupt, *New York Times*, 2 December 1971, p. 45; Julian Moynahan, *Book World*, 5 December 1971, p. 26; Paul Scott, *Country Life*, 152 (1972), 1010; G. Tindall, *New Statesman*, 84 (1972), 520; William Heyen, *Saturday Review*, 55 (15 January 1972), 42; John Gardner, *New York Times Book Review*, 30 January 1972, p. 3, 22; Anne Clark, *JJLCS*, No. 10 (Spring 1972), pp. 5–7; [J. R. Christopher], *Choice*, 9, No. 4 (June 1972), 507; Minette Marrin, *Spectator*, 229 (9 December 1972), 930; Daniel J. Casey, *The English Record*, 23, No. 2 (Winter 1972), 99–100; *Times Literary Supplement*, 15 December 1972, p. 1525; Robert Greaschen, *Books and Bookmen*, 18, No. 4 (January 1973), 99–100; George Soule, *The Carleton Miscellany*, 13, No. 1 (Fall / Winter 1972 / 73), 102–8; Lavinia Marina Learmont, *Books and Bookmen*, 19, No. 8 (May 1974), 95–96; Nina Demurova, *Sovremennaya Khudozhestvennaya Litera-*

*tura za Rubezhon*, No. 1 (1974), 95–98; Benny Green, *Spectator*, 8 February 1976, p. 158; Dieter Petzold, *Anglia*, 93 (1975), 550–52; Paul Turner, *Notes and Queries*, n.s. 23, No. 9 (September 1976), 419–20.

**C71:25]** Pierre, José. "Les Dessins de Lewis Carroll." In *L'abécédaire*. Paris: Eric Losfeld, 1971, pp. 151–57.

The transcript of a radio interview with Pierre who finds Carroll's artistic skills limited, but Carroll inspired reaching poetic heights in some of his drawings.
   Published in English as "The Drawings of Lewis Carroll." Translated by John Lyle. *Surrealist Transforma(c)tion* (Devon, England), 5 (Spring 1973).

**C71:26]** Richmond, John. "Happy Birthday Alice." *Montreal Star*, 24 December 1971, p. E1.

A note on the centenary of *Through the Looking-Glass*.

**C71:27]** Taylor, Alexander. "Talk Given to the Lewis Carroll Society of London, 6th October 1971." *JJLCS*, No. 9 (Winter 1971), 1–5.

Taylor relates how he came to write *The White Knight* and some of his discoveries in the *Alices* that particularly intrigued him.

**C71:28]** Vitner, Ian. "Antimimezis: Lumea de dincolo de oglindă." In *Semnele romanului*. Bucharest: Cartea Românească, 1971. Pp. 136–37.

Translation of the Rumanian title of the article is "Antimimesis: The World beyond the Mirror." In *Novel Guide Marks*. Not seen.

## 1972

**C72:1]** Aiken, Joan. "Between Family and Fantasy." *The Quarterly Journal of the Library of Congress*, 29, No. 4 (October 1972), 308–26.

Carroll is among the fantasy writers discussed. "Instead of controlling his fantasies, I feel that Carroll let them roll away from him at random; it was this sense of undirected force . . . which distressed me as a child. . . ."

**C72:2]**  Anderson, William, and Patrick Groff. *A New Look at Children's Literature*. Belmont, California: Wadsworth, 1972.

A general analysis of the *Alices* as dream fantasy appears on pages 69–73. A secondary or postsecondary textbook. See index.

**C72:3]**  Arbuthnot, May Hill, and Zena Sutherland. *Children and Books*. 4th ed. Glenview, Illinois: Scott, Foresman, 1972.

Carroll's life and work are discussed on pages 248–51 et passim. Postsecondary text. Previous editions in 1947, 1957, and 1964.

**C72:4]**  Arnoldi, Richard. "Parallels between *Our Mutual Friend* and the Alice Books." *Children's Literature: The Great Excluded*, 1 (1972), 54–57.

While composing *Through the Looking-Glass* Carroll was reading *Our Mutual Friend*. "Carroll saw this novel as Dickens' cleverest, and it is not surprising that the affinity which he felt for *Our Mutual Friend* led Carroll to echo some of its passages in his own classic fantasy of childhood." Dickens and Carroll "shared certain interests and images." Parallels between *Our Mutual Friend* and the *Alice* books are identified.

**C72:5]**  Bartley III, W. W. "Lewis Carroll's Lost Book on Logic." *Scientific American*, 227, No. 1 ( July 1972), 38–46.

Surveys the contents and merits of the recently reconstructed Part II of Carroll's *Symbolic Logic*, and argues that Carroll's work in logic was highly original.

**C72:6]**  Bowman, Isa. *Lewis Carroll as I Knew Him*. Introduction by Morton N. Cohen. New York: Dover, 1972. Pp. xiv + 132 + [xviii].

Modern reprint, with a new introduction, of the 1899 *The Story of Lewis Carroll Told for Young People by the Real Alice in Wonderland*, published by J. M. Dent, London (*WMG* III; 1979 ed., 503).

Another modern reprint retaining the original title and based on the 1900 edition (*WMG* III; 1979 ed., 503) was published by Finch Press, 197?

Reviewed by Anne Clark, *JJLCS*, No. 13 (Winter 1972), pp. 4–5.

**C72:7]**  Clark, Anne. "Miracles from Badcock's Yard: Account of a Lecture Given to the [Lewis Carroll] Society [England] by

Graham Ovenden." *JJLCS*, No. 11 (Summer 1972), pp. 28–29.

A discussion of Carroll's photography and an account of a presentation which included seventy slides plus an assortment of original Carroll photographs.

**C72:8]**  Cornwell, Charles L. "From Self to the Shire: Studies in Victorian Fantasy." *Dissertation Abstracts*, 33 (1972), 1163–64A (Virginia).

Through an analysis of selected works of four nineteenth-century fantasists, including Carroll and his *Alices*, Cornwell attempts "to distinguish Victorian fantasy from Tolkienian fantasy and to describe the uniqueness of the works. . . . Lewis Carroll's *Alice* books explore the problems of adjusting to an ordered but rigid adult world. . . . Carroll's Wonderland is a series of adult attitudes that threaten to destroy Alice's self, defined as the childlike."

**C72:9]**  Davies, Rev. Ivor. "Lewis Carroll as a Churchman." *JJLCS*, No. 10 (Spring 1972), pp. 9–12.

Dodgson "was a sincere Christian of a typically English kind. His churchmanship was orthodox without being stiff, his attitude to moral and social problems old fashioned rather than inflexible. . . . Charles was not afraid to embrace some of the liberal views current in mid-Victorian Oxford." Reprinted with slight revisions in C73:32.

**C72:10]**  De la Mare, Walter. *Lewis Carroll*. Philadelphia: R. West; [Folcroft, Pennsylvania]: Folcroft; Port Washington, New York: Haskell; Finch Press, 1972; Norwood, Pennsylvania: Norwood Editions, 1976.

Reprints of the 1932 edition published by Faber & Faber, London (*WMG* IX; 1979 ed., 509a).

**C72:11]**  Eagleton, Terry. "Alice and Anarchy." *New Blackfriars*, 53, No. 629 (October 1972), 447–55.

An investigation of the Wonderland world of games and chaos from a largely philosophical perspective. "It would be wrong to see Wonderland merely as a world of indeterminate, dangerously whimsical, shiftily improvised rules, a game which changes elusively in the act of being played. For the point about the place, just as much, is its authoritarian, snappishly dogmatic character, its remorseless absolutism. It's an anarchic society but also a stiflingly oppressive one, and this combination constitutes its peculiarly menacing quality."

**C72:12]** Goodacre, Selwyn. "Correspondence." *JJLCS*, No. 10 (Spring 1972), p. 27.

Suggests Carroll had the White King send 4207 men to "put Humpty Dumpty in his place again" since 4207 is another manifestation of Carroll's favorite number 42.

**C72:13]** _____ . "The Illnesses of Lewis Carroll." *The Practitioner*, 209 (August 1972), 230–39.

Lewis Carroll's complete medical history reconstructed by a British physician. See C74:14.

**C72:14]** Green, Roger Lancelyn. "Haigha Hunting." *JJLCS*, No. 10 (Spring 1972), p. 12.

Suggests possible inspiration for Haigha in *Through the Looking-Glass*.

**C72:15]** _____ . "More Aspects of Alice." *JJLCS*, No. 13 (Winter 1972), pp. 9–14.

Text of a speech delivered at the Institute of Contemporary Arts in London on 6 October 1972. Discussion of R. Philip's *Aspects of Alice* (C71:24).
    Alexander L. Taylor comments in a letter, *JJLCS*, 2, No. 1 (Spring 1973), 20–21.

**C72:16]** Hankey, May. "Tea with Lewis Carroll." *Daily Telegraph*, 15 December 1972, p. 15.

A brief reminiscence.

**C72:17]** Hillman, Ellis S. "Who Was Humpty Dumpty?" *JJLCS*, No. 12 (Autumn 1972), pp. 18–21.

Argues that if George Hudson, the Victorian railroad tycoon, was not an inspiration for Carroll's rendering of the traditional character in the famous nursery rhyme, he at least shared some of Humpty's characteristics and misfortunes.

**C72:18]** Hudson, Derek. "Correspondence." *JJLCS*, 11 (Summer 1972), pp. 24–25.

Refutes assertions made in Gernsheim's 1969 preface to *Lewis Carroll Photographer* concerning Lewis Carroll's "love life," and the missing diaries. Hudson states that there is no evidence that the diaries were destroyed by S. D. Collingwood; that Dodgson was not in love with Alice Liddell in a romantic sense, nor is it likely that he suffered a disappointment in love over Ellen Terry.

**C72:19]** _____ . *Lewis Carroll.* Westport, Connecticut: Greenwood Press; Philadelphia: R. West, 1972.

Reprints of the 1954 edition published by Constable, London (*WMG* XXV; 1979 ed., 525).

**C72:20]** Johnson, Paula. "Alice Among the Analysts." *Hartford Studies in Literature* 4, No. 2 (1972), 114–22.

Surveys the psychoanalytic criticism of the *Alice* books and finds that most of it "is marred by a confusion between the writer, the work, and the reader; the most helpful studies are those which recognize and preserve these distinctions: Greenacre's biography, Empson's literary discussion." A modified Freudian approach, the guidelines of which have been drawn by Norman Holland, should help to resolve the contradictory evaluations by psychoanalysts and lead to a better understanding of the books.
    Reviewed by Denis Crutch in *JJLCS*, No. 12 (Autumn 1972), pp. 10–12.

**C72:25]** Leonard, A. "Ordination Certification." *JJLCS*, No. 10 (Spring 1972), p. 9.

Reprint of the certification—now in the Guildford Museum—given to C. L. Dodgson at his ordination.

**C72:26]** "Lewis Carroll Remembered." *Listener,* 76 (4 August 1972), p. 1962.

Ethel Hatch's remembrances of Lewis Carroll, recorded first in "Woman's Hour" (a BBC radio program), are excerpted.

**C72:27]** Livesley, Brian. "The Alice in Wonderland Syndrome." *Update,* December 1972, pp. 1326–29.

Discusses the effects of Carroll's health problems on the writing of the *Alice* books.

**C72:28]** Martens, Francis. "Sage comme une image / Perinde as cadaver." *Revue de Psychologie et des Sciences de l'Education,* 7, No. 3 (1972), 363–71.

Lewis Carroll, considered a precursor of surrealism and a patrician of dream logic, had a great interest in mirrors and in photographic composition, and both permeate his work. In a psychoanalytic study, Martens discusses the uses of the mirror and superstitions about the relationships of mirrors to misfortune or death and analyzes the various images in *Through the Looking-Glass*. Martens also considers the element of reflection in Rogerian psychotherapy. In French.

**C72:29]** Morgan, Stuart B. "Correspondence." *JJLCS*, No. 12 (Autumn 1972), p. 25.

Points out that the climax of William Morris's "The Blue Closet" in his *Defense of Guenevere* (1858) employs the same meter as Carroll's "The Walrus and the Carpenter."

**C72:30]** Petzold, Dieter. *Formen und Funktionen der englischen Nonsense-Dichtung im 19. Jahrhundert*. Nurnberg: Hans Carl, 1972.

Study of nineteen-century British nonsense focusing on the work of Carroll and Lear.
   Reviewed by Christian W. Thomsen, *Anglia*, 93 (1975), 546–49.

**C72:31]** Rogers, Byron. "Alice is Back to the Front and Looking New." *Daily Telegraph Magazine*, 3 November 1972, pp. 60–63.

A review essay treating Carroll's current popularity, Steadman's new illustrations for *Through the Looking-Glass* (A72:30) which "are often truer to Carroll than Tenniel's revered originals," and Josef Shaftel's film version of *Alice in Wonderland*. Illustrated.

**C72:32]** Sapire, D. "*Alice in Wonderland:* A Work of Intellect." *English Studies in Africa*, 15, No. 1 (1972), 53–62.

An examination of "the logico-metaphysical constraints" in the construction of *Alice*. Carroll is a philosophically inclined logician, and much of the humor in *Alice* has a logical basis. Carroll draws his readers into Alice's imaginary world through a logical device—from a false proposition one can deduce any other proposition one likes—rather than through identification with Alice. Also briefly discusses Carroll and Kant as "explorers who extend the boundaries of human experience."

**C72:33]**   Shaberman, R. B. "Lewis Carroll and the Society for Psychical Research." *JJLCS*, No. 11 (Summer 1972), pp. 4–7.

Carroll maintained a long-term interest in the occult. His library contained many books with occult themes; he was a member of the Society for Psychical Research from its foundation in 1882 until his death; occult and otherwise "magical" elements appear in his works.

**C72:34]**   _____, and Denis Crutch. *Under the Quizzing Glass.* London: Magpie Press, © 1971, 1972. Pp. 58.

"A Lewis Carroll Miscellany" containing new studies of Carroll's life and work and reprints of some rare primary works. Shaberman offers a study of the Carroll / Dodgson dualism and readings of Carroll's works. Crutch offers an imaginary conversation about the inconsistencies of plot in the *Alices* and bibliographical studies of *Rhyme? and Reason?* and *Alice*-type books. A Carroll parody is printed for the first time; the Prospectus for *Symbolic Logic* and a Latin parody are reprinted. Limited to 400 copies.
    Reviewed by: *Times Literary Supplement,* 7 April 1972, p. 402; Selwyn Goodacre, *JJLCS*, No. 12 (Spring 1972), pp. 8–9.

**C72:35]**   Shaw, John M. "Who Wrote 'Speak Gently?' " *JJLCS*, No. 11 (Summer 1972), 13–20.

What is the poem Lewis Carroll intended to parody with the Duchess's version of a lullaby, "Speak roughly"? It could be a version of "Speak Gently" by Carney, or Bates, or Langford, or Reed. See also C76:18, and *JJLCS*, 4, No. 1 (Winter 1975), 20; and *JJLCS*, 7, No. 2 (Spring 1978), 50, for letters from A. Leonard.

**C72:36]**   Stern, Jeffrey. "Lewis Carroll and 'The Lady of the Lilacs.' " *JJLCS*, No. 10 (Spring 1972), pp. 16–17.

Suggests Pre-Raphaelite influence on Carroll's art. See C73:38, C76:18.

**C72:37]**   Stewart, Seumas. *Book Collecting: A Beginner's Guide.* Newton Abbot: David & Charles, 1972, pp. 127–30.

Suggests a passage from *The Child's Guide to Knowledge* (1828) as the origin for the Queen's catechism of Alice in *Through the Looking-Glass.* Also see index.

**C72:38]**   *"Through the Looking-Glass:* Some Hints for Travellers from a Lecture Delivered to the [Lewis Carroll] Society [London] by Mr. Denis Crutch." *JJLCS*, No. 11 (Summer 1972), pp. 1–3.

Review of a wide-ranging talk in which Crutch raises a series of questions about the action in and design of *Through the Looking-Glass.*

**C72:39]** Tuckerman, Charles S. "Carroll's *Jabberwocky*, 23." *Explicator* 31, No. 3 (November 1972), Item 16.

Suggests that as an educated Englishman Carroll had studied Greek and probably had the Greek "callooh, callay," ("good") in mind when he was composing "Jabberwocky."

**C72:40]** Vajda, Miklós. "Carroll, Lewis." In *Világirodalmi Lexikon*. Budapest: Akadémiai Könyvkiadó, 1972, I, pp. 85–86.

Encyclopedia entry on Carroll, arguing that the special charm of Carroll's work is due to a kind of intellectual humor close to the child's imagination and to fantasy. It is a bold application of distorting logic with pseudo-serious tone, precise elaboration, and stylistic virtuosity. In Hungarian.

**C72:41]** Walters, Jennifer, R. "The Disquieting Worlds of Lewis Carroll and Boris Vian." *Revue de Littérature Comparée,* 46 (1972), 284–94.

Both Carroll and Vian "created unreal worlds which were similar in many ways." Similarities are identified and discussed. "Rational man lives in a verbal structure which has, of its very nature, produced a more sophisticated system of logic than the human mind normally uses. Carroll and Vian exploit this systematically and show, with terrifying clarity, how fully words control sense and how easily they can distort it."

## 1973

**C73:1]** Anderson, Irmgard Z. "From Tweedledum and Tweedledee to Zap and Zepo." *Romance Notes,* 15, No. 2 (Winter 1973), 217–20.

Records Fernando Arrabal's debt to Lewis Carroll. The "Tweedledum and Tweedledee" chapter of *Through the Looking-Glass* supplied Arrabal with the entire vital substance of *Pique-nique en campagne*. There is a close, unmistakable correspondence between the ideas and the actions of Carroll's characters and those created by Arrabal.

**C73:2]**   Auerbach, Nina. "Alice and Wonderland: A Curious Child." *Victorian Studies*, 17 (September 1973), 31–47.

*Alice's Adventures in Wonderland* presents a complex portrait of the Victorian child. Alice does not possess Wordsworthian innocence and is not the Victorian idealization of both child and woman; she is less passive, more savage and cruel. Alice's curiosity, sympathy, and appetite are examined from several perspectives. Reading *Alice in Wonderland* one witnesses the tracing of a female psyche.

**C73:3]**   Bartley, W. W., III. "Lewis Carroll as Logician." *Times Literary Supplement*, 15 June 1973, pp. 655–56.

A discussion and reassessment of Carroll as a logician based, in large part, on the then unpublished Part II of *Symbolic Logic*. "The second part confirms the opinions of Bertrand Russell and Eric Temple Bell that Dodgson 'had in him the stuff of a great mathematical logician.' One finds in his unpublished work what one might expect of a first-class logician working just seven years before Russell published his *Principles of Mathematics* (1903)."

**C73:4]**   Baum, Alwin Louis, III. "Toward a Pragmatics of Paradox: A Structural Approach to the Absurd *Récit*." *Dissertation Abstracts International*, 33 (1973), 3574A (U. Cal.—San Diego).

Carroll is discussed in part because his *récits* "are structured on the functional base of paradoxical communication which tends toward the neutralization of 'message-value' in the text, thus forcing the protagonist (and the reading consciousness) onto a plane of pure association which can only be decoded through adequate metacommunication.

   In the *Alice* narratives, particularly, the code of conventional language is insistently subverted by the inhabitants of the 'imaginary,' such as Humpty-Dumpty, who, in questioning Alice's identity, affirms that 'names must mean something' in Wonderland. 'Other words can mean anything.' This reversal of the normal sign-functions would serve to liberate the individual's *parole* only at the expense of nullifying communication, and thus the psychosocial existence of the subject."

**C73:5]**   Benham, Philip S. "Left Hand?—Right Hand?" *JJLCS*, 3, No. 1 (Winter 1973), 7–8.

Alice passed through the looking-glass without any physical transformations.

**C73:6]**   Brassaï. "Lewis Carroll Photographe." *Zoom* (Paris), No. 11 (1973), pp. 74-81.

See C71:23. In French.

**C73:7]**   Carbó, Nicholás A. "Fragmentos de realidad en 'El gato de Cheshire.'" In *Homenaje a Enrique Anderson Imbert*. Ed. Helmy F. Giacoman. Long Island City, New York: Anaya / Las Americas, 1973, pp. 211-25.

An analysis of Imbert's *El gato de Cheshire* (The Cheshire cat). To appreciate the aesthetics of this book, in which Imbert expresses his theory of the relativity of the world, one must know *Alice in Wonderland* and understand Carroll's art. The Cheshire cat's grin is a permanent allusion throughout the work. In Spanish.

See also pages 229-31 for the section in an essay by Guillermo Ara on *El gato de Cheshire*, which similarly cites the importance of *Alice in Wonderland* to Imbert's work.

**C73:8]**   Christopher, J. R. *"The Hunting of the Snark* as a Romantic Ballad." *Orcrist, A Journal of Fantasy in the Arts*, No. 7 (Summer 1973), pp. 30-32.

A reprise and discussion of W. H. Auden's commentary on the *Snark* which appeared in *The Enchafèd Flood* (1950).

**C73:9]**   Crutch, Denis. "Lewis Carroll and the Marionette Theatre." *JJLCS*, 2, No. 1 (Spring 1973), 1-9.

Text of a talk delivered at a meeting of the Daresbury Branch of the Lewis Carroll Society (England) on 17 May 1972. A toy marionette theatre described in auction catalogues as being used and partly made by the young Carroll is *not* the one Carroll played with as a boy. Carroll's marionette play "La Guida di Braglia" has survived from his youth.

**C73:10]**   Danilov, Yu. A. "Logics in Wonderland." *Knowledge is Strength*, No. 12 (1973), pp. 26-29.

A general essay on Carroll's work on logic with frequent quotations from the primary works translated into Russian. Title and article in Russian.

Questions posed in this article are answered in *Knowledge is Strength*, No. 5 (1974), p. 45.

**C73:11]**  Davies, Ivor. "Alice Unveiled." *JJLCS*, 2, No. 1 (Spring 1973), 9–12.

"Consciously or unconsciously Carroll called up his characters from the Tarot Pack." Considers Wonderland parallels with Tarot cards.
  Privately reprinted as a booklet.

**C73:12]**  ———. "Queen Alice." *JJLCS*, 2, No. 3 (Autumn 1973), 10–11.

*"Through the Looking-Glass* must surely owe something to the old game of chess with a Marked Pawn. . . . " The game is described in a book owned by Carroll at the time of his death.

**C73:13]**  De Keyser, J. "The Stuttering of Lewis Carroll." In *Neurolinguistic Approaches to Stuttering.* Eds. Yvan Lebrun and Richard Hoops. The Hague: Mouton, 1973, pp. 32–36.

"While Carroll's stammering largely accounts for his failure as a teacher and priest, it was instrumental in making him a famous writer. In fact, Carroll's celebrated *portmanteau*-words seem to have taken their origin in the blendings of synonyms which he made as a stutterer." A common denominator in the explanation of his portmanteau-words is the telescopy of synonyms.

**C73:14]**  Doherty, H. B. "The Mirror-Image Relationship Between *Alice in Wonderland* and *Through the Looking-Glass.*" *JJLCS*, 2, No. 2 (Summer 1973), 18–21.

"A large number of the characters and incidents in the two stories bear an unmistakably close resemblance to each other." Correspondences are cited in a listing. See also C71:22, C73:16.

**C73:15]**  Furniss, Harry. "Confessions of an Illustrator." *JJLCS*, 2, No. 3 (Autumn 1973), 11–21.

Reprint of Furniss's account of his relationship with Carroll, which first appeared in *Confessions of a Caricaturist* (1901).

**C73:16]**  Goodacre, Selwyn. "The Parallels Between the *Alice* Books—A Corrective." *JJLCS*, 3, No. 1 (Winter 1973), 20–22.

In response to H. B. Doherty's proposed list of mirror images between the *Alice* books, Goodacre, looking on a broader basis, offers eleven similar sequences between the books. For Doherty's response and Goodacre's reply see *JJLCS*, 3, No. 3 (Summer 1974), 18–19; *JJCLS*, 4, No. 1 (Winter 1975), 20.

**C73:17]** Graham, Neilson. "Sanity, Madness and Alice." *Ariel*, 4, No. 2 (1973), 80–89.

Linguistically, insanity involves an absence of discernible motive in the speaker and consequent loss of contact. We see this in the utterances of the Mock Turtle and the Gryphon, the Hare and the Hatter, and the Caterpillar, yet we do not think of them as lunatics because so much of their intellectual and affective behavior makes obvious good sense, even ultimately their "insane" utterances. At the root of all anticommunicative behavior is fear, and it is fear — chiefly of Alice — which underlies the linguistic aberrations of the creatures.

**C73:18]** Green, Roger Lancelyn. "Correspondence." *JJLCS*, 2, No. 2 (Autumn 1973), 22–23.

Carroll's earliest recorded portmanteau word is fluff, probably a combination of flurry and huff. Appears as "went off in a fluff " in "Crundle Castle."

**C73:19]** Haviland, Virginia, ed. *Children and Literature: Views and Reviews*. Glenville, Illinois: Scott, Foresman and Company, 1973; London: The Bodley Head, 1974.

Includes M. Gatty's review of *Alice's Adventures in Wonderland* from *Aunt Judy's Magazine*, page 20; a condensed reprint of Walter de la Mare's "Lewis Carroll" from the 1 September 1930 issue of *Fortnightly Review*, pages 57–63. Also see index.

**C73:20]** Hays, R. W. "A Note about Lewis Carroll." *Armchair Detective*, 7, No. 2 (1973), 95–96.

There is only one passage in Carroll's writing that shows an interest in the work of the detective. It is the answer to Knot VII of "A Tangled Tale," which also displays the influence of Dickens, both in style and in the use of the name "Bill Sykes."

**C73:21]** Henkle, Roger B. "The Mad Hatter's World." *Virginia Quarterly Review*, 49, No. 1 (Winter 1973), 99–117.

"Within the Alice books are explorations of an adult life that venture as far as Carroll could risk going toward freedom from duties, responsibilities, and arid self-limitations of modern society—and in this aspect we may discover the immediacy of their appeal to contemporary readers." Carroll's need to retreat to personal patterns of play and whim is rendered in fragments of a desired lifestyle with the freedoms and satisfactions of adult play. His books show the reluctant conclusion that totally independent life patterns are impossible and even dangerous.

**C73:22]**   Hickley, Katherine. "Lewis Carroll at Whitburn" (letter). *Country Life,* 153 (3 May 1973), 1232, 1234.

**C73:23]**   Hillman, Ellis. "Who was the Mad Hatter?" *JJLCS*, 3, No. 1 (Winter 1973), 12–14.

Reviews possible sources of the Mad Hatter, and proposes a new candidate, Charles Babbage, the controversial Cambridge mathematician and mechanician.

**C73:24]**   Jones, Enid Huws. *Mrs. Humphrey Ward.* London: Heinemann, 1973.

See index for references to Carroll. A Carroll photograph is reproduced.

**C73:25]**   Kendrick, Myra. "English Country Churches—No. 2—The 'Alice in Wonderland' Parishes." *This England,* 6, No. 4 (1973), 44.

Discusses today's All Saints, Daresbury, and St. Peter, Croft-on-Tees—the parishes which were the successive livings of Carroll's father and where the boy grew up.

**C73:26]**   Kincaid, James R. "Alice's Invasion of Wonderland." *Publications of the Modern Language Association,* 88, No. 1 (January 1973), 92–99.

"By rejecting Wonderland and the world behind the looking-glass, Alice is rejecting not only the horrifying chaos of meaninglessness but the liberating chaos of comedy as well." The tone of the *Alice* books is ambivalent in relation to the protagonist, and it is this "tonal ambivalence which makes these books so baffling and complex."

**C73:27]**   Komar, Michal. "Carroll Jego Gry." *Literatura na Świecie,* No. 5 (1973), pp. 308–28.

A background essay on Carroll's life and work and a wide-ranging critical reading of the *Alices* with some emphasis on the reader's response. The title translates as "Carroll, His Game." A game is being played in the stories between the reader and the text (author); the mystery of the adventures emerges from the moment of contact between the printed page and the reader. In Polish.

**C73:28]**   Laporte, Henri. *Alice au pays des merveilles: Structures Logiques et Représentations du Désir*. France: Mame, 1973. Pp. 103.

A structural approach to *Alice in Wonderland*. Argues that Alice's physical and intellectual reactions have little to do with our daily experience of reality. Carroll's first objective seems to be to escape from common experience and repressive norms. Looks at the logical realities Alice faces during her adventures since Carroll organizes Alice's initiation according to mathematical-logical criteria. Finds that logic in Wonderland is repressive and leads only to false liberation. Includes an investigation of the elements which evoke a sense of imprisonment in *Alice,* and a look at how Carroll introduces actions of time and desire. In French.
    Reviewed by Anne Villelaur, *La Quinzaine Littéraire*, No. 183 (15 March 1974), pp. 13–15.

**C73:29]**   "The Late 'Lewis Carroll.' " *JJLCS*, 3, No. 1 (Winter 1973), 14–15.

Reprint of an obituary that appeared in 1898 in the *Eastbourne Gazette*.

**C73:30]**   Mann, Nancy, E. D. "George MacDonald and the Tradition of Victorian Fantasy." *Dissertation Abstracts International*, 34 (1973), 3413A–14A (Stanford).

In a study of George MacDonald, Carroll is discussed as one of four writers in the second half of the nineteenth century producing works of prose fiction belonging to the subgenre called fantasy.

**C73:31]**   Matheson, Brenda Dane. *The Tender Years: Lewis Carroll Around the North*. Darlington, England: Nordales (Five Counties) Publications, [1973].

Brief biography containing the sustained argument that Carroll's early years with his family in the North of England had a preeminent influence on his literary creations. Photographs. Short selection of poems.
    Reviewed by A. Leonard, *JJLCS*, 3, No. 2 (Spring 1974), 7.

**C73:32]**  *Mr. Dodgson: Nine Lewis Carroll Studies*. Introduction by Denis Crutch. London: The Lewis Carroll Society (England), 1973.

Contains the following essays: "Lewis Carroll and the Dodgson Lineage" by Philip Dodgson Jaques (pp. 7–9) traces the Dodgson family history to the present by Carroll's great-nephew; "Three Faces of Alice" by Anne Clark (pp. 10–14) discusses the life of Alice P. Liddell with respect to Lewis Carroll; "Lewis Carroll the Creative Writer" by Selwyn N. Goodacre (pp. 15–22) discusses all of Carroll's creative literature, but primarily *Alice in Wonderland*—genesis, nature and significance, publication, and early editions; "The Revd. Mr. Dodgson, by Ivor Davies (pp. 23–25) discusses Carroll's religious views and practices; "C. L. Dodgson: Mathematician" by Tony Beale (pp. 26–33) reassesses Carroll as a mathematician; "Lewis Carroll: Linguist of Wonderland" by Denis Crutch (pp. 34–37) reviews *Alice* from a linguistic perspective—portmanteau words, puns, imaginative word uses and abuses [Crutch adds a note in a letter in *JJLCS*, 5, No. 1 (Winter 1976), 32]; "C. L. Dodgson, Photographer and Artist" by Graham Ovenden (pp. 38–39) reassesses Carroll generally as an artist and photographer; "Mr. Dodgson, Man About Town" by Mary Crutch (pp. 40–42) looks at Carroll at the sea-side, visiting friends for Sunday tea, and going to the theatre; "Artists in Wonderland" by John Davis (pp. 43–48) discusses the many illustrated versions of Alice that followed Tenniel's. Also contains *A Companion-Guide to "Alice at Longleat"* (B73:2).
    Reviewed by Brian Sibley, *JJLCS*, 3, No. 1 (Winter 1973), 2-4.

**C73:33]**  Oultram, Ken. "The Cheshire Cat and Its Origins." *JJLCS*, 3, No. 1 (Winter 1973), 8–14.

Traces the origin of the notion of "the grinning Cheshire Cat." Reprints various old and obscure explanations.

**C73:34]**  Rackin, Donald. "What You Always Wanted to Know About Alice but Were Afraid to Ask." *Victorian Newsletter*, No. 44 (Fall 1973), pp. 1–5.

"Although the *Alice* books do have sexual implications, they are not books about sex." If we read sexuality into them, "we introduce an element that destroys their 'invented' organic completeness and interferes with their deepest purposes—aesthetic and philosophical," and "we deny ourselves the sovereign chance to accompany Alice on those trips of the unimpeded intellect into lands beyond matter and change and death."

**C73:35]** Reinstein, Phyllis G. "Alice in Context: A Study of Children's Literature and the Dominant Culture in Eighteenth and Nineteenth Centuries." *Dissertation Abstracts,* 34 (1973), 285A (Yale).

Although the *Alice* books "have generally been considered revolutionary, in reality they rise from, and in some measure depend upon, previous children's literature and the cultural and social environment of the Victorian period." The development of juvenile literature is traced "from its inception in the late eighteenth century to the publication of the *Alice* books, attempting to establish a background for understanding Carroll's novels."

**C73:36]** Schedler, Melchior. *Schlachtet die blauen Elefanten: Bemerkungen über das Kinderstück.* Weinheim and Basel: Beltz, 1973.

See pages 23–37 for a study of nonsense which includes a discussion of Carroll and *Alice in Wonderland.* Carroll, like Lear, uses children's literature as an escape. Rules and social and literary conventions are the inner themes of nonsense. Since 1972, nonsense has been in vogue in German children's books and in the theatre, where there was a popular new dramatization of *Alice in Wonderland.* In German.

**C73:37]** Schrey, Helmut. *Grundzüge einer Literaturdidaktik des Englischen.* Ratingen: A Henn Verlag, 1973.

Schrey's essay on English nonsense poetry (C66:18) is reprinted on pages 67–86, and further remarks on nonsense in general and Carroll in particular appear on pages 61–66 and 91–111. In German.

**C73:38]** Stern, Jeffrey. "Approaches to Lewis Carroll." Dissertation University of York, 1973.

Introduction: ". . . it is only if seen in isolation that Carroll and his work seem eccentric; in relationship to certain other key figures he can be seen as having connections with a number of significant traditions. The ultimate aim . . . is to attempt to re-evaluate Carroll . . . by approaching him from various seemingly heterogeneous viewpoints . . . the literary aspect will be made taking examples for the 17th, 18th, and 19th centuries, followed by examples from the visual arts of the 19th and 20th centuries."

**C73:39]** Stickney, Charles Jacob. "The Distorted Word: Word

Distortion in Modern British and American Literature." *Dissertation Abstracts International,* 33 (1973), 6933A (C.U.N.Y.).

Primarily a study of the purposes and processes of word distortion in modern British and American literature. In chapter 2 a series of analytic processes are applied to various "classics" of word distortion, including *Alice in Wonderland.*

**C73:40]** Stiller, Robert. "Powrót do Carrolla." *Literatura na Świecie,* No 5 (1973), pp. 330-63.

A background essay on and critical discussion of Carroll's work on the occasion of the first translation of *Through the Looking-Glass* into Polish. The problems of translating / adapting Carroll's works into Polish are discussed; four Polish translations of *Alice in Wonderland* are compared; and the first Polish translation of *Through the Looking-Glass* (1972) is analyzed. The critical discussion is focused on aspects of language. The title translates as "Back to Carroll." We are returning to Carroll following Joyce and his followers because Carroll took the first step. In Polish.

**C73:41]** Tabbert, Reinbert. "Humpty Dumpty oder die Kunst Lewis Carrolls." *Literatur in Wissenschaft und Unterricht* (Kiel), 6 (1973), 176–87.

Humpty Dumpty is perhaps the most complex character in children's literature. He is a unique creature—a fictional character who is artful, ingenious, comical, and full of pride. He has attracted not just children but writers and philologists. In German.

**C73:42]** Takahashi, Yasunari, ed. *Arisu no Ehon.* Tokyo: Bokushinsha, 1973.

Title translates as *Picturebook of Alice.* Contains several illustrations and essays on the image of Alice. Includes Japanese translations of Allen Tate's "Last Days of Alice," W. H. Auden's "Today's Wonder-world' needs Alice" (part), L. Aragon's "Lewis Carroll in 1931," M. Grotjahn's "About the Symbolism . . . ," and T. Fensch's "Alice in Acidland."

**C73:43]** Trevor-Roper, Hugh. *Christ Church Oxford.* [Oxford]: Published by authority of the Governing Board of Christ Church, 1973.

See pages 29, 32, 35, and 36 for references to Lewis Carroll.

## 1974

**C74:1]**  Arbasimo, Alberto. "La Mostra Delle Fotographie di Lewis Carroll a Londra: Con l'obiettivo puntato su Alice." *Corriere Della Sera*, 2 February 1974.

The author of *Alice in Wonderland* enjoyed all sorts of gadgets and was a passionate photographer. He produced extraordinary portraits of Victorians, especially Oxford academicians, and children's photographs. In Italian.

**C74:2]**  Benham, Philip S. "Sonnet Illuminate." *JJLCS*, 3, No. 3 (Summer 1974), 1–3.

Discusses Carroll's "Anagrammatic Sonnet," pointing out errors in past solutions, and proposes an "improved" solution. For corrections see *JJLCS*, 4, No. 1 (Winter 1975), 19.

**C74:3]**  Berman, Ruth. *Patterns of Unification in Sylvie & Bruno*. Baltimore: [T-K Graphics] 1974. Pp. 23.

Argues that the Outland-Fairyland and England plots are unified too closely, thematically and structurally, to make it possible to separate the superior fantasy from the inferior realism.

**C74:4]**  Blake, Kathleen. *Play, Games, and Sport: The Literary Works of Lewis Carroll*. London and Ithaca, New York: Cornell Univ. Press, 1974.

See C71:2.

Reviewed by: R. L. Brooks, *Library Journal*, 99 (1 April 1974), 1390; Anthony Quinton, *Times Literary Supplement*, 20 December 1974, p. 1436; (J. R. Christopher), *Choice*, 11, No. 11 (January 1975), 1626; Benny Green, *Spectator*, 8 February 1975, p. 158; Alvin C. Kibel, *Victorian Studies*, 18, No. 3 (March 1975), 370–72; Richard A. Lanham, *Nineteenth-Century Fiction*, 29, No. 4 (March 1975), 480–83; Edward Guiliano, *Children's Literature*, 4 (1975), 186–91; C. C. Barfoot, *English Studies*, 56 (1975), 448; Jeffrey Stern, *JJLCS*, 4, No. 1 (Winter 1975), 12–13; James Fraser, *Phaedrus*, 2, No. 1 (Fall 1976), 44–45. Phyllis Greenacre, *Psychoanalytic Quarterly*, 45, No. 1 (1976), 162–64; Elizabeth Sewell, *Novel*, 9, No. 3 (Spring 1976), 283–85; J. Gattégno, *Etudes Anglaises*, 24 (1976), 620–21; C. Miller, *Southern Humanities Review*, 10 (1976),

198–99; J. Mezciems, *Yearbook of English Studies*, 6 (1976), 322–23; S. Pickering, *Saturday Review*, 84 (1976), lii–lvi.

**C74:5]** Blount, Margaret. *Animal Land: The Creatures of Children's Fiction*. London: Hutchinson, 1974; New York: William Morrow and Company, 1975.

Includes a comparison of Carroll's work with Lear's and a discussion of Sylvie and Bruno's visit to Dogland.
Reviewed by Brian Sibley, *JJLCS*, 4, No. 1 (Winter 1975), 14–15.

**C74:6]** Bradbury, Ray. "Because, because. . . ." Introduction to Raylyn Moore, *Wonderful Wizard Marvelous Land*. Bowling Green, Ohio: Bowling Green Univ. Popular Press, 1974, pp. xi–xviii.

Contains a comparison of Wonderland with Oz.

**C74:7]** Cohen, Morton N. "The Wonderful Day Gertrude met the Snark." *The Times* (London), 20 July 1974, p. 12.

A brief look on the one-hundredth anniversary of the *Snark*'s conception at the poem's genesis and subsequent reception. Includes the reprinting of a little-known acrostic poem to Alice Crompton.

**C74:8]** Danilov, Yu. A. "The Man Who Created 'Alice'." *Literaturnaya Gazeta*, 21 September 1974.

A short biographical study. Title and text in Russian.

**C74:9]** Doherty, H. B. "The Genesis of *Alice in Wonderland*." *JJLCS*, 3, No. 2 (Spring 1974), 18–26.

"The story was suggested to Lewis Carroll by two of Alice Liddell's school-books, probably also by a third. We can identify the first two, and there is every reason to believe they were the principal ones."

**C74:10]** Empson, William. "Alice i eventryrland: barnet som hyrdeskikkelse." Trans. Per Olsen. *Meddelelser fra Dansklaererforeningen*, No. 4 (1974), pp. 533–47.

Danish translation of Empson's 1935 essay on *Alice in Wonderland*.

**C74:11]**  Füger, Wilhelm. "Stephen in Wonderland? A Note on the Beginning of Joyce's *Portrait.*" *Archiv für das Studium der neueren Sprachen,* 211, No. 1 (July 1974), 72–75.

Discusses similarities between the works of Carroll and Joyce, and compares, in particular, the opening of *The Nursery 'Alice'* with the opening of Joyce's *Portrait.* A side-glance at *The Nursery 'Alice'* rewards us with a better understanding of the opening technique applied in the *Portrait.* Finds, for one example, that the "rabbit has a similar function for Alice as the moocow has for Stephen."

**C74:12]**  Gattégno, Jean. *Lewis Carroll: une vie d'Alice à Zénon d'Elée.* Paris: Seuil, 1974.

A biography consisting of a series of thirty-seven brief and diverse essays on aspects of Carroll's life and art. For English translation see C76:15.

Reviewed by: Anne Villelaur, *La Quinzaine Littéraire,* No. 183 (15 March 1974), pp. 13–15; Jean-Clause Dietsch, *Etudes Anglaises* (June 1974), p. 138; Robert Benayoun, *Le Point,* 14 January 1975, p. 76; Hubert Juin, *Le Monde,* 8 February 1974, pp. 11, 14; Catherine David, *Le Nouvel Observateur,* 4 March 1974; Edward Guiliano, *Children's Literature* (1975), 186–91.

**C74:13]**  Goodacre, Selwyn H. "Humpty Dumpty's Song—A Possible Origin." *JJLCS,* 3, No. 2 (Spring 1975), 17–18.

Suggests Sara Coleridge's "The Months" (1834) as a source.

**C74:14]**  _____. "Lewis Carroll and Hypnogogic Phenomena." *World Medicine,* 28 August 1974, p. 9.

Carroll experienced hypnogogic phenomena from an early age and turned them to creative use in his fiction writing.

**C74:15]**  G[reen], R[oger] L[ancelyn]. "Lewis Carroll." *Encyclopedia Britanica: Macropaedia,* 1974 ed., pp. 966–68.

Biographical sketch, headed by the Rejlander portrait of Carroll, in which *Sylvie and Bruno* is defended as presenting "the truest available portrait of the man," and intense attempts at interpreting *Alice* are disparaged.

**C74:16]**  Heath, Peter. "Alice and the Philosophers." *JJLCS,* 3, No. 4 (Autumn 1974), 3–8.

Publication of a talk given before the Lewis Carroll Society (England) as an introduction to *The Philosopher's Alice;* see A74:13.

**C74:17]**  Helson, Raveena. "The Psychological Origins of Fantasy for Children in Mid-Victorian England." *Children's Literature,* 3 (1974), 67–76.

*Alice in Wonderland* is among the children's books discussed. Its publication was "a revolutionary event because it brought the pursuit of pleasure for its own sake into children's books. Alice represents a reaction not so much against ego-defensive selfishness and greed as against the tyranny of the ego processes themselves — logic, reason, schooling, propriety, all the cultural purposiveness which gradually shuts off one's capacity to experience freshly and playfully, and to be aware of one's grotesque, incongruous 'id' characteristics."

**C74:18]**  Joyce, James. "Lolita in Humberland." *Studies in the Novel,* 6, No. 3 (Fall 1974), 339–48.

Allusions to the *Alice* books "have structural and thematic purpose, and thus important consequences for understanding the novel" *Lolita.*

**C74:19]**  Kibel, Alvin C. "Logic and Satire in *Alice in Wonderland.*" *American Scholar,* 43, No. 4 (1974), 605–29.

Wide-ranging discussion of Carroll and the *Alices* with some emphasis on the reader response of children and adults to the books, and on the nature of the logic evidenced in them. "Uniquely, Dodgson discovered an intellectual legitimacy in the childish viewpoint, making it available to both childish and adult intelligences. . . . The Alices are eccentric performances about the child's need to deal with an eccentric world, and an ideal of courtesy is at their center."

**C74:20]**  Manley, K. A. "Dodgson v. Carroll: The Case of the Bodleian Catalogue." *Times Literary Supplement,* 28 June 1974, p. 691.

Summarizes Dodgson's successful attempt to prevent the publication of his name linked with Lewis Carroll in the *Dictionary of Anonymous and Pseudonymous Literature of Great Britain* in the 1880s and his later failure to remove the link in the Bodleian Catalogue. Includes the first publication of letters to Falconer Madan (6 December 1880 and 8 December 1880) and to E. B. Nicholson (25 April 1882). Morton N. Cohen and Denis Crutch responded to Manley's piece with letters, 19 July 1974, p. 769. Cohen states that "any suggestion that Dodgson opposed Carroll or that he suffered from a split personality is simply not supported by the facts." See also Selwyn Goodacre's letter, *JJLCS*, 6, No. 3 (Summer 1977), 87–88.

**C74:21]**   Miller, Edmund. "Lewis Carroll Genealogical Oversight in 'The Tangled Tale.' " *English Language Notes*, 12, No. 2 (December 1974), 109–11.

In Knot II Carroll's answer of "one guest" is not the mathematically parsimonious answer for the number of guests at the Governor of Kgovjni's *very* small dinner party. Miller provides two solutions which yield zero guests plus the governor.

**C74:22]**   Otten, Terry. "Steppenwolf and Alice—In and Out of Wonderland." *Studies in the Humanities*, 4, No. 1 (March 1974), 28–34.

Compares and contrasts *Alice* with Herman Hesse's *Steppenwolf*. Both Alice and Steppenwolf "journey into mad Wonderlands similarly depicted through the use of terrors, sudden evaporation of scenes, disregard of time and space, disappearance of characters, association of savagery and cruelty, images of childhood and lost innocence, and various other common elements." Even more significant is that both Alice's and Steppenwolf's flights "become a measure of their humanity, a means by which their 'beingness' is defined."

**C74:23]**   Praz, Mario. "Two Masters of the Absurd: Grandville and Carroll." In *The Artist and Writer in France: Essays in honour of Jean Seznec*. Ed. Francis Haskell, Anthony Levi, and Robert Shackleton, Oxford: Clarendon, 1974, pp. 134–37.

Comparison of the "logical organization of the absurd" in the work of Grandville and Carroll.

**C74:24]**   Razova, V. *"Lewis Carroll." Children's Literature Abroad: A textbook for college libraries*. Moscow: Prosveshcshenie Publishers, 1974, pp. 57–59.

A brief account of Carroll's life and work. Title and text in Russian.

**C74:25]**   Reichert, Klaus. *Lewis Carroll—Studien zum literarischen Unsinn*. Munich: Carl Hanser Verlag, 1974. Pp. 216, paperback.

A philosophical and linguistic analysis of Carroll's nonsense largely from biographical and sociological standpoints. In German.

Reviewed by: Gertrud Mander, *Die Zeit,* 6 December 1974; D. Petzold, *Anglia,* 94 (1976), 542–45.

**C74:26]**   Robinson, A. H. "The March Hare's Origin" (letter). *The Field,* 7 November 1974, p. 1042.

Suggests possible models for Tenniel's March Hare.

**C74:27]**   Schulmann, Kuno. " 'Hear the Tolling of the Bells': Lewis Carroll's *The Hunting of the Snark.*" In *Miscellanea Anglo-Americana: Festschrift für Helmut Viebrock.* Ed. Kuno Schulmann, Wilhelm Hortmann, and Armin P. Frank.

*The Hunting of the Snark* should be read as a modern poem. As a poem, it does not communicate with the reader, it provokes the reader. Answers are not given through *content* but through *construction.* This nonsense poem does not follow the rules of poetic-stylish images, but the laws of language and aesthetic autonomy. Carroll, like Poe, trusts the power of words. In German.

**C74:28]**   Taylor, Alexander L. *The White Knight: A Study of C. L. Dodgson (Lewis Carroll).* [Folcroft, Pennsylvania]: Folcroft Library Editions, 1974; Norwood, Pennsylvania: Norwood Editions, 1976.

Reprints of 1952 edition published by Oliver & Boyd, Edinburgh (*WMG* XXIII; 1979 ed., 523).

**C74:29]**   Townsend, John Rowe. *Written for Children.* Harmondsworth: Kestrel Books, 1974; Philadelphia and New York: J. B. Lippincott Company 1975.

Revised and expanded edition of book originally published in 1965. See index for references to Carroll.

**C74:30]**   White, Daniel N. "Lewis Carroll, Photographer." *Princeton Alumni Weekly,* 28 May 1974, pp. 10–14.

A summary of Carroll's career as a photographer. Six well-known photographs from the Parrish Collection are reproduced with accompanying commentaries.

**C74:31]**   Wisdom, William A. "Lewis Carroll's Infinite Regress." *Mind,* 83 (1974), 571–73.

A contribution to the controversy about inference inaugurated by Carroll's article "What the Tortoise said to Achilles," in *Mind* (December 1894).

# 1975

**C75:1]** Anastaplo, George. "Lewis Carroll, C. L. Dodgson, and their Alices." *The University of Chicago Magazine,* 68, No. 2 (Winter 1975), 26–32.

Wide-ranging discussion on Carroll and the art, poetry, calculation, and dreams evidenced in the *Alices.*

**C75:2]** Binder, Lucia. "Die phantastische Erzählung." In *Jugendschriftenkunde.* Ed. Richard Bamberger. (Schriften zur Jugendlektüre.) Vienna: Jugend und Volk, 1975.

Fantasy came late to children's literature in German. It appeared earlier in other countries, especially England. *Alice in Wonderland* and other works of this genre are analyzed. They brought laughter, fun and games, and moments of surprise to children's literature and have allowed adults to explore children's literature and consider it seriously as an art form. In German.

**C75:3]** Bratton, J. S. *The Victorian Popular Ballad.* London: Macmillan, 1975.

In a chapter entitled "Comic Ballads in the Drawing Room, pp. 207–50," the comic ballads of Gilbert and Carroll are compared and contrasted. Also discussed are "Phantasmagoria" and *The Hunting of the Snark*—Carroll's "cerebral game of words and literary associations."

**C75:4]** Breitkruez, Hartmut. "Alice im Wunderland." In *Enzyklopädie des Märchens.* Ed. Kurt Ranke. Berlin and New York: Walter de Gruyter and Co., 1975, I, cols. 311–14.

Literary encyclopedia entry on *Alice in Wonderland.* In German.

**C75:5]** Carlson, Richard S. *The Benign Humorists.* Hamden, Connecticut: Archon Books, 1975.

Carroll is one of seven writers discussed extensively in this study of late nineteenth and early twentieth-century literary humorists. See pages 32–37 (Carroll as nonsense humorist), 80–85 (Carroll's language of benign humor), and index.

**C75:6]**   Ciardi, John, and Miller Williams. *How Does A Poem Mean?* 2nd ed. Boston: Houghton Mifflin, 1975.

Chapter 2, "A Burble through the Tulgey Wood," includes a discussion of Carroll as a comic poet, parodist, and nonsense writer. There is an extended analysis of "Jabberwocky" and briefer analyses of "Father William" and "The Crocodile."
   First edition appeared in 1959.

**C75:7]**   Cohen, Morton N. "Lewis Carroll Comes to School." *Ad Lucem* [alumnae magazine at the Oxford High School for Girls], (1975), pp. 7–8.

Concerns Lewis Carroll's association with the Oxford High School for Girls as a logic instructor and as a friend to students and staff members.
   Reprinted with slight alterations in *JJLCS*, 5, No. 1 (Winter 1976), 25–27.

**C75:8]**   _____. "Miss Ethel Hatch." *The Times* (London), 9 April 1975, p. 16.

Obituary notice of one of Carroll's last surviving child friends.

**C75:9]**   Crutch, Denis. "*Alice* for the Little Ones." *JJLCS*, 4, No. 4 (Autumn 1975), 87–89.

A history and review of *The Nursery 'Alice.'*

**C75:10]**   _____. "*Sylvie and Bruno:* An Introduction." *JJLCS*, 4, No. 3 (Summer 1975), 47–50.

Brief recounting of the genesis, structure, and limitations of the *Sylvie and Bruno* books.

**C75:11]**   Crutch, Mary. "An *Alice* for Today's Nursery." *JJLCS*, 4, No. 4 (Autumn 1975), 90–91.

Discussion of appeal and appropriateness of *The Nursery 'Alice'* for "today's little ones."

**C75:12]**   Dakin, D. Martin. "Alice and the Queen." *JJLCS*, 4, No. 1 (Winter 1975), 11.

Queen Elizabeth II is distantly related to Alice Liddell. Includes genealogical chart. In *JJLCS,* 4, No. 3 (Summer 1975), 84, the relationship is fixed at third cousin three times removed.

**C75:13]**   Danilov, Yu. A. "Food for the Mind." *Priroda,* 9, No. 5 (1975), 125–28.

Introduction to and general discussion of "Feeding the Mind." Title and text in Russian.

**C75:14]**   _____. "Lewis Carroll and his 'Eight or Nine Words on Letter Writing.' " *Knowledge Is Strength,* No. 2 (1975), pp. 46–48.

Title and text in Russian.

**C75:15]**   Davis, J. N. S. "E. Gertrude Thomson, Illustrator, 1850–1929." *JJLCS,* 4, No. 4 (Autumn 1975), 96–99.

Brief history of the relationship between Carroll and his artist-friend E. Gertrude Thomson.

**C75:16]**   _____. "The Salisbury Correspondence." *JJLCS,* 4, No. 3 (Summer 1975), 59–65.

Summarizes twenty-seven letters, currently in the Library of Hatfield House, by Lewis Carroll to the Third Marquess of Salisbury written during the 1874–97 period and covering a wide variety of topics. Also contains minimal background information.

**C75:17]**   De La Roche, Wayne W. "Privacy and Community in the Writings of Lewis Carroll." *Dissertation Abstracts International,* 36 (1975), 3683A (Columbia).

"This dissertation explores in chronological order the various techniques with which Carroll experimented until he finally balanced his public and private identities, and found a legitimate place for imagination in Victorian society. It attempts to reconcile the hidden conflicts of the man and his times." Argues that Carroll epitomizes "the kind of artist who cannot bear isolation, yet whose powers of invention alienate him from his contemporaries." His *Alice* books provided him with an "outlet for games and fantasy and satisfied his desire for intimacy. . . ." They also provided him with a safe forum to comment on the social problems of his age.

**C75:18]**   Fisher, Margery. *Who's Who in Children's Books: A Treasury of Familiar Characters of Childhood.* London: Weidenfeld & Nicholson, 1975.

The rules and regulations in Carroll's fictive world are noted in the entry on Alice, pages 13–17. The entry is illustrated with pictures by Carroll, Tenniel, Steadman, Rackham, Claveloux, and Jansson; and photographs of Carroll and Jonathan Miller's TV *Alice.* Also contains entries on Sylvie and Bruno (p. 337) and Prince Uggug (p. 365).

**C75:19]**   Garner, Philippe. "Looking at Victorian Photographs." *Antique Dealer and Collector's Guide,* July 1975, pp. 78–81.

In a brief survey of British creative photographers in the nineteenth century, Carroll is ranked "amongst the foremost portraitists of the period." A Carroll photograph of a young girl is reproduced.

**C75:20]**   Goodacre, Selwyn H. "In Search of Alice's Brother's Latin Grammar." *JJLCS,* 4, No. 2 (Spring 1975), 27–30.

Progress report on search for a Latin Grammar which uses "Mouse" as a declension example and which could have inspired Carroll's "A mouse—of a mouse—to a mouse—a mouse—O mouse!"
    In a letter, *JJLCS,* 6, No. 2 (Spring 1977), 59–60, August A. Imholtz, Jr., suggests Carroll was punning on the Greek noun.

**C75:21]**   Guiliano, Edward. "Academic Wonderlands." *Children's Literature,* 4 (1975), 186–91.

Discusses Carroll's emergence on university campuses, and reviews three books by academicians, A74:13, C74:4, C74:12.

**C75:22]**   _____. "Correspondence." *JJLCS,* 4, No. 3 (Summer 1975), 79–80.

Proposes a list of items needed for a real advance in Carroll studies.

**C75:23]**   Hardy, Barbara. *Tellers and Listeners: The Narrative Imagination.* London: Athlone, 1975.

The *Alices* are discussed extensively in a section on fantasy and dream. See pages 33–45, and index.

**C75:24]** Heath, Peter. "Correspondence." *JJLCS,* 4, No. 3 (Summer 1975), 78–79.

Concerns the validity of literary criticism of Carroll's works. Written in response to reviews of Kathleen Blake's *Play, Games and Sport* (C74:4) and Heath's *The Philosopher's Alice* (A74:13). Includes reviewers' replies.

**C75:25]** Hillman, Ellis. "The Walrus and the Carpenter." *Ghost Dance Times,* 20 June 1975, p. 2.

Suggests that Bismark was the model for the Walrus, Count Cavour for the Carpenter, and Austria for the ill-fated oysters.

**C75:26]** Hoglund, Ken. "Charles Dodgson and George Mac-Donald: A Friendship Observed." *Myrddin Two,* 1, No. 2 (August 1975), 35–38.

Brief biographical account.

**C75:27]** Horgas, Béla. "Csodák, ötletek." *Élet és Irodadom,* 19, No. 21 (1975), 11.

A review of *Alice's Adventures in Wonderland.* Hungarian children will hardly enjoy the world of nonsense humor Carroll creates. The characteristically English heroes who play with the impossible are alien to them. Horgas suspects that in all probability Carroll's surrealism will only meet with fragmentary understanding and appreciation in Hungary. In Hungarian.

**C75:28]** Ippolitova, V. V. "V mire Snarka (o poeme L. Carrolla *Okhota na Snarka)." Sbornik trudor MOPI* (Moscow), 19 / 20 (1975), 116–23.

Contains an account of the genesis of *The Hunting of the Snark,* a discussion of the difficulties in interpreting it rationally, a brief survey of Carroll's and others' interpretation of it, an attempt to place it into a social and literary context, and also a comparison with *Moby-Dick.*

**C75:29]** "Knot to Be Undone." *Bandersnatch: The Lewis Carroll Society* [England] *Newsletter,* No. 12 (October 1975), p. [4].

Notes on *A Tangled Tale* including the identification of some of Carroll's opening quotations.

**C75:30]**  Little, Edmund. "Some Observations on the Biography and Work of Lewis Carroll and Nikolai Gogol." *Forum for Modern Language Studies,* 11, No. 1 (January 1975), 74–92.

Points out many similarities in the lives and works of Carroll and Gogol. In these "two authors who made merry with the norms and conventions of the waking world but were nevertheless realists in a higher sense of the world, with a better claim than Dostoyevsky to this honour!"

**C75:31]**  Livingston, Myra Cohn. "But Is It Poetry?" *Horn Book,* 51, No. 6 (December 1975), 571–80.

On Carroll's "Poeta Fit, Non Nascitur" and children's poetry today.

**C75:32]**  Loughbridge, J. Michael. "Alice [im Wunderland]." In *Lexikon der Kinder- und Jugendliteratur.* Ed. Klaus Doderer. Weinheim / Basel / Berlin: Beltz, 1975, I, cols. 22–25.

A history and critical survey of *Alice in Wonderland.* Discussed are the genesis and history of the publication; Carroll's letters to his child friends; the themes in *Alice*—especially the escape from reality theme; Carroll's literary style—especially use of riddles, parodies, and wordplay; modern interpretations of *Alice; Alice's* current worldwide popularity and influence; and Carroll's interest in math as reflected in the work. In German.

**C75:33]**  ———. "Carroll, Lewis." In *Lexikon der Kinder- und Jugendliteratur.* Ed. Klaus Doderer. Weinhem / Basel / Berlin: Beltz, 1975, I, cols. 244–45.

Children's literature encyclopedia entry on Carroll's life and work with a German / English bibliography of primary and secondary works. In German.

**C75:34]**  Morrow, Patrick. "Yossarian in Wonderland: Bureaucracy, the *Alice* Books, and *Catch-22.*" *North Dakota Quarterly,* 43 (Spring), 50–57.

*Catch-22* has important literary ancestors in Lewis Carroll's *Alice* books. Numerous parallels between the *Alices* and *Catch-22* are identified and discussed.

**C75:35]**  Peccoud, Robert. "Alice Carroll, ou les mémoires d'une jeune fille droguée." *Temps Modernes,* 31, No. 352 (November 1975), 643–61.

Compares Alice's journey to a drug trip. Alice's story is both the story of initiation to a psychedelic trip and the dialectic, long-term cultural integration / disintegration provoked by the repeated use of a halucinatory drug. In the first chapters of *Alice,* for one example, the metaphoric representation applies to the effects of drugs rather than to the drug itself. Relates how perspectives are changed today as in Alice's trip. In French.

**C75:36]**   Plett, Heinrich F. *Textwissenschaft und Textanalyse.* Heidelberg: Quelle & Meyer, 1975.

A linguistic analysis, in German, of the English "Jabberwocky" appears on pages 196–201.

**C75:37]**   Prideaux, Tom. *Love or Nothing: The Life & Times of Ellen Terry.* New York: Scribner, 1975.

See index for references to Carroll and the Terrys.

**C75:38]**   Prioleau, Elizabeth. "Humbert Humbert Through the *Looking-Glass." Twentieth Century Literature,* 21, No. 4 (December 1975), 428–37.

Similarities between *Lolita* and *Through the Looking-Glass* are identified. "Seen together, Humbert's whole narration has a "Looking-Glass world" perspective: time and space move backward, doubles proliferate, language fractures into new combination." At the same time, within Humbert's story itself, there is a concurrent dramatization of Humbert's struggle to penetrate the looking-glass.

**C75:39]**   Richardson, Joanna. "Dodgson in Wonderland." *History Today,* 25, No. 2 (February 1975), 110–117.

A wide-ranging popular discussion of the *Alices.*

**C75:40]**   Rodrigues, Jaime. "Literatura Policial, Nonsense e Lewis Carroll." *Minas Gerais (Suplemento Litérario),* 10 May 1975, pp. 8–9.

The nature and history of detective fiction are analyzed, and Rodrigues argues that detective literature could be considered as a typical *nonsense* literature in the sense that it exposes facts and situations that attack the social order, seeking, in this way, to repair the logical thread (that has been broken at some point) in the name of legality. Several parallels with Carroll's nonsense are drawn. In Portuguese.

**C75:41]** Rose, Kenneth. *The Later Cecils*. London: Weidenfeld & Nicholson, 1975.

Carroll's relationship with the Cecils is discussed briefly, and three of his photographs of the Cecil children are reproduced for the first time.

**C75:42]** Rosivach, Vincent J. "A Borrowed Vorpal Blade (letter)." *JJLCS*, 4, No. 2 (Spring 1975), 41.

On the etymology of "vorpal blade," which prior to "Jabberwocky" clearly had a sexual sense.

**C75:43]** Satty, Glenn. "An Alice Collage." *Lawrentian*, 39, No. 4 (March 1975), 21–26.

An excerpt from "A Chivers Lecture" given at the Lawrenceville School which touches on Carroll's biography, logic and nonsense, and *Through the Looking-Glass*.

**C75:44]** ˙ley, Brian. "Correspondence." *Dickensian*, 71, No. 377, part ɔ (1975), 169–70.

In *Sylvie and Bruno* Lady Muriel offers a chair to a ghost as does Scrooge in Dickens' *A Christmas Carol*.

**C75:45]** ———. "The Nursery '*Alice*' Illustrations." *JJLCS*, 4, No. 4 (Autumn 1975), 92–95.

A history and evaluation of the illustrations. Includes a discussion of the pictoral variants of *The Nursery 'Alice'* with *Alice in Wonderland*.

**C75:46]** ———. "The Poems to *Sylvie and Bruno*." *JJLCS*, 4, No. 3 (Summer 1975), 51–58.

"The verses in the two volumes of *Sylvie and Bruno* represent an important stage in Carroll's development as a poet; for their roots are buried deep within the book, and grow from the text in a highly original fashion. . . . The *Sylvie and Bruno* books contain some of Carroll's best—and some of his worst—versifying: some of his most brilliant pieces of construction, triumphant foolery and wildest surrealism; and some of his most uncontrolled, sentimental whimsy."

**C75:47]** Tabbert, Reinbert. "Zum literarischen Nonsense: Versuch einer Orientierung." *Der Deutschunterricht* (Stuttgart), 27, No. 5 (1975), 5–22.

A discussion of the origin, current definition, value and treatment in education, and the interpretation of nonsense. Carroll is cited as a nonsense writer, and "Jabberwocky" is evaluated. In German.

**C75:48]** Wolff, Robert Lee. "An 1862 Alice: 'Cross Purposes' or, *Which Dreamed it?" Harvard Library Bulletin,* 23, No. 2 (April 1975), 199–202.

George MacDonald's "Cross Purposes," with a heroine named Alice, thought to have been first published in 1867 and to contain a passage imitating *Alice in Wonderland,* was first published in 1862. Carroll could have known the piece, "and he must have been astonished, on reading 'Cross Purposes' to find his friend independently working the same vein of fantasy."

# 1976

**C76:1]** Almansi, Guido. "Come scrivere ad Alice." *Verri,* 3 (1976), 33–52.

Lewis Carroll had no difficulty communicating with children. His letters to children can be read from an adult's perspective and from a children's perspective. When we read them as adults we appreciate the logical paradoxes, the word play and the nonsense in them; however, we can sometimes miss the re-actions children can experience—surprise, laughter, and embarrassment. Numerous examples of Carroll's letters are offered and analyzed. In Italian.

Published in French as "Ecrire à Alice," trans. Jacques Carré. *Poétique,* 25 (1976), 36-48.

**C76:2]** Beckwith, Osmond. "The Oddness of Oz." *Children's Literature,* 5 (1976), 74–91.

Contains a comparison of Oz with Wonderland.

**C76:3]** Cohen, Morton N. "Correspondence." *JJLCS,* 5, No. 4 (Autumn 1976), 130–31.

Reprints article about Carroll that appeared in the *Illustrated London News* in 1891, which links the name Carroll with Dodgson. See C74:20.

**C76:4]** _____. "The electric pen." *Illustrated London News,* Christmas Number 1976, pp. 33, 35.

Lewis Carroll's fascination with and use of the electric pen, a primitive version of the mimeograph invented by Thomas Edison, is discussed. Includes facsimile examples of two Carroll letters written with the pen.

**C76:5]** Crutch, Denis. *"The Hunting of the Snark:* A Study in Fits and Starts." *JJLCS,* 5, No. 4 (Autumn 1976), 103–9.

General factual discussion. The poem, at first just three fits, was intended for *Sylvie and Bruno,* perhaps first to be privately printed, but it grew to eight fits and a small book. Suggests some sources and explanations.

**C76:6]** Davies, Ivor. "Archdeacon Dodgson." *JJLCS,* 5, No. 2 (Spring 1976), 46–49.

An account of the religious beliefs and career of Lewis Carroll's father.

**C76:7]** Dickins, A. S. M. "Alice in Fairyland." *JJLCS,* 5, No. 1 (Winter 1976), 3–24.

An adaptation of a talk given by an International Judge of the World Chess Federation on Fairy Chess, the *Looking-Glass Chess Problem,* the universal appeal of *Through the Looking-Glass,* and the significance of *Through the Looking-Glass* in the history of chess literature—it is a parody of a Chess Morality.

For a continued discussion see two letters and Dickins's reply in *JJLCS,* 5, No. 3 (Summer 1976), 95–99. See also C76:42.

Privately printed as a booklet.

**C76:8]** Dixon, F. E. "Correspondence." *JJLCS,* 5, No. 2 (Spring 1976), 61–62.

Lewis Carroll did not invent the transferable-vote system.

**C76:9]** Dupont, V. "Le monde et les personnages animaux dans 'Alice au pays des merveilles.' " *Caliban,* No. 3 (1966), 133–73.

Refutes Freudian interpretations applied to the animals in *Alice in Wonderland* and shows the reality and importance of the animal presence in *Alice.* Although Alice is the main character, all the animals participate in the action through dialogue. The animals love no one and tire Alice, yet produce a comic effect. The animals' features and gestures are human, and they possess literary and poetic values and interests. In French.

**C76:10]** Ede, Lisa Susan. "The Nonsense Literature of Edward Lear and Lewis Carroll." *Dissertation Abstracts International,* 36 (1976), 5314A (Ohio State).

An examination of the nonsense literature of Lear and Carroll with critical analyses of their major works. *"In Through the Looking-Glass* and 'The Hunting of the Snark,' Carroll utilizes similar external structural devices, such as the chess game, Looking-Glass reversals, and the 'rule of three,' to give the reader a sense of control and safety. In *Alice in Wonderland,* however, this dialectic is internalized and presented as a split in Alice's own character. . . . Lear's and Carroll's nonsense is subversive. . . . At perhaps its most profound, Lear's and Carroll's nonsense reforms its terms to reveal the non-human nightmare of logic, and the surreal logic of dreams."

**C76:11]** Englebreston, George. "A Note on the Sense of 'Jabberwocky.' " *JJLCS,* 5, No. 3 (Summer 1976), 93–94.

In "Jabberwocky" the content words almost always have either no sense, or unclear senses, or vague senses, or ambiguous senses. . . . almost all the burden of sense is carried by form rather than content. . . . Carroll seems to have had a keen and clear picture of the morpheme structure of the English language."

**C76:12]** ———, and Nora Gilday. "Lewis Carroll and the Logic of Negation." *JJLCS,* 5, No. 2 (Spring 1976), 42–45.

An investigation of Carroll's theory of negation—one small but important aspect of his logic—concludes that Carroll's theory is flawed and that Carroll was neither a theoretical nor a practical logician. "For Carroll logic was play, mental exercise. . . . Nevertheless, Carroll was aware of theoretical issues, especially those involving paradox."

**C76:13]** Fraser, Morris. *The Death of Narcissus.* London: Secker and Warburg, 1976.

Argues that narcissism breeds introverted and unpleasant relationships between mature adults and prepubertal children. Carroll, with his "disorder" known as paedophilia, is among the writers discussed, receiving one chapter, ". . . And After That the Snark."

**C76:14]** Furniss, Harry. "Recollections of Lewis Carroll." Edited with an introduction by Lance Salway. *Signal,* No. 19 (January 1976), 45–50.

Edited reprint of article which appeared in the *Strand Magazine,* 35, (January 1908).

**C76:15]**   Gattégno, Jean. *Lewis Carroll: Fragments of a Looking-Glass.* Translation by Rosemary Sheed. New York: Crowell, 1976.

Translation of C74:12.
   Reviewed by: P. L. Adams, *Atlantic,* 237 (March 1976), 108; Victor Howes, *Christian Science Monitor,* 4 March 1976, p. 22; G. B. Cross, *Library Journal,* 101 (1 April 1976), 901; John Russell, *New York Times Book Review,* 18 July 1976, p. 6; *New Yorker,* 52 (16 August 1976), 92; J. P. Lovering, *Best Seller,* 36 (October 1976), 218; *Choice,* 13, (October 1976), 812; Peter Heath, *Virginia Quarterly Review,* 53, No. 3 (Summer 1977), 534–40; Nina Auerbach, *Nineteenth-Century Fiction,* 32, No. 2 (September 1977), 222–25; N. Miller, *Antioch Review,* 35 (1977), 120; J. R. Wilson, *CEA Critic,* 20, No. 3 (1978), 32–33; Geoffrey Grigson, *Country Life,* 163 (23 February 1978), 491–92; Nicholas Richardson, *New Society,* 43 (2 March 1978), 502–3; D. J. Enright, *Listener,* 99 (18 May 1978), 649.

**C76:16]**   Goodacre, Selwyn H. "An Unrecognized Lewis Carroll Parody." *JJLCS,* 5, No. 2 (Spring 1976), 52–56.

Carroll's *Hints for Etiquette: or Dining Out Made Easy* (1855) is a parody of the bestselling *Hints on Etiquette and the Usages of Society: with a Glance at bad habits* (1834; 26th rev. ed. 1849).

**C76:17]**   Grotine, Martin. "Al Olam ha-Smalin shel *Aliza be-Eretz ha-Plaot.*" *Keshet,* 70 (1976), 149–54.

Psychoanalytic analysis of *Alice.* In Hebrew.

**C76:18]**   Guiliano, Edward, ed. *Lewis Carroll Observed: A Collection of Unpublished Photographs, Drawings, Poetry, and New Essays.* New York: Potter, 1976.

Contains the following essays (listed in order of appearance): "Laughing and Grief: What's So Funny About *Alice in Wonderland?*" by Donald Rackin (pp. 1–18) demonstrates by examination of the text and illustrations that *Alice in Wonderland*'s complex humor depends heavily on much that cannot be called "funny," that might indeed be better called "horrifying"; "Speak Roughly" by Martin Gardner (pp. 19–30) looks at the parodies in the *Alice* books and at the question of who wrote the poem that "Speak Roughly" parodies; "Arthur Rackham's Adventures in Wonderland" by Michael Patrick Hearn (pp. 31–44) discusses the background to Rackham's 1907 illustrated edition of *Alice* and compares its distinguished artistic merits with those of Tenniel's and Carroll's drawings; "Lewis Carroll as Photographer: A Series of Photographs of Young Girls" introduced by Edward Guiliano (pp. 45–59) contains a dozen photographs published for the first time and a background and critical introduction; "The Nonsense System in Lewis Carroll's Work and in Today's World" by Elizabeth Sewell (pp. 60–67) argues that Carroll's nonsense developed in the *Alices*, when viewed as a system of mental relations, closely analogizes certain real-life systems in today's society; "High Art and Low Amusements" in Roger Henkle (pp. 68–73) explores the curious fact that Carroll was not a "literary figure" and that his most avid "literary" preoccupation was with the popular theatre, the most trivial cultural expression of his time; "Assessing Lewis Carroll" by Jean Gattégno (pp. 74–80), translated for the first time by Mireille Bedestroffer and Edward Guiliano, see C71:23; "Carroll's 'The Ligniad': An Early Mock Epic in Facsimile" introduced by Roger Lancelyn Green (pp. 81–91) contains the first publication of an 1851 mock epic and a background and critical introduction; "Hark the Snark" by Morton Cohen (pp. 92–110) recreates the events in Dodgson's life during the summer of 1874, when he first heard the line "the Snark *was* a Boojum you see" and reprints contemporary reviews of *The Hunting of the Snark* (1876); "Whale or Boojum: An Agony" by Harold Beaver (pp. 111–31) argues that Melville's *Moby-Dick* is a close analogue of *The Hunting of the Snark;* "The *Sylvie and Bruno* Books as Victorian Novel" by Edmund Miller (pp. 132–44) argues that the *Sylvie and Bruno* books (one continuous novel) show us that reality and nonsense are not easily separable and that we learn about the nature of love by moving from one world to the other through dream; "Lewis Carroll as Artist: Fifteen Unpublished Sketches for the *Sylvie and Bruno* Books" introduced by Edward Guiliano (pp. 145–60) contains the hitherto unpublished drawings and a background and critical introduction; "Lewis Carroll and Pre-Raphaelite 'Fainting in Coils' " by Jeffrey Stern (pp. 161–80) investigates Carroll's relationships with Pre-Raphaelites Arthur Hughes and D. G. Rossetti and the influence their art had upon Carroll's; "The Game of Logic; A Game of Universes" by Ernest Coumet (pp. 181–95), translated for the first time by Peter Heath, see C71:23; "The Film Collector's Alice: An Essay and Checklist" by David H. Schaefer (pp. 196–207) records and briefly discusses the many film adaptations of the *Alice* books.

Reviewed by: *Kirkus Reviews,* 1 August 1976; *Publisher's Weekly,* 23 August 1976, p. 62; Charles Bishop, *Library Journal,* 15 September 1976, p. 1857; *ALA Booklist,* 1 December 1976, p. 515; *Chicago Daily News,* December 4–5, 1976; Victor Howes, *The Christian Science Monitor,* 17 December 1976, p. 23; *New Yorker,* 20 December 1976, p. 119; Anne-Marie De Moret, *St. Louis Globe-Democrat,* 6 February 1977; *Choice,* March 1977; Robert Phillips, *Commonweal,* 104, No. 14 (8 July 1977), 439–41; Peter Heath, *Virginia Quarterly Review,* 53,

No. 3 (Summer 1977), 534-40, Selwyn Goodacre, *JJLCS,* 6 No. 3 (Summer 1977), 78-82; Myra Cohn Livingston, *Horn Book,* August 1977, p. 462; Nina Auerbach, *Nineteenth-Century Fiction,* 32, No. 2 (September 1977), 222-23; Francis Huxley, *Times Literary Supplement,* 13 January 1978, p. 26.

**C76:19]**   Henkle, Roger B. "Spitting Blood and Writing Comic: Mid-Century British Humor." *Mosaic,* 4 (1976), 77-90.

A survey of British literary humor in the 1850s and 1860s. Carroll is discussed in conjunction with Hood and Gilbert. "Carroll remains within the peculiar tradition of Hood and Gilbert. For all three begin with grievances that are probably social in origin, but immediately cast them into forms that seem to be more intensely personal. They launch directly into artistic caprice: into plays on words, into curious fantasies, into exotic variations."

**C76:20]**   Hillman, Ellis. "Hunting the Boojum." *JJLCS,* 5, No. 4 (Autumn 1976), 125-26.

On the etymology of Boojum.

**C76:21]**   Hudson, Derek. *Fushigi no kuni no Sugakusha: Ruisu Kyaroru.* Trans. by H. Takayama. Tokyo: Tokyo-Tosho, 1976.

Japanese translation of Hudson's 1954 biography of Carroll. Title reads: *A Mathematician in Wonderland: The Life of Lewis Carroll.*

**C76:22]**   _____. *Lewis Carroll: An Illustrated Biography.* London: Constable, 1976; New York: Potter, 1977.

Revised edition of biography first published in 1954 by Constable, London. Contains two hundred illustrations.

Reviewed by: Geoffrey Grigson, *Guardian,* 25 November 1976; Woodrow Wyatt, *Sunday Times* (London), 28 November 1976, p. 38; Robert Melville, New Statesman, 3 December 1976, p. 804; Margaret Lane, *Daily Telegraph,* 30 December 1976; Brian Alderson, *Times* (London), 17 February 1977, p. 8; J. S. Atherton, *Times Literary Supplement,* 25 February 1977, p. 217; Roger Lancelyn Green, *Books and Bookmen,* February 1977, pp. 50-51; *New Yorker,* 26 September 1977, p. 147; Doris Grubach, *New York Times Book Review,* 16 October 1977, p. 18; Edward Guiliano, *Phaedrus,* 4 (Fall 1977), 45; Jerome Bump, *Victorian Studies,* 21, No. 4 (Summer 1978), 521-23; A. L. Taylor, *JJLCS,* 7, No. 4 (Autumn 1978), 102-4; James R. Kincaid, *Nineteenth-Century Fiction,* 33 (1978), 272-76.

**C76:23]**   Huxley, Francis. *The Raven and the Writing Desk*. London: Thames & Hudson; New York: Harper & Row, 1976.

Reviewed by I. Stewart, *Country Life*, 160, (1976), 160; Woodrow Wyatt, *Sunday Times* (London), 28 November 1976, p. 38; Eric Korn, *New Statesman*, 92 (3 December 1976), 802–3; John Fuller, *Listener*, 96 (9 December 1976), 754; Roger Lancelyn Green, *Books & Bookmen*, February 1977, p. 50; *New Yorker*, 52 (14 February 1977), 124; Brian Alderson, *The Times* (London), 17 February 1977, p. 8; J. S. Atherton, *Times Literary Supplement*, 25 February 1977, p. 217; Charles Bishop, *Library Journal*, 102 (1 March 1977), 609; *Choice*, 14, No. 3 (May 1977), 372; Peter Heath, *Virginia Quarterly Review*, 53, No. 3 (Summer 1977), 534–40; Jerome Bump, *Victorian Studies*, 21, No. 4 (Summer 1978), 521–23; James R. Kincaid, *Nineteenth-Century Fiction*, 33 (1978), 272–76.

**C76:24]**   Ippolitova, V. V. "Dva vozrasta Lewis Carrolla." *Sbornik trudov MOPI* (Moscow), 22 (1976), 125–35.

The "two ages of Lewis Carroll." A brief review of Carroll's life and work and an analysis of the child and grown-up in his mental makeup.

**C76:25]**   Iszlai, Zoltán. "Két angol klasszikus." *Óvodai Nevelés*, 29, No. 4 (1976), 157.

Review of two classics of English children's literature. *Alice* and *Winnie the Pooh*. *Alice* is an infinite stream of ideas and happenings, a mixture of lingual and logical humor, and of deep understanding of man. It is a source for modern authors writing humorous tales. In Hungarian.

**C76:26]**   Little, Judith. "Liberated Alice: Dodgson's Female Hero as Domestic Rebel." *Women's Studies*, 3, No. 2 (1976), 195–205.

"Alice's two dream adventures are almost a comic compendium of feminist issues." In the *Alice* books there is "a literally 'underground' image of a woman resisting the 'system.'" In her adventures Alice resists the role of social "queen," and mother, and discovers the paternalistic knight's fallibility. The *Alice* books "are a particularly rich context of image and symbol which can illuminate the pattern of protest and self-discovery" in subsequent fiction.

**C76:27]**   McGillis, Roderick F. "Tenniel's Turned Rabbit: A Reading of *Alice* with Tenniel's Help." In *Proceedings of the Sixth National Convention of the Popular Culture Association, St. Louis,*

*Missouri, March 20–24, 1976.* Bowling Green: Bowling Green State Univ. Popular Pr., pp. 1528–48 [microfilm].

See C77:20.

**C76:28]** McLuhan, Marshall. "Empedocles and T.S. Eliot." In Helle Lambridis, *Empedocles.* University, Alabama: Univ. of Alabama Press, 1976,vi–xv.

The space-time vision of Empedocles may have made its entrance into English literature via Lewis Carroll rather than Mathew Arnold, in the image of Humpty Dumpty.

**C76:29]** Maloy, Barbara, "The Light of Alice's World," *Linguistics in Literature,* 1, No. 2 (1976), 69–86.

Identifies parallels to the *Alice* books in Hemingway's "The Light of the World."

**C76:30]** Manning, Jack. "Photography Has Long Been Part of History." *New York Times,* 31 October 1976, Arts & Leisure Section, pp. 40, 42–43.

An essay on the history of photography and photography in history. Carroll is discussed briefly as the most outstanding photographer of children in the nineteenth century, and the final page of *Alice's Adventures Under Ground* with the photographic medallian of Alice Liddell is reproduced prominently.

**C76:31]** Massey, Irving. *The Gaping Pig: Literature and Metamorphosis.* Berkeley: Univ. of California Press, 1976.

Chapter 6, pages 76–97, is an examination of six aspects of metamorphosis evidenced in the *Alice* books: "(1) natural metamorphoses (2) metamorphoses of antithesis or dialectic (3) metamorphoses related to language, especially at the beginning and end of each book (4) the revolt of words (5) the metamorphosis of the character into the author (6) an antimetamorphic principle." See also index.

**C76:32]** Mathews, Oliver. "The Snark was a Boojum." *The Lady,* 15 April 1976, pp. 667, 669.

Recounts the *Snark's* genesis and gives a synopsis of the saga.

**C76:33]**  Mitchell, Jeremy Corlett. "Electoral Strategy Under Open Voting: Evidence from England 1832–1880." *Public Choice,* 28 (Winter 1976), 17–35.

Discusses the historical context of Carroll's *The Principles of Parliamentary Representation.* The system that Duncan Black has described for 1880–1885 in his reinterpretations of Carroll's booklet "shared many features with one existing from 1832–1880." Discusses "those features and the 'fit' between the Carroll-Black game theoristic model and the electoral realities of the earlier period."

**C76:34]**  Pattison, Robert B. "The Little Victims: The Child Figure and Original Sin in English Literature." *Dissertation. Abstracts International,* 37 (1976), 3647A (Columbia, 1974).

Lewis Carroll is treated in the section of examples of children in children's literature.

Published as a book, *The Child Figure in English Literature.* Athens, Georgia: Univ. of Georgia Press, © 1977, 1978.

**C76:35]**  Poole, Gordon. "Il 'nonsense' di Lewis Carroll." *Verri,* 3 (1976), 53–72.

On the Nonsense of Lewis Carroll. In Italian.

**C76:36]**  Priestley, J[ohn] B[oynton]. *English Humor.* London: Heinemann; New York: Stein & Day, 1976.

Includes a discussion of Lear and Carroll and critical reviews of *Alice* and *The Hunting of the Snark.*

**C76:37]**  Pudney, John. *Lewis Carroll and His World.* London: Thames & Hudson; New York: Charles Scribner's Sons, 1976.

Pictorial biography.

Reviewed by: I. Stewart, *Country Life,* 160 (1976), 999, 1001; Benny Green, *Spectator,* 25 September 1976, pp. 20–21; Margaret Lane, *Daily Telegraph,* 30 December 1975; Keith Gaberian, *Montreal Gazette,* 8 January 1977, p. 39; Brian Alderson, *The Times* (London), 17 February 1977, p. 8; Roger Lancelyn Green, *Books & Bookmen,* February 1977, pp. 50–51; Anne Clark, *JJLCS,* 6, No. 2 (Spring 1977), 48–50; Robert Phillips, *Commonweal,* 104, No. 14 (8 July 1977), 439; M. S. Congrave, *Horn Book,* 53 (1977), 200; Charles Bishop, *Library Jour-*

*nal,* 102 (1977), 110; Jerome Bump, *Victorian Studies,* 21, No. 4 (Summer 1978), 521–23; James R. Kincaid, *Nineteenth-Century Fiction,* 33 (1978), 272–76.

**C76:38]**   Rabkin, Eric S. *The Fantastic in Literature.* Princeton: Princeton Univ. Press, 1976.

A study of the nature and uses of the fantastic with frequent mentions of Lewis Carroll and his works.

**C76:39]**   Reed, Langford. *The Life of Lewis Carroll.* Norwood, Pennsylvania: Norwood Editions, 1976.

Reprint of 1932 edition published by W. & G. Foyle, London (*WMG* XI; 1979 ed., 511).

**C76:40]**   Rivers, Katharine. "Memories of Lewis Carroll." [McMaster University] *Library Research News,* 3, No. 4 (January 1976). Pp. [28].

Entire issue devoted to publication of unpublished reminiscence in the Library's special collections. Miss Rivers was the youngest daughter of Reverend Henry Rivers who treated Carroll for stammering. Introduced by Richard Slobodin.

**C76:41]**   Salway, Lance, ed. *A Peculiar Gift: Nineteenth Century Writings on Books for Children.* Harmondsworth: Kestrel Books, 1976.

See index. Carroll and Alice are mentioned in various contexts by divers nineteenth-century writers.

**C76:42]**   Shaberman, R. "Correspondence." *JJLCS,* 5, No. 4 (Autumn 1976), 132.

Speculates on the origin of Carroll's misquotation of "loved" in place of "nurs'd" in "The Dear Gazelle."
    Also discusses Carroll's composition of puzzles based on chess. See C76:7.

**C76:43]**   _____. "Lewis Carroll and George MacDonald." *JJLCS,* 5, No. 3 (Summer 1976), 67–88.

Section 1 of this three-part essay is a discussion of Carroll's friendship with George MacDonald and his family. In section 2 MacDonald's influence upon Carroll's art is studied. "Certain passages in *Phantastes* undoubtedly influenced the *Alice* books. . . . ." Section 3 is a comparison of the fairy tales of the two authors, revealing "certain common elements of symbolism and association."

**C76:44]**  Sibley, Brian. "End Game." *JJLCS,* 5, No. 4 (Autumn 1976), 119–24.

A critical reading of *The Hunting of the Snark.* The crew are certainly playing *some* sort of game. "The *real* game is the game of not recognizing the game which is *really* being played!"

**C76:45]**  Takahasi, Yasunari, ed. *Arisu Genso.* Tokyo: Subaru-shobo, 1976.

Anthology entitled *Images of Alice.* Contains several photographs by Carroll, illustrations, and divers critical essays. In Japanese.

**C76:46]**  Tucker, Nicholas, ed. *Suitable for Children? Controversies in Children's Literature.* Berkeley and Los Angeles: Univ. of California Press, 1976.

The *Alices,* a contrast to prevalent Victorian thought and writing, are "in many ways a commentary on the author himself." The great appeal of the *Alices* "might only have been possible because Carroll originally thought of the story in terms of a child audience" (p. 21).

**C76:47]**  Vogeler, Martha S., and Albert R. Vogeler. "Gissing's Friends: More Light on the Gaussens." *Gissing Newsletter,* 12, No. 4 (October 1976), 6–14.

An account based largely upon unpublished entries in Carroll's diary of his interactions with two of George Gissing's close acquaintances, Mr. Frederic Harrison and Mrs. Gaussen. "The entries illuminate, if obliquely, a corner of Gissing's early life."

## 1977

**C77:1]**  Baum, Alwin L. "Carroll's *Alices:* The Semiotics of Paradox." *American Imago,* 34, No. 1 (Spring 1977), 86–108.

An analysis of the dreamwork and the linguistic structure of the *Alice* narratives. In part, the *Alices* are "metacommentaries on the nonsense of conventional English usage," and one finds in them major parameters of dream codification instrumental to their structure as well as other mechanisms of dreamwork.

**C77:2]**   Bishop, Charles. " 'The Mouse's Tale' and the First Stanza of 'Jabberwocky'—A Matched Pair." *JJLCS*, 6, No. 3 (Summer 1977), 72–74.

Identifies several historical and technical correspondences between "The Mouse's Tale" and "Jabberwocky." They are a "matched pair" in which Carroll's strong sense of visual coincided with his abiding interest in language and his love of symetry. . . ."

**C77:3]**   Clark, Anne. "The Griffin and the Gryphon." *JJLCS*, 6, No. 1 (Winter 1977), 3–15.

A historical description of the griffin, the imaginary creature that would be forgotten today except for "its widespread adoption in heraldry, and its inclusion by Carroll in *Alice's Adventures in Wonderland.*"

**C77:4]**   ———. "Hassard Hume Dodgson and The Oxford Union Society." *JJLCS*, 6, No. 2 (Spring 1977), 40–42.

Biographical account of Carroll's Uncle Hassard's early years. He was very active in debating societies at Oxford in the mid 1820s.

**C77:5]**   Cohen, Morton N. "Alice Under Ground." *New York Times Book Review*, 9 October 1977, pp. 3, 32.

Announces discovery of drawing by Carroll of Alice Liddell beneath Alice's photograph at the end of the *Under Ground* manuscript.

**C77:6]**   Crutch, Denis. "Familiar Chat with Bird and Beast." *JJLCS*, 6, No. 1 (Winter 1977), 18–19.

A brief discussion of the proliferation of animals in the *Alices*. All of them speak except the puppy. ". . . he is an intruder from the 'real' world who blundered into Alice's dream, bringing her close to waking."

**C77:7]**   Durán, Manuel. "¿Quevedo precursor de Lewis Car-

roll?" In *The Two Hesperias: Literary Studies in Honor of Joseph
Fucilla on the Occasion of His 80th Birthday.* Ed. Americo Bugliani.
(Studia Humanitas.) Madrid: Porrúa, 1977, pp. 143–59.

A comparison and contrast of the words of Quevedo, D. Luis de Gónzora, and
Carroll. Despite different backgrounds, traditions, and literary affinities, all
three were great creators of words, and their writings invite their readers to
think. Quevedo, Góngora, and Carroll used parody for simultaneously con-
structive and destructive ends. They create words but destroy myths. Title
translates as "Is Quevedo a prescursor of Lewis Carroll?" In Spanish.

**C77:8]**  Faimberg, Haydée. "The Snark was a Boojum." *International Review of Psychoanalysis,* 4 (1977), 243–49.

An explication of *The Hunting of the Snark.* "This poem is the retroactive construction of a poetical-prophetic end where, through the literary adventure of
creation of 'nonsense,' the disappearance of the subject is effected through the
absolute encounter of two significants: Snark—Boojum. Either of them becomes the meaning of the other one, and thus the incessant search for signifi-
cances that make it possible for this subject to live in a symbolic world is
stopped, once and for all."

**C77:9]**  Goodacre, Selwyn H. "On Alice's Changes of Size in
Wonderland." *JJLCS,* 6, No. 1 (Winter 1977), 20–24.

An analysis of Alice's twelve distinct size changes in *Wonderland* and ten in
*Alice's Adventures Under Ground.* "In 120 years, no artist has yet portrayed the
changes in size accurately and consistently."

**C77:10]**  Hillman, Ellis. "Correspondence." *JJLCS,* 6, No. 3
(Summer 1977), 85–86.

Discusses Carroll's anagrams for William Ewart Gladstone. Lists several anagrams of Carroll's name as well.
    See letter by Kevin Thacker, *JJLCS,* 7, No. 2 (Spring 1978), 47.

**C77:11]**  ———. "Dinah, The Cheshire Cat, and Humpty
Dumpty." *JJLCS,* 6, No. 1 (Winter 1977), 290.

Speculations on the connections between Dinah and Humpty Dumpty; both
are mentioned in an odd paragraph in the concluding chapter of *Through the
Looking-Glass.*

**C77:12]** _____. "A Lewis Carroll Visit to a Synagogue."
*JJLCS*, 6, No. 2 (Spring 1977), 43–44.

Recalls Carroll's visit to a synagogue in Berlin in 1867. It is identified as the
Great Reform Synagogue destroyed in World War II.

**C77:13]** Hoehling, Hans. "Stolen Waters: A Reconsideration."
*JJLCS*, 6, No. 4 (Autumn 1977), 91–100.

An explication, including close textual analysis, of Carroll's serious poem "Stolen Waters." *"Stolen Waters* is a devotional poem; it paints, in the fashionable
colours of the time, a picture of the fallen state of man once he has left the path
of chastity, and of the possible means of redemption. . . . The poem gains a
certain effort from the way in which mythological, biblical and folklore material are combined with nature imagery (the sunset), and in which the 'action'
that takes place *inside* the youth is mirrored in the changing light of the dying
day."

**C77:14]** Kelly, Richard. *Lewis Carroll*. Boston: Twayne (a division of G. K. Hall), 1977.

A critical introduction to Carroll's life and works.

**C77:15]** Kemeny, Tomaso. *"Alice nel Paese delle Meraviglie:*
L'oscillazione tra senso e nonsenso." *Verri*, 6 (1977), 68–79.

An analysis of *Alice in Wonderland* focused on how sense and nonsense emerge
and function in the novel. As part of the analysis, the way in which semantic
reactions shape the work, identity as a leitmotif, and the tension between
dream and the state of being awake are discussed. Title translates as *"Alice in
Wonderland:* The oscillation between sense and nonsense." In Italian.

**C77:16]** Klimovitch, L. *"Alice's Adventures in Wonderland* in
Russian." In *Proceedings of the Russian Colloquium, University of
Melbourne, August 26–27, 1976.* Ed. Nina Christesen and Jill
Scurfield. Melbourne: Russian Dept., Univ. of Melbourne,
1977, pp. 40–46.

Critical review of Russian translations of *Alice in Wonderland* by Oleníč-Gne-
nenko (A60:17), Demurova (A67:11), and Zakhoder (A75:32).

**C77:17]** Leonard, A. "Correspondence." *JJLCS*, 6, No. 3
(Summer 1977), 86.

Argues that Carroll may have known about "treacle-mines."

**C77:18]**   Livingston, Myra Cohn, ed. "Introduction," *O Frabjous Day!* (A Margaret K. McElderry Book.) New York: Atheneum, 1977.

"Jabberwocky," Carroll's "unsurpassed nonsense poem," is briefly discussed.

**C77:19]**   Luchinsky, Ellen A. "Alice: Child or Adult." *JJLCS,* 6, No. 3 (Summer 1977), 63–71.

The *Alices* are "original, witty, and beautifully told stories designed for children but equally valuable for adults." They have been "wildly over-interpreted," although they do contain some philosophy and are full of in-jokes, symbolism, and comments on the day. And there has been too much "psychoanalysis-in-the-past-tense of Dodgson."
    See letter by Denis Crutch, *JJLCS,* 7, No. 2 (Series 1978), 49.

**C77:20]**   McGillis, Roderick F. "Tenniel's Turned Rabbit: A Reading of *Alice* with Tenniel's Help." *English Studies in Canada* (Toronto), 3 (1977), 326–35.

In his illustrations Tenniel examines all the ambiguities of *Alice's Adventures in Wonderland.* He "faithfully visualizes Carroll's scene while commenting on it, and what he reveals is a complex of social, sexual, and solipsistic themes that run throughout the book."

**C77:21]**   Nagy, István. "Négy nagy meseregény." *Könyv és Nevelés,* 19, No. 6 (November / December 1977), 246–51.

*Alice in Wonderland* is one of several famous works for children that are analyzed. *Alice* is a caricature of Victorian England, therefore it is only partly understandable to Hungarian children. But Carroll's peculiar humor makes *Alice* enjoyable to both children and adults. Carroll understood the world of a child better than any other writer. In Hungarian.

**C77:22]**   Preston, Eileen. "Cat With a Smile"; continued by J. E. Machen, "Alice's Cat?"; and by B. Ball, "The Original Cheshire Cat." *Country Life,* 161 (1977), 1378, 1748; 162 (1977), 436.

A Norman carving of a cat at Cranleigh, Surrey, is reputed to have inspired Carroll's Cheshire cat. The connection is open to doubt.

**C77:23]**   Queneau, Raymond. "Concerning Some Imaginary Animal Languages, Particularly The Dog Language in *Sylvie and Bruno.*" Trans. Don Sherwin. *JJLCS,* 6, No. 1 (Winter 1977), 25–28.

Translation from French; for original see C71:23.

**C77:24]**   Rea, John A. "A Bit of Lewis Carroll in *Ulysses.*" *James Joyce Quarterly,* 15 (1977), 86–89.

The ultimate source of Bloom's "I never loved a dear gazelle but it was sure to . . ." is not Thomas Moore's *Lalla Rookh* but Carroll's parody of it, "The Dear Gazelle: Arranged with Variations." This allusion demonstrates that Joyce knew Carroll's work prior to 1927, the date Joyce acknowledged.

**C77:25]**   Rest, Jaime. "La locura y el método." *Escritura,* 4 (1977), 195–206.

Not seen. Title translates as "Madness and Method." In Spanish.

**C77:26]**   Schwartz, Narda Lacey. "The Dodo and the Caucus Race." *JJLCS,* 6, No. 1 (Winter 1977), 3–15.

Discusses how Carroll may have learned of the dodo and why he decided to use it in *Alice.* Surveys historical, pictorial, and bibliographical sources of Carroll's dodo. The dodo has come to symbolize the extinction of species. . . . Carroll has preserved the dodo and added to it, its inclusion into the fabulous, giving it its rightful place in a fairy-tale laced with reality."
    See letter by Brian Sibley, *JJLCS,* 6, No. 2 (Spring 1977), 58.

**C77:27]**   Tabbert, Reinbert. "Nonsense." In *Lexikon der Kinder-und Jugendliteratur.* Ed. Klaus Doderer. Weinheim / Basel / Berlin: Beltz Verlag, 1977. Vol. I.

Carroll is treated extensively and critically in this literary encyclopedia survey of English nonsense literature. Also contains German / English bibliography of primary and secondary works. In German.

**C77:28]**   Takahashi, Yasunari. *Nonsensu Taizen.* Tokyo: Shobunsha, 1977.

Anthology of essays on nonsense writers entitled *Anthology of Nonsense.* Carroll is discussed frequently, and the volume contains illustrations by Carroll, Tenniel, and Furniss. In Japanese.

**C77:29]** Wakeling, Edward. "What I Tell You Forty-Two Times Is True." *JJLCS*, 6, No. 4 (Autumn 1977), 101–106.

Carroll's favorite number was forty-two. Its appearances—intentional and coincidental—in Carroll's life and works are identified.

**C77:30]** Walker, Peter. "Ali Swear." *JJLCS*, 6, No. 3 (Summer 1977), 75–77.

Speculates that Carroll may have been "a little hard of hearing." This might explain the genesis of some of the "word-confusion" in his works.

# Section D.   *Miscellaneous—Including Dramatic and Pictorial Adaptations and Discussions of Translation*

## 1960

**D60:1]**   Le Gallienne, Eva, and Florida Friebus. *Alice in Wonderland*. Foreword by Eva Le Gallienne. New York: Samuel French, 1960.

Reprint of stage adaptation first published in 1932 by Samuel French, New York.

**D60:2]**   Macdonald, Dwight, ed. *Parodies: An Anthology from Chaucer to Beerbohm—and After*. New York: Random House, 1960.

Contains a selection of "nonsense" poems from the *Alices* along with the original poems that they either burlesque or parody. The section on Carroll, pages 277–92, begins with a brief critical introduction to Carroll's poems.

**D60:3]**   Wolf, Edwin, and John Fleming. *Rosenbach, A Biography*. Cleveland: World Publishing; London: Weidenfeld & Nicolson, 1960.

A. S. W. Rosenbach of Philadelphia twice bought the manuscript of *Alice*. For references to the manuscript and to rare editions, see index.

## 1961

**D61:1]**   Blumenthal, Walter Hart. "Once Upon a Time: Collecting That Keeps the Heart Young." *The American Book Collector*, 12, No. 1 (September 1961), 15–18.

On collecting children's books. Carroll and his works are mentioned frequently.

## 1962

**D62:1]** Kirk, Daniel F. "A Day in Dodgsonland." *Colby Library Quarterly,* 6 (1962), 158–68.

Events and impressions of a recent visit to Carroll's Oxford.

## 1963

**D63:1]** Etkind, E. *Poeziia i perevod.* Leningrad: [?], 1963.

Etkind discusses the translations of Carroll's verse parodies into Russian by Polyxena Soloviova, Aleksandr Olenič-Gnenenko and Samual Marshak on pages 346–51. In Russian.

## 1964

**D64:1]** Lösel, F. "The first German translation of *Alice in Wonderland.*" *Hermathena,* 99 (1964), 66–79.

Treats the 1869 Zimmermann translation of *Alice,* and the general problems a translator of *Alice* must face. Argues that Zimmermann's lack of contemporary success is because *Alice* is bounded by limitations and determinants of a cultural background that cannot be simply transferred into the patterns of another national experience, and because Zimmermann's preconceived, abstract fairy-tale approach "obscures essential features of the original."

## 1965

**D65:1]** Ernst, Morris L. *Pandect of C. L. D.,* Mount Vernon, New York: privately printed at the Peter Pauper Press, 1965.

An imaginary recounting by Carroll in 1892 of the genesis and contents of *Alice* poking fun at overly ambitious critics.

**D65:2]**   Evans, Luther H. "The Return of 'Alice's Adventures Under Ground.' " *Columbia Library Columns,* 15 (November 1965), 29–35.

The behind-the-scenes story of the return of the manuscript of *Alice's Adventures Under Ground* to England in 1948 by the Library of Congress administrator who coordinated the effort. Also see "Alice at Columbia," pages 36–37.

**D65:3]**   Martens, Anne Coulter. *Alice in Wonderland.* Chicago: Dramatic Publishing Co., 1965. Pp. 124.

Stage adaptation.

**D65:4]**   Nicholson, Margaret A. "On the Track of the Jabberwock." *English Journal,* 54, No. 1 (January 1965), 45–47.

Results of a high school writing assignment. Honor students were asked to analyze "Jabberwocky" "so that in content and tone your interpretation will satirize the structured analyses of poetry and other genre done earlier. . . ." A paper comparing "Jabberwocky" and *Hamlet* is reprinted.

**D65:5]**   Robb, Brian. "Tenniel's Illustrations to the 'Alice' Books." *Listener,* 74 (26 August 1965), 310–11.

Discussion of Tenniel and his collaboration with Carroll on the *Alices,* including a brief critical discussion of the success of Tenniel's illustrations. "Tenniel's unique qualification lay, it seems, in his dispassionate attitude to the irrational that triumphantly brings out demonic logic of his author."

See letters to editor by Derek Hudson, 74 (9 September 1965), 386, and 74 (7 October 1965), 503; and by Helen Pepin, 74 (16 September 1965), 422.

# 1966

**D66:1]**   "At Last, an Alice Unspoiled." *Life,* 61 (25 November 1966), 96A–98.

On the Jonathan Miller BBC TV / film of *Alice in Wonderland*. Illustrated with still pictures.

**D66:2]** Bruxner, David. "Alice: A Suitable Case for Treatment?" *Guardian* (Manchester), 9 July 1966, p. 7.

Discusses Jonathan Miller's concept of *Alice* with regard to his television adaptation, and some of the plans for his film then in production.

**D66:3]** Coleman, John. "Dishevelled Dreamscape." *New Statesman*, 72 (23 December 1966), 947.

Favorable review of Jonathan Miller's BBC TV / film of *Alice in Wonderland*.

**D66:4]** Edes, Mary Elizabeth. "Alice Liddell of Wonderland." In *Readings About Children's Literature*. Ed. Evelyn R. Robinson. New York: David McKay, 1966, pp. 304–10.

Biographical account of Alice Liddell, later Mrs. Reginald Gervis Hargreaves. She died in 1934.

**D66:5]** " 'I do wonder what *can* have happened to me,' said Alice. . . ." *Illustrated London News*, 249 (3 December 1966), 22–23.

Concerns the forthcoming television version of *Alice* by Jonathan Miller. Illustrated with stills and Tenniel drawings.

**D66:6]** Judson, Horace. " 'I had this sense of lurking magic.' " *Life*, 61 (25 November 1966), 98, 100.

Discussion of Jonathan Miller's BBC TV / film of *Alice in Wonderland*.

**D66:7]** Miller, Jonathan. "Alice in Wonderland." *Vogue*, 148 (December 1966), 240–47.

Miller discusses the inspiration for and genesis of his television version of *Alice in Wonderland*.

**D66:8]** Muggeridge, Malcolm. "Alice, Where Art Thou?" *New Statesman*, 72, No. 1867 (23 December 1966), 933.

Muggeridge, who played the Gryphon in Jonathan Miller's television version of *Alice,* discusses Miller's conception of *Alice* as well as his own and comments on the success of this production.

    Reprinted, with illustrations from the film, in *Muggeridge Through the Microphone.* London: B.B.C., 1967.


# 1967


**D67:1]**   Cavallone, Franco. "Uno specchio per Alice." *Linus,* 3, No. 33 (December 1967), 1–7.

A brief history and discussion of illustrations for *Alice in Wonderland* from Carroll through Steadman. Illustrations. In Italian.

**D67:2]**   Hill, Rochelle. "Alice in Wonderland." *Plays,* 26, No. 4 (January 1967), 81–91.

Stage adaptation.
    Reprinted: *Plays,* 31, No. 7 (April 1972), 51-60.

**D67:3]**   Lynch, Alexander. "Alice in a Window Glass" (letter). *Country Life,* 142 (30 November 1967), 1412.

Description of stained-glass window in Daresbury Parish Church, Cheshire, depicting Alice and the Wonderland creatures. Discussion continued in a letter by Kathleen Gregson, 14 December 1967, pages 1617–18, which also lists sources for Carroll's Cheshire Cat.


# 1968


**D68:1]**   Demurova, Nina. "Alice's New Life." *Literaturnaya Gazeta,* 26 March 1968, p. 8.

An account by a Russian translator of her new translation of the *Alices* and the problems she faced in rendering the style, jokes, and parodies of these unusually difficult-to-translate books. Title and text in Russian.

**D68:2]** Lösel, Franz. "Alice im Wunderland." *Beiträge zur Kinder- und Jugendliteratur* (East Berlin), 12 (1968), 81–87.

Extended favorable analysis and interpretation of Lieselotte Remanés's "Germanization" of *Alice in Wonderland* (A67:18). In German.

**D68:3]** Pisu, Silverio, trans. *Alice nel paese delle meraviglie.* Illustrations by Lima and Sani. Milan: Fabbri, 1968. Pp. 256, two volumes + sixteen records, color illustrations.

Text and recording of an Italian play version of *Alice in Wonderland.*

**D68:4]** Schickel, Richard. *The Disney Version.* New York: Simon & Schuster, 1968.

See pages 178, 284, and 295–96 for material concerning Disney's film of *Alice in Wonderland.*

# 1969

**D69:1]** Jaques, Philip. "A Special Appeal on Behalf of Future Research." *JJLCS,* No. 2 (December 1969), p. 3.

Appeal to establish Guildford Museum as research center devoted to Lewis Carroll. The Dodgson Family Collection of Carrolliana is on loan to the Museum.

**D69:2]** Lösel, Franz. "Die erste deutsche Übersetzung von 'Alice im Wunderland.'" *Beiträge zur Kinder- und Jugendliteratur* (East Berlin), 13 (1969), 111–17.

Analysis of Antonie Zimmermann's first German translation of *Alice in Wonderland.* Discusses the difficulty of finding German equivalents for puns and plays on words, and finds that when Zimmermann does not try to translate literally, but uses her own interpretation, she achieves her best results. In German.

**D69:3]** "Press Notices." *JJLCS* [No. 1 (1969)], pp. 3–4.

Reprints of newspaper notices concerning the formation and first meeting of the Lewis Carroll Society (England) on 15 May 1969.

**D69:4]** Rollins, Ronald G. "Carroll and Osborne: Alice and Alison in Wild Wonderlands." *Forum,* 7 (Summer 1969), 16–20.

John Osborne in his 1956 play *Look Back in Anger* adroitly uses *Alice in Wonderland* "as an archaic prototype, as an analogy which frequently duplicates and illuminates the action recorded in *Look Back in Anger.* Demonstrates "how Osborne consciously derives character, conduct, landscape, themes, and imagery from Carroll's classic."

**D69:5]** Shepard, Richard F. "Take Carroll, Add Soul. . . ." *New York Times,* 24 April 1969, p. 40.

Favorable review of "But Never Jam Today," an Afro-American musical adaptation of the *Alice* books.

# 1970

**D70:1]** "Abstract of a Talk Delivered by Dr. Selwyn Goodacre to The Lewis Carroll Society [England]." *JJLCS,* No. 4 (Summer 1970), pp. 14–15.

Report of slide show / discussion / which treated various visual changes in the many editions of *Alice in Wonderland* from the shape of the mouse's tale to impressions of Salvador Dali.

**D70:2]** Demurova, Nina. "The Voice and the Violin." In *The Art of Translation, Book Seven.* Moscow: Sovetsky Pisatel, 1970, pp. 150–85.

A detailed account of the problems which the translator had to face while completing her *Alices* and her solution to these problems. Title and text in Russian.

**D70:3]** Gilmore, Maeve. *A World Away: A Memoir of Mervyn Peake.* London: Gollancz, 1970.

See index for references to *Alice* illustrations.

**D70:4]**   Gregory, André. "Alice in Wonderland (photos)." *The Drama Review*, 14, No. 4 (1970), 94–104.

Photo essay on Gregory's Manhattan Project stage version of the *Alice books*.

**D70:5]**   Harries, Lyndon. "Translating Classical Literature into Swahili. *Swahili: Journal of the Institute of Swahili Research*, 40, No. 1 (March 1970), 28–31.

A brief analysis of the problems involved in translating *Alice in Wonderland* into Swahili is included in this discussion of the reasons for and problems in translation in East Africa.

**D70:6]**   Hunt, Henry J. "Looking Back on Alice." *JJLCS*, No. 4 (Summer 1970), pp. 5–6.

Reminiscence on Carroll in the popular culture of England in the twentieth century.

**D70:7]**   Huxley, Julian. *Memoirs*. London: Allen and Unwin, 1970.

See index for reference to Carroll and previously published photograph.

**D70:8]**   Jaques, Irene. "Recollections of My Father." *JJLCS*, No. 6 (Winter 1970), pp. 2–3.

Lewis Carroll's brother Skeffington remembered briefly by his daughter.

**D70:9]**   Kalem, T. E. "To a Laughing Hell." *Time*, 26 October 1970, p. 93.

Favorable review of André Gregory's Manhattan Project play version of *Alice in Wonderland*.

**D70:10]**   Karlinsky, Simon. "Anya in Wonderland: Nabokov Russified Lewis Carroll." *TriQuarterly*, No. 17 (Winter 1970), pp. 310–15.

A review of the early Russian translations focusing on Nabokov's 1923 translation—"it is by far the best one that exists in Russian." Russian translation problems and strategies are considered.
   This issue of *TriQuarterly* was reprinted in England as a book: *Nabokov: Crit-*

*icism, Reminiscences, Translations and Tributes.* Ed. Alfred Appel, Jr., and Charles Newman. London: Weidenfeld & Nicolson, 1971.

**D70:11]**   Kerr, Walter. "Carroll Knew the Dark Side First." *New York Times,* 18 October 1970, section D, p. 3.

Unfavorable review of André Gregory's Manhattan Project play version of *Alice in Wonderland.*

**D70:12]**   Lahr, John. "Playing with Alice." *Evergreen Review,* 14 (1970), 59–64.

Discussion of André Gregory's Manhattan Project stage version of *Alice.*

**D70:13]**   Lester, Elenore. "Taking a Trip with André and his 'Alice.' " *New York Times,* 1 November 1970, section D, p. 3.

Gives background to André Gregory's Manhattan Project play version of *Alice in Wonderland.*

**D70:14]**   Robbie, Dorothy. *Lewis Carroll's Alice in Wonderland: A Musical Version.* Book and lyrics by Dorothy Robbie. Music by Desmond Hand. Edited by Arthur E. McGuiness. Dixon, California: Proscenium Press, [1970].

# 1971

**D71:1]**   Demurova, N[ina]. "Moscow Lewis Carroll Fans." *The Soviet Woman Magazine,* 7 (1971), 32–33.

The story of a Lewis Carroll Club that existed for several years at a Moscow school. Nina Demurova, an accomplished translator of Carroll's works into Russian, visited the club to judge and advise translators of "Advice from the Caterpillar" in a competition. In English.

**D71:2]**   "Eventyr og antireklame i rød fløyel: Klaus Hangerups 'Alice i Underverdenen' pa Amfi." *Dagbladet,* 1 January 1971.

Review of Klaus Hangerups's Norwegian threatrical adaptation of *Alice's Adventures Under Ground.* In Norwegian.

**D71:3]**   Goodacre, Selwyn. "Alice at the Edinburgh Festival."
*JJLCS,* No. 9 (Winter 1971), pp. 13–14.

Unfavorable review of performance of André Gregory's Manhattan Project
version of *Alice* given at the 1970 Edinburgh Festival; also mentions an exhibition given of the folio prints of the Dali *Alice.*

**D71:4]**   Lambert, William B. *"The Annotated Alice and the Three
Bears." JJLCS,* No. 9 (Winter 1971), pp. 14–24.

Source study, including reprint, of the Southey version of "The story of the
Three Bears."

**D71:5]**   Robinson, J. Denton. "Lewis Carroll" (letter). *Country
Life,* 150 (5 August 1971), 341.

Concerns stained-glass window in memory of Lewis Carroll in Daresbury
Church. A photograph of the window is reproduced. See D67:3.

**D71:6]**   Sandier, Gilles. "Gymnastique et militantisme." *La
Quinzaine Littéraire,* No. 127 (15 October 1971), pp. 26–27.

Favorable review of André Gregory's Manhattan Project version of *Alice in
Wonderland* played at L'Espace Cardin in Paris.

**D71:7]**   Smith, Ruth L. *Alice in Wonderland Cook Book.* Muncie,
Indiana: Der Drucker, 1971. Pp. [64], paperback in folder.

Facsimile reprint, limited to 600 numbered copies, of unique copy of a book
published by Bowman Publishing Company prior to 1922. Three-color illustrations. Recipes spring from food references in the *Alices.*
   Discussed by Anne Clark, "For Wonderland Cooks" in *JJLCS,* No. 11
(Summer 1972), pp. 29–30.

## 1972

**D72:1]**   "Alice in Wonderland Card Game." *JJLCS,* No. 11
(Summer 1972), pp. 20–21.

Facsimile reprint of rules to the Wonderland Card Game. See *JJLCS,* No. 12
(Autumn 1972), pp. 25–26, for a bibliographical description of variants.

**D72:2]**   Anderson, Verily. *The Last of the Eccentrics: A Life of Rosslyn Bruce*. London: Hodder & Stoughton, 1972.

Contains a short account of the performance of *Alice* at Worcester College in 1894.

**D72:3]**   Clark, Anne. "Steadman's Alice Drawings." *JJLCS*, No. 13 (Winter 1972), p. 15.

Summary of a talk given by Ralph Steadman on 13 December 1972 concerning his approach to illustrating *Through the Looking-Glass*.

**D72:4]**   Crutch, Denis. "Two Recent Carroll Productions." *JJLCS*, No. 10 (Spring 1972), pp. 2–3.

Favorable reviews of a pantomime production of *The Hunting of the Snark* by the Tavistock Repertory Company, Canonbury, and of a version of *Alice* by the Pip Simmons Group.

**D72:5]**   Davis, John N. S. "*Alice in Wonderland* Film." *JJLCS*, No. 13 (Winter 1972), p. 7.

Unfavorable review of 1972 Shaftel film version of *Alice*. See also D72:11.

**D72:6]**   Goodacre, Selwyn. "Cyril Fletcher Reads *Alice*." *JJLCS*, No. 11 (Summer 1972), p. 8.

Favorable review of "Lewis Carroll Through the Looking-Glass," a play /reading starring Cyril Fletcher.

**D72:7]**   Lennon, Florence Becker. "Alice on the Grass." *JJLCS*, No. 12 (Autumn 1972), pp. 1–4.

Favorable review of a performance of *Alice Through the Looking-Glass* given on Roger Lancelyn Green's estate in Bebington, Cheshire.

**D72:8]**   "Lewis Carroll Memorial at Croft." *JJLCS*, No. 11 (Summer 1972), p. 12.

Wall-plaque memorial to Lewis Carroll dedicated at St. Peter's Church, Croft.

**D72:9]**   Panov, M. V. "About Russian Translations of Carroll's 'Jabberwocky.'" In *Development of Modern Russian*. Moscow: Nauka Publishers, pp. 239–48.

A Moscow University Russian language and poetry professor discusses three different translations of "Jabberwocky." Title and text in Russian.

**D72:10]**   Poltanees, Welleran. *All Mirrors Are Magic Mirrors: Reflections on Pictures Found in Children's Books.* LaJolla, California: Green Tiger Press, 1972.

Contains a brief discussion of Tenniel's and Rackham's illustrations for *Alice.*

**D72:11]**   Sibley, Brian. "Curiouser and Curiouser!" *JJLCS,* No. 13 (Winter 1972), pp. 5–6.

Unfavorable review of 1972 Shaftel film version of *Alice's Adventures in Wonderland.* See also D72:5.

**D72:12]**   Svensson, Georg. "Mervyn Peake" (letter). *Times Literary Supplement,* 17 March 1972, p. 308.

On Mervyn Peake's 1945 illustrations for the Zephyr Books (Sweden) edition of the *Alices.*

# 1973

**D73:1]**   Arbus, Doon. *Alice in Wonderland: The Forming of a Company and the Making of a Play.* New York: Merlin House, 1973.

Full text of André Gregory's *Alice,* with a discussion of the genesis of the Manhattan Project Acting Company. Contains more than one hundred photographs of the production by Richard Avedon.

**D73:2]**   Bull, Peter. *Life is a Cucumber.* London: Peter Davies, 1973.

Peter Bull, who played the Duchess, offers a behind-the-scenes discussion of Jonathan Miller's film version of *Alice* on pages 203–9.

**D73:3]**   Cary, Joseph. "Tertiary Worlds," *Children's Literature: The Great Excluded,* 2 (1973), 213–15.

Review of *Jabberwocky: The Journal of The Lewis Carroll Society* (England).

**D73:4]** Crutch, Denis. "Two Stage Versions of 'Alice.' " *JJLCS*, 2, No. 1 (Spring 1973), 15–16.

Favorable review of an adaptation of *Alice* given by the Dulwich Players, and an unfavorable review of James Barton's presentation of *Alice* as it might be interpreted by an Oriental playwright.

**D73:5]** Davis, John N. S. "Through the Looking-Glass and what Alice found there." *JJLCS*, 2, No. 1 (Spring 1973), 18.

Mixed review of Felicity Douglas's adaptation of *Through the Looking-Glass* given at the Ashcroft Theatre, Croydon (England).

**D73:6]** Gardner, Martin. *The Snark Puzzle Book*. New York: Simon and Schuster, 1973. Pp. 124.

Seventy-five questions, "Snarkteasers" with answers, alongside the text of *The Hunting of the Snark* with Henry Holiday's illustrations. "Jabberwocky" with Tenniel's illustrations is also reprinted.
  Reviewed by: *Kirkus Reviews,* 41 (15 October 1973), 1165; *Publishers Weekly,* 204 (22 October 1973), 111; Anne Clark, *JJLCS,* 3, No. 1 (Winter 1973), 2; Benny Green, *Spectator,* No. 7603 (16 March 1974), pp. 232–36; *Library Journal,* 99 (15 April 1974), 12.

**D73:7]** Goodacre, Selwyn H. " 'Alice' at Stradford-on-Avon." *JJLCS*, 2, No. 1 (Spring 1973), 15.

Unfavorable review of 1972 Christmas production of *Alice in Wonderland* by Triumph Theatre Productions at the Royal Shakespeare Theatre.

**D73:8]** Jackson, Elizabeth, adapter. *Alice in Wonderland: A Play Adapted from Lewis Carroll's Book.* Music by June Woods. London: Heinemann, 1973.

**D73:9]** Jones, Kenneth. "Alas, in Wonderland." *English Journal,* 62, No. 4 (April 1973), 577–78.

A high school teacher relates his experience teaching *Alice in Wonderland* for the first time.

**D73:10]** Lennon, Florence Becker. "Alice Off-Off-Broadway." *JJLCS*, 2, No. 3 (Autumn 1973), 6–7.

Favorable reviews of the Manhattan Project theatre production of *Alice in Won-*

*derland* given at New York University, and the 1972 Shepperton Studios (England) movie version of *Alice*.

**D73:11]**  Lennon, Peter. "Television." *The Sunday Times* (London), 30 December 1973, p. 23, col. 2.

Favorable review of James MacTaggart's TV production of *Alice Through the Looking-Glass*.

**D73:12]**  Maltin, Leonard. *The Disney Films*. London: Thomas Nelson; New York: Crown, 1973.

Contains a history and description of the Disney movie version of *Alice* on pages 101–4, and cartoon shorts on pages 279–80. Illustrations.

**D73:13]**  Ovenden, Graham, ed. *The Illustrators of Alice*. Introduction by John Davis. London: Academy; New York: St. Martin's, 1972.

A compendium of selected illustrations by divers illustrators for each chapter of *Alice in Wonderland;* some reproduced in color. In his introduction, John Davis recounts the history of the *Alice* books and their many illustrated editions. Includes a bibliography of illustrated English-language editions.
     Revised paperback edition published in 1979, London: Academy; New York: St. Martin's.
     Reviewed by: R. R. Harris, *Library Journal*, 98 (1972), 2072; Anne Clark, *JJLCS,* No. 13 (Winter 1972), pp. 2, 4; *Choice,* 10 (1973), 1538; Ruari McLean, *Connoisseur*, 183 (1973), 152; Corrine Robbins, *New York Times Book Review,* 6 January 1973, pp. 2–3; J. R. Christopher, *Mythprint*, 12, No. 2 (August 1975), 6–7.

**D73:14]**  Schaefer, David. "Mrs. Hargreaves in America." *JJLCS*, 3, No. 1 (Winter 1973), 15–16.

Description and transcription of a 1932 newsreel of "Alice's" arrival in New York.

**D73:15]**  Sibley, Brian. "A Californian Yankee at the Court of Queen Alice." *JJLCS*, 2, No. 2 (Summer 1973), 5–14.

Discussion of the Disney movie version of *Alice*.

**D73:16]**  ———. "Correspondence." *JJLCS*, 2, No. 2 (Autumn 1973), 23–24.

Concerns Florence Becker Lennon's discussion of the Disney film version of
*Alice* in her revised edition of *The Life of Lewis Carroll.*

**D73:17]**   Stern, Jeffrey. "Correspondence." *JJLCS,* 2, No. 1
(Spring 1973), 22–23.

A query about the contents of a letter, reproduced for the first time, from Reginald Hargeaves concerning his forthcoming marriage to Alice Liddell. A second query concerns a set of colored lantern slides.

For a reply to the question regarding the slides see John Davis's letter in
*JJLCS,* 2, No. 3 (Autumn 1973), 23.

**D73:18]**   Takahashi, Yasunari, trans. *Syojo Arisu.* Photographs
by Hajime Sawatari. Tokyo: Kawadeshobo-shinsha, 1973. Pp.
[60].

Photo essay inspired by *Alice in Wonderland.* Contains fifty-seven photographs
of an English girl posed as Alice and Japanese translations of "Alice Remem-
bers," "Letters to Child friends," "Photography Extraordinary," and "A Photographer's Log in England." Also published as *Alice.*

# 1974

**D74:1]**   Danilov, Yu. A. "Lewis Carroll in Russia." *Knowledge
Is Strength,* No. 9 (1974), pp. 44–47.

Title and text in Russian.

**D74:2]**   Davis, John N. S. "Alice Through the Looking-Glass."
*JJLCS,* 3, No. 2 (Spring 1974), 6–7.

Brief review of Felicity Douglas's theatrical adaptations of *Through the Looking-
Glass* presented on 25 December 1974 at the Mercury Theatre at Colchester,
England.

**D74:3]**   De Prez, Edna. "Where the Sun Comes Peeping in at
Morn." *Cheshire Life,* 40, No. 5 (May 1974), 81.

An account of the history of Daresbury Rectory, Lewis Carroll's birthplace.

**D74:4]**   Dierickx, J. "Some Belated Remarks on the Frenchification of Snarks." *Revue des Langues Vivantes* (Brussels), 40, No. 5 (1974), 466–73.

A comparison and contrast review of three translations of *The Hunting of the Snark* (Parisot, A62:14, Gilliam and Mano, A70:11, Parisot A71:22), and a general discussion of the problems of translation.

**D74:5]**   Galloway, Myron. "Alice in Wonderland." *Montreal Star,* 21 May 1974, p. B10.

Note on the rerelease of the 1951 Disney film version of *Alice.*

**D74:6]**   Gilmore, Maeve, and Shelagh Johnson. *Mervyn Peake: Writings and Drawings.* London: Academy Editions, 1974.

Contains an illustration from the *Snark* and seven from *Alice.*

**D74:7]**   Hardwick, Mollie. *Alice in Wonderland.* London: Davis-Poynter, 1974.

Playscript.

**D74:8]**   Harmetz, Aljean. " 'Alice' Returns, Curiouser and Curiouser." *New York Times Arts & Leisure Section,* 21 April 1974, pp. 1, 11.

Discussion of the rerelease of the 1951 Disney film version of *Alice.*

**D74:9]**   Humphreys, Tim. "Kids Follow Mad Hatter to a Dollard Wonderland." *Montreal Star,* p. D15.

Report on a production of *Alice in Wonderland* by 1400 children in a Montreal park.

**D74:10]**   Johnson, E. R. Fenimore. *His Master's Voice Was Eldridge R. Johnson.* Milford, Delaware: State Media, 1974.

Johnson's interest in collecting *Alice* books—he owned the manuscript of *Alice's Adventures Under Ground*—is discussed on page 127.

**D74:11]**   Lennon, Florence Becker. "Carrolling at Princeton." *JJLCS,* 3, No. 2 (Spring 1974), 1.

Report on the founding of the Lewis Carroll Society of North America.

**D74:12]** "Lewis Carroll Society." *Publications of the Modern Language Society of America,* 89, No. 5 (October 1974), 1130.

Announcement of the founding of the Lewis Carroll Society of North America.

**D74:13]** Mahlmann, Lewis. "Alice's Adventures in Wonderland: Dramatization from Story by Lewis Carroll." *Plays,* 33 (March 1974), 77–83.

Puppet play.

**D74:14]** Mango, Susan A. "Alice in Two Wonderlands: Lewis Carroll in German." *Dissertation Abstracts International,* 35 (1974), 2232A (American Univ.).

". . . examines Christian Enzenberger's translation of *Alice in Wonderland* and *Through the Looking-Glass* from the point of an English reader. . . . although Enzenberger shows utmost ingenuity and brilliance in his handling of the poems, puns and verbal play, the overall tone and feeling of the translated work suffer because of the changes in syntactic structure."
    Reprinted in: *Sub-stance* 16 (1977), 63–84.

**D74:15]** Pastor, Constance. "The New Alice in Wonderland." *School Arts,* 73, No. 10 (June 1974), 14–15.

An account, with photographs, of a "modern" marionette versions of *Alice* adapted and produced at the John Sherman Junior High School, Mansfield, Ohio.

**D74:16]** Sibley, Brian. "The BBC's Christmas Greeting to Every Child Who Loves 'Alice.' " *JJLCS,* 3, No. 2 (Spring 1974), 1–5.

Review of Anthony Cornish's radio production of *Alice's Adventures in Wonderland* and James MacTaggart's television production of *Through the Looking-Glass*. Both were aired by the BBC on 25 December 1973. See D74:20.

**D74:17]** ———. "Mr. Dodgson and the Dodo." *JJLCS,* 3, No. 2 (Spring 1974), 9–15.

Historical account of the extinct Dodo; contains a bibliography and two engravings, one of which may have been used as a reference by Tenniel.

**D74:18]**    _____. *Microscopes & Megaloscopes or Alice in Pictures-that-move and Pictures-that-stand-still.* Kent., England: privately printed, 1974.

A survey of the film adaptations of *Alice*. Begins with a brief discussion of book illustrators' attempts, particularly Tenniel's, at visually presenting *Alice*. Limited edition of one hundred numbered and signed.
    Rev. by Selwyn Goodacre, *JJLCS*, 3, No. 4 (Autumn 1974), 21–22.

**D74:19]**   Spurling, Hilary. *The Drawings of Mervyn Peake.* London: Davis-Poynter, 1974.

Includes thirteen of Peake's drawings for the *Alice* books.

**D74:20]**   Walker, Peter F. "Cardboard Tenniel." *JJLCS*, 3, No. 2 (Spring 1974), 2–5.

Review of James MacTaggart's television production of *Through the Looking-Glass.* See D74:16.

**D74:21]**   Whalley, Joyce Irene. *Cobwebs to Catch Flies.* London: Elek Books Ltd., 1974.

An illustrated account of illustrated books for the nursery and schoolroom, 1700–1900. See index.

## 1975

**D75:1]**   Ellis, Sarah. "Alice in Wonderland—Typography and Illustration." *Amphora*, 19, No. 1 (1975), 13–30.

The wedding of two elements of book design, typography and illustration, analyzed in ten editions of *Alice in Wonderland*.

**D75:2]**   Fisher, John. *Alice's Cook Book: A Culinary Diversion.* London: Frederick Muller, 1975; also published as *The Alice in Wonderland Cookbook: A Culinary Diversion.* New York: Clarkson N. Potter, 1976.

Thirty-seven recipes with titles from the *Alices,* accompanied by extracts from the books and Tenniel's illustrations. Includes Carroll's "Feeeding the Mind" and "Hints for Etiquette."

**D75:3]**   Ford, Henry. "A Christmas Carroll." *Antique Collector,* 46 (December 1975), 18–19.

Notes a few editions of *The Hunting of the Snark* the new collector might buy. Illustrations.

**D75:4]**   Goodacre, Selwyn H. "A GP Helps Keep the Lewis Carroll Legend Alive"; "Medics Prominent among Carroll-philes." *Doctor,* 10 April and 24 April 1975.

A two-part article covering the life of Carroll, the peculiar joys of collecting, and life in the Lewis Carroll Society and the Newcastle Snark Club.

**D75:5]**   Gussow, Mel. "Stage: Musical 'Alice' with Puppets." *New York Times,* 14 March 1975, p. 30.

Favorable review of Bill Baird's musical, puppet version of *Alice in Wonderland* presented at the Bill Baird Theater in New York City.

**D75:6]**   Peppin, Brigid. *Fantasy: Book Illustration 1860–1920.* London: Studio Vista, 1975.

Includes four Tenniel *Alice* pictures; see index.

**D75:7]**   Rickard, Peter. "*Alice* in France or Can Lewis Carroll Be Translated?" *Comparative Literature Studies,* 12, No. 1 (March 1975), 45–66.

A comparison of some of the numerous French translations of the *Alice* books. "While all the translators could be said to have conveyed something of the wonder and fascination of the originals, the most successful of them were those who understood their text most fully and sensitively and who proved resourceful and imaginative in sustaining the spirit, while at the same time echoing the letter of the original, by subtle adaptation and by the devising of ingenious equivalents."

**D75:8]**   Supree, Burt. "Oz Bodkins." *Village Voice,* 31 March 1975, p. 91.

Favorable review of a stage version of *Through the Looking-Glass* presented by the Meri Mini Teen Company in New York City.

## 1976

**D76:1]**  Hegdal, Magne. "Men Staten var ingen 'Boojum.'"
*Dagbladet,* 13 January 1976.

Review of Norwegian television performance of a musical adaptation of *The
Hunting of the Snark* featuring trombonist A. Brevig. In Norwegian.

**D76:2]**  Schaefer, David and Maxine. "The First 'Alice' Motion
Picture." *JJLCS,* 5, No. 2 (Spring 1976), 50–51.

A description and discussion of Cecil Hepworth's 1903 film version of *Alice in
Wonderland.*

**D76:3]**  Schenk, Lenie, C. Reedijk, and A. Kossman. *Het Kook-
boek van Alice in Wonderland.* Illustrations by John Tenniel. Rotterdam: Ad. Donker; Baarn: H. Meulenhot, 1976.

A Dutch *Alice in Wonderland* cookbook.

**D76:4]**  Sibley, Brian. "Five Degrees of Frost." *JJLCS,* 5, No.
2 (Spring 1976), 35–41.

A critical overview of A. B. Frost's illustration to Carroll's work and a discussion of his working relationship with Lewis Carroll. "Frost's illustrations to
Carroll's work have been overrated, but they mischievously reflect the disrup-
tive elements of derision and irony in Carroll's poems, which are frequently
overlooked." Illustrated.

**D76:5]**  ———. "Peaks and Chasms." *The Mervyn Peake Society
Newsletter,* No. 2 (Spring 1976), pp. 17, 20–22.

Concerns Mervyn Peake's illustrations for *The Hunting of the Snark.* Finds the
members of the crew "a motley company of silent comics caught busily ignor-
ing imminent disaster," whom Peake draws as a "seedy, moth-eaten lot."

**D76:6]**  Sparrow, Joan. Review of "Crocodiles in Cream: a Portrait of Lewis Carroll," by David Horlock and Michael Roth-
well. *Bandersnatch: The Lewis Carroll Society* [England] *Newsletter,*
No. 16 (October 1976), p. [2].

Favorable review of play presented by the Bristol Old Vic Company at the
Mermaid Theater, 4–28 August 1976.

A list of press reviews and coverage is appended to the review.

**D76:7]**  Watney, John. *Mervyn Peake*. London: Michael Joseph,
1976.

See index.

# 1977

**D77:1]**  Brunner, Frank. *Alice in Wonderland*. Denver: Hirshfield
Press Golden Graphics, 1977.

Six illustrations issued in a limited edition of one thousand signed and numbered portfolios.

**D77:2]**  Davis J[ohn] N. S. *"Alice in Wonderland." JJLCS,* 6,
No. 2 (Spring 1977), 51–52.

Mixed review of Mervyn Lloyd's adaptation, rich in Victorian allusions and
subplots, given at the Minack Theatre, Cornwall.

**D77:3]**  Downes, Edward. "Notes on the Program: *Final Alice.*"
*Stagebill,* 4, No. 7 (March 1977), pp. [11–13] + 4p. insert.

Program for the March 24, 25, 26, 29 performances of David Del Tredici's *Final Alice* by the New York Philharmonic at Lincoln Center. Includes a discussion by Del Tredici.

The work was given its world-premiere performance by the Chicago Sym-
phony Orchestra on October 7, 8, 9, 1976. The program for the Chicago performance includes a biography of Del Tredici and his discussion of *Final Alice.*

The New York Philharmonic performance was reviewed by Raymond
Ericson, *New York Times,* 26 March 1977; Frank Rich, *New York,* 18 April
1977, p. 89.

**D77:4]**  Motter, Dean. "Alice. Alice. Alice. . . ." Afterword by
Eric McLuhan. [ Toronto ?]: Iconoclast Imageworks, 1977.

Ten drawings, one in color. Limited edition of one thousand signed and numbered portfolios.

**D77:5]**   Nilsen, Alleen Pace. "Children's Literature & Media." *School Library Journal,* 23, No. 7 (March 1977), 106–9.

Reports the result of an investigation of the influence of children's literature on the language of the mass media. "Of the longer pieces of literature, the one most often referred to was Lewis Carroll's *Alice in Wonderland* and its companion *Through the Looking-Glass.*"

**D77:6]**   Supree, Burt. "Alice Down the Hobbithole." *Village Voice* (New York), 20 June 1977, p. 81.

Mixed review of the Fourth Wall's *Alice in Wonderland,* a stage adaptation which combines elements of the *Alice* books, performed in the Provincetown Playhouse, New York City.

**D77:7]**   Williams, Janice. " 'Alice in Wonderland' comes to Houston." *Texas: Houston Chronicle Magazine.* 6 February 1977, pp. 18, 19, 22, 23.

A discussion of Byron and Susan Sewell's interest in collecting Lewis Carroll material, on the occasion of an exhibition of their holdings in the Houston Public Library; see B77:7.

# Index

EDWARD GUILIANO is Assistant Professor of English at New York Institute of Technology. He is the Managing Editor of *Dickens Studies Annual* and Editor of *Carroll Studies*.